Advanced Programming

WILEY SERIES IN COMPUTING

Consulting Editor
Professor D. W. Barron
Department of Computer Studies, University of Southampton, U.K.

Advanced Programming
A Practical Course

D. W. Barron
Department of Computer Studies
University of Southampton, UK

and

J. M. Bishop
Computer Science Department
University of the Witwatersrand
South Africa

A Wiley–Interscience Publication

JOHN WILEY & SONS

Chichester · New York · Brisbane · Toronto · Singapore

Copyright © 1984 by John Wiley & Sons Ltd.

Library of Congress Cataloging in Publication Data:

Barron, D. W. (David William), 1935–
    Advanced programming.
    (Wiley series in computing)
    1. Electronic digital computers—Programming.
I. Bishop, J. M.   II. Title.   III. Series.
QA76.6.B.368   **1984**   001.64′2   83-17060

ISBN 0 471 90319 1

British Library Cataloguing in Publication Data:

Barron, D. W.
    Advanced programming.—(Wiley series in computing)
    1. Electronic digital computers—Programming
    I. Title   II. Bishop, J. M.
    001.64′24   QA76.6

ISBN 0 471 90319 1

Typeset by Pintail Studios Ltd., Ringwood, Hampshire
Printed by Page Bros. (Norwich) Ltd., Norwich.

Preface

It has been recognized in recent years that learning a programming language is not the same as learning programming. The best introductory texts now reflect this, teaching not only the language but also techniques of problem solving, emphasizing program *design* and *construction* rather than just program *writing*. Nevertheless, the rules of a language must loom large in an introductory course, and most of the examples must be of the 'drill' variety, reinforcing understanding of elementary programming concepts. Thus the student emerges from the course with a good grasp of what we may describe as *programming in the small*.

This book takes over where the elementary courses leave off, introducing the ideas of *programming in the large*. We aim to teach the student how to design non-trivial programs that are correct, reliable, robust, and reasonably efficient. Building such programs involves three components: design of algorithms, design of data structures, and the design of input–output. These three threads are explored systematically in the main part of the book, using practical requirements to motivate the study of each new technique or concept as it arises. Interactions between the different aspects of design are emphasized, and we stress the need to do a sound engineering job, balancing requirements against constraints and choosing an effective compromise. Thus the book will serve as a good foundation for software engineering courses.

We have chosen Pascal as the language to use, because it incorporates many of the features required for teaching systematic programming, and because it is the language most likely to be known by the intended reader. However, the underlying ideas are not special to Pascal, and in a concluding chapter we briefly discuss Ada, and relate Ada facilities to the material already presented.

This is a practical text: it includes three substantial 'comprehensions' which require the student to understand and then modify an existing program, thus introducing the ideas of software maintenance, so often neglected in academic courses but so important in real life. In addition we include two major projects, each of which is sufficient to keep a student occupied for a whole semester.

These projects are class-tested, as indeed is the whole book. The material in the book is derived from a course called 'Advanced Programming', given to second- and third-year honours-level undergraduates. A recognizable ancestor of the course was first given at Southampton University over eight years ago, and it has been given every year since. For the last five years the course has also been given (in identical form) at the University of the Witwatersrand, Johannesburg. Thus the whole approach, the assignments and the comprehensions, incorporate the experience of teaching programming at this level to many generations of students. Complete solutions to the projects and comprehensions will be made available to *bona fide* teachers. Provision of this material in machine-readable form is under consideration.

D. W. BARRON
Southampton
J. M. BISHOP
Johannesburg
May 1983

About the Practical Work

For the guidance of teachers, we describe how the practical work has been used in our courses, which last ten to twelve weeks at second-year level.

The *Assignment* is given to students on day one and is designed to bring the class to a uniform level of good Pascal programming. It stresses the features which might not have been covered in a first course, such as proper use of procedures, records, subranges and enumerated scalars. The assignment is submitted after two weeks and specimen solutions are provided.

A *Project* follows immediately after the assignment, with Play Structure (Chapter 3) and Family Tree (Chapter 6) being given in alternate years. Each project starts off with two straightforward tasks concerned with defining a fairly complex data structure, then reading into it and writing it out. This takes three weeks and again the students hand in their work and are given specimen solutions. Students are encouraged to use the procedures in the solutions for the rest of the project, it being emphasized that there is no stigma attached to replacing one's efforts with better versions. Parts 2, 3, and 4 of the project are concerned with manipulating the data structure and are deliberately phrased so as to be open-ended. These parts are completed in six to seven weeks, and we are continually amazed at the excellent and innovative work produced. The final programs are between 800 and 1200 lines of well laid-out Pascal.

In the years when we use the Family Tree, the order of the material is slightly altered by doing Section 6.1 (Introducing Trees) straight after Section 3.1 (Dynamic Variables). We have found that there is nothing that makes trees inherently more difficult than linear lists, and the students from the different years fare equally well.

The *Comprehensions* are set as tutorial material in afternoon sessions. Unless one wishes the students to actually run the amended programs, an hour and a half is sufficient to complete the questions. Fruitful discussion usually arises, and we emphasize that while there is no one solution to each of the problems, there is a right way of going about it!

The questions on *Analysis* of methods at the end of Chapter 5 are taken from past examination papers and the intention is to give students practice in this kind of work. These are tackled at home.

List of Figures

Contents

Chapter 1

Introduction

1.1 Programming for Real

This second course in programming is addressed to those who have already completed an introductory course. It is a course about programming for real—the design and construction of programs to solve real problems in the real world, as opposed to the toy programs that one writes in a beginners' course.

In an introductory course, the main emphasis is on learning the rules of the language, and the student gains experience in the language by seeing and doing lots of small programming examples. All he or she is doing at this stage is *coding*—the problem is such that there is only one sensible way of doing it. The instructor will probably have explained this method, and all the student has to do is to express it in the particular programming language being taught. Programming in the big world is different. For one thing, one is programming in the large, and putting together a large program has its own problems, quite separate from those of programming in the small. What is more, the method to use is rarely clear-cut. There will be more than one possible algorithm, and more than one possible data structure. Each will have its own benefits and its own drawbacks—one choice may optimize running time at the expense of memory usage, while another choice may reduce the memory occupied at the expense of the running time. There will be constraints on both of these resources, and so the construction of the program is a matter of *design*, choosing a combination of algorithm and data structure that comes nearest to meeting all the constraints. It is a fault of many educators that they always present students with clear-cut solutions to problems. Life isn't like that: it is fuzzy. There is rarely a 'best' solution to a problem, certainly never an unqualified best—the most we can hope to achieve is an approach to an optimum solution that gets near to satisfying all the (probably mutually contradictory) constraints. Finding such solutions is the hallmark of a good engineer, and advanced programming as we shall present it is very definitely an engineering discipline.

Real programs, then, are large and complex, and hedged around by constraints. What other characteristics do they have? Most important, the specification—the user's requirements—will not be cut-and-dried. Even if we do manage to get a precise specification of the requirements, these will change with time. More probably the initial specifications will not be totally precise, and will evolve as the

1

program develops. Thus we must accept that programs are dynamic objects with a life-cycle of their own. This has substantial implications for the way we build them.

We can now set out some of the characteristic features of a real program.

1. It must *work*: that is, it must do what its specification says it should do. This is vital—a program that doesn't work to specification is just so much garbage.
2. It must work *within specified constraints* of for example, memory and processor utilization or response time to the user. At least it must provide an acceptable compromise between conflicting requirements.
3. It must be *robust* and *resilient*: it must behave sensibly when confronted by nonsensical inputs, and it must never, **never** 'crash', whatever the user may do.
4. Since the specification is likely to change, it must be *modifiable* (in the trade we call it *maintainable*).
5. Since the original programmer will probably not be around to do the modifications, the program must be *readable*, at least in the sense that a mathematics textbook is readable.

Advanced programming is a discipline that leads towards programs which have these characteristics. Achieving them is a difficult task and we should always have clearly in our minds the unparalleled capacity of the computer to magnify our errors:

> To err is human: to make a thorough mess of things you need a computer.'

Design Methodology

Given these requirements, how can they be satisfied? Before going into detail, we need to establish a methodology, some general rules to guide our approach. The first thing to realize is that constructing a program is a piece of engineering design, and that the process is an iterative one. In elementary programming courses one goes more-or-less direct to a solution. Real programming is different: just as an engineer proceeds from rough sketches on the back of an envelope to working drawings before actually constructing anything, so the design of a program goes through a number of stages before one gets it right.

Programming in the Large

The major problem in a large-scale program is to keep control of complexity, since there is a (quite small) limit to the amount of detail that a programmer can comprehend at any one time. The ideal is to break up the problem into 'bite-sized chunks', each of which is small enough to be readily comprehended—a good target is modules that are small enough to fit on one sheet of paper, or to be displayed as one screenful on a VDU. Of course, such decomposition is only of use if the modules fit together in a systematic way, and the correct decomposition of a problem into modules is a substantial part of the design process.

This is what is known as *top-down design*. We start with a statement of the problem, thus:

and we subdivide it into smaller problems, thus:

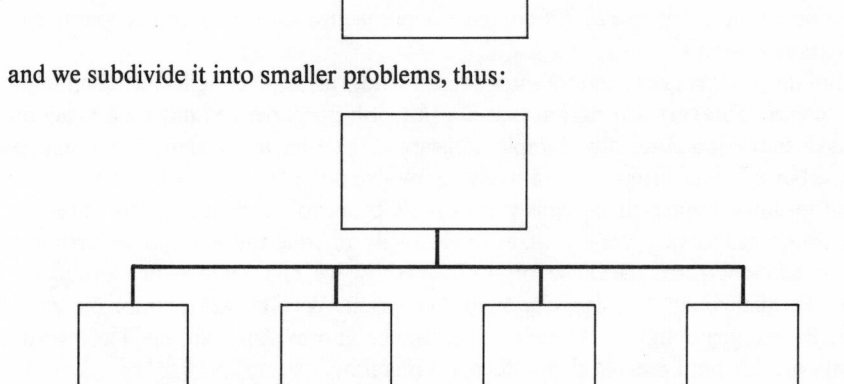

We then apply the subdivision process to each sub-problem, and apply this technique repeatedly until the modules we have got satisfy the 'one-page' rule. This design methodology offers many advantages. A major benefit is in terms of quality assurance. Each time we break up a task into smaller components we can satisfy ourselves that if the components work as specified, then the task in question will work correctly. In this way the correctness 'proof' is distributed throughout the design.

The decomposition technique also has benefits at program testing time. It is well known that (unlikely) special cases require a disproportionate amount of programming effort, and there is a great temptation to leave them out 'till later'. Using the decomposition techniques of program construction, the processing of a special case will appear as a self-contained module at some level, and for testing purposes this can be replaced by a *stub*—a dummy module that merely prints out a message to say what has happened. Once the main logic of the program has been debugged these stubs can be replaced by appropriate pieces of code. Another benefit is in the area of maintainability: for example, if at some level there is a module that has to sort items into some special order, this can be replaced by a more efficient sort without disturbing the rest of the program.

If the lower-level modules are likened to bricks, there must be a systematic way of putting them together. The programming structure that facilitates this is the *procedure*. Ideally, each module would be implemented as a procedure that communicates with its environment solely through its parameters, i.e. it would have no non-local variables. If this rule can be maintained, a module really is a plug-in unit which, with its local workspace, is a genuinely independent entity. In practice this is an impossible ideal, so we try to minimize the use of global variables to enhance the interchangeability of modules. It should be apparent that a procedure-based language facilitates this kind of decomposition: the hierarchy of procedures will exactly match the top-down design tree. In principle the procedure declarations will be nested to correspond to the levels of the design tree: non-local variables can then be declared for a sub-tree of related procedures, however, experience shows that deeply nested procedure declarations are difficult to follow, and we tend not to nest very deep. (Of course, the procedure *calls* may and probably will be deeply nested.)

Building a program out of procedures helps us to reconcile the conflicting objectives of having a program that does the job properly and having a program that does the job efficiently. Simple programs are easier to get right than complex ones, but efficient programs are likely to involve complex and tricky code. Using the top-down approach we first write simple procedures. When we are sure that the program works correctly we can selectively re-code the vital procedures in a more efficient form. Because of the hierarchy we can replace one procedure without disturbing anything else in the program. We can also assure ourselves that the program still works before we replace another procedure. This way we contain errors and prevent their effects propagating.

The alternative approach to program construction is to start *bottom-up*. It would be foolish to assert that either method should be used exclusively, since real programming is a pragmatic combination of the two. For example, if we are developing a word-processing system that involves a lot of character-string manipulation, it is sensible to start by developing a set of procedures for the common string manipulations and then to construct, in a top-down manner, a program that uses these procedures. We may observe that the procedure calls define the primitives of an abstract machine that is more convenient for string manipulation, and the top-down design generates a program for this abstract machine. This is a very powerful technique; in programming we see the truth of Mr Polly's discovery:

> 'If the world does not please you,
> *you can change it.*'

In practice one uses a mixture of top-down and bottom-up design. Another technique sometimes useful is *modular decomposition* in which self-contained sections of a program are recognized and developed independently. Most important, the whole design process is iterative. Although textbook problems may exhibit clear-cut top-down structure, real life is not usually so helpful. Even if we proceed top-down, the decomposition is rarely unique and often we find that problems arising some distance down the tree structure cause us to reconsider the way in which we decomposed the problem higher up.

The Programming Triangle

When we first learn to program, most of our effort goes into achieving the right flow of control. A language like Pascal gives us the ability to specify control flow in a natural manner, so that in some sense the structure of the program represents the structure of the problem. Control flow is, however, only part of the program. Whereas the programmer using FORTRAN or BASIC has to browbeat his problem until it can be described in terms of arrays of reals and integers, the Pascal programmer can employ a richer variety of data types and structures: records, sets, sequences, enumerated types, etc. An important part of the design process is to choose appropriate data structures that mirror the structure inherent in the problem. The choice of data structure is often dependent on the control structure, and vice versa. For example, when we look up a number in the telephone directory we use an informal algorithm that depends heavily on the alphabetic organization of the directory. If we wanted to find the name corresponding to a given number, we would find a different directory organization more convenient. The choice of data structure and choice of control structure are interlinked, and in a real design process they are developed and refined in parallel.

In the design of a real program there is yet another factor: the input–output. Real programs have to communicate with people, and the design of an interface that meets the needs of people rather than the convenience of the program is a tricky and difficult exercise. We can thus view programming as a triangle:

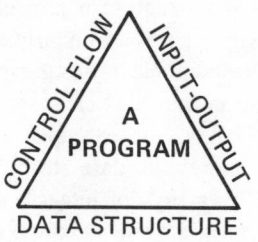

The triangle is equilateral: it rests equally on any of its sides, and all three sides are of equal importance at different stages in the design process, as we shall see as this course progresses.

Use of the techniques outlined so far will contribute to our aim of producing a clear, efficient, working program. However, despite all our efforts our programs will still contain bugs when we first write them, and the final aspect of programming-for-real is that we accept this as an inescapable fact of life. We try to minimize the occurrence of bugs and to facilitate their eradication by systematic design, but they will still be there. One of the greatest computer scientists, the late Christopher Strachey, summed it up in 1966:

"Although programming techniques have improved immensely since the early days, the process of finding and correcting errors in programming—known graphically if inelegantly as 'debugging'—still remains a most difficult, confused and unsatisfactory operation. The chief impact of this state of affairs is psychological. Although we are happy to pay lip-service to the adage that to err is human, most of us like to make a small private reservation about our own performance on special occasions when we really try. It is somewhat deflating to be shown publicly and incontrovertibly by a machine that even when we do try, we in fact make just as many mistakes as other people. If your pride cannot recover from this blow, you will never make a programmer."

1.2   About Pascal

When high-level languages were first introduced they were regarded as convenient ways of conveying instructions to the computer; indeed, the earliest languages were called *autocodes*. With increasing maturity we see that the language is a means of expressing our intentions: it is then up to the computer system to realize these. We thus stay at a high level of abstraction from the computer, which we regard as a machine capable of carrying out any operation we like to specify on data held in memory in some arrangement convenient to us.

Programming can be carried out in many languages, and the choice of language may be constrained by external circumstances. If we have a free choice, we shall do best with a language that allows us to express our designs conveniently; that is, a language whose operations and structure mirror closely the kinds of operation and structure used in our design process. Similarly, if we are able to define data structures and forms that correspond closely to those occurring in the problem we shall get a natural representation that aids clear thought and accurate programming. On this basis, FORTRAN, for example, is not a good language. In FORTRAN the multifarious variety of data structure occurring in the problem world has to be represented by arrays of integers and reals, and the mappings required to achieve this make programs obscure and error-prone.

At the other extreme, on these criteria Pascal is a good language. It also has the attraction of being widely available, and its expository powers are attested by a goodly fund of experience in its use. We have therefore chosen Pascal as the language for this book, and in this section we give a brief overview of the language. You should read this section even if you already know Pascal, since our view of Pascal may differ from what you have been taught, and we want to start illustrating the important features of Pascal style right from this early stage.

With Pascal, as with any other language, we can separate the description into two parts: the data objects that can be operated upon and the control structures that determine the sequence in which operations are carried out. We start by looking at the data objects.

Declarations and Types

Data objects in Pascal are identified by a name, and must be completely defined before they are used. This definition is achieved by a *declaration* which introduces both the new name and the type of the associated data object, i.e. what kind of data object it is. Data objects may be *constants* or *variables*. Integer, character, and real constants may be declared, e.g.:

```
CONST linelength = 74;
         asterisk = '*';
               pi = 3.1415926536;
```

The type of a constant is apparent from its value. When we declare a variable, we have to specify its type, e.g.:

```
VAR   x: real;
        i: integer;
      ch: char;
```

Pascal includes real, integer, and character (char) as primitive data types: a fourth primitive type is boolean (possible values true and false). However, the primitive data types play a relatively minor role in Pascal, since we can (and almost always do) define our own types to suit the problem.

Data Types

In mathematics the concept of 'type' embraces both the nature of the object and the operations that can be carried out on it. In older programming languages the same is true, since the only types available are the primitive or 'built-in' types with their associated built-in operations. Modern languages such as Pascal allow us to define our own types, but the definition of a type is limited for the most part to defining the kind of object, and not the available operations, which must be defined separately.

When we define a type we specify a pattern, but we do not allocate storage. Thus the declaration

```
TYPE thing = . . .;
```

tells the compiler what a thing is, for future reference. When we declare a variable

```
VAR something: thing;
```

the compiler uses its knowledge of the properties of thing to allocate an appropriate amount of storage. It will also use its knowledge of the properties of thing to check that the operations we specify to be performed on the variable something are self-consistent. This is a most valuable feature, since it protects us from many of the consequences of carelessness in programming.

A type declaration specifies the properties of a class of objects; the var declaration creates objects within that class. If there is only one such object we can use a useful shorthand, e.g.:

VAR anotherthing: *definition of the type*;

The shorthand notation can be useful, but in general it is better to develop the habit of using named types for everything. That way you avoid being tripped up by some of the more subtle rules of type-compatibility. We now look at some useful data types.

1. Integer subranges

e.g. TYPE smallinteger = 0 .. 63;
　　　 positiveinteger = 1 .. maxint;

(The notation *m* .. *n* means the integers from *m* to *n* inclusive. maxint is a constant denoting the largest integer that can be stored.)

The built-in type integer is far too blunt a weapon for most purposes. Good style suggests the use of an appropriate subrange whenever an integer value is needed. If the problem specifies a positive integer, use the type positiveinteger defined above. If you have a count that will never exceed 100, use

VAR count: 1 .. 100;

in preference to

VAR count: integer;

Why? Partly because thinking about the possible range of values helps you to understand the problem. Partly because using subranges makes the program self-documenting—if you write

VAR i: positiveinteger;

you don't need to write

{i is a positive integer}

Finally, using subranges helps the compiler to detect programming errors. Given

VAR count: 1 .. 100;
　　...
count := 0;

the error will be picked up by the compiler before the program has even been run.

The primitive operations for an integer subrange are the same as those for an integer provided that the result of the operation lies within the subrange. Thus given

```
VAR i: 1 .. 63;
...
i := i + 1;
```

the assignment would be in error if i had the value 63, and a run-time error would be generated when the program was executed.

2. Enumerated types

An enumerated type is one whose domain is defined by an explicit enumeration, e.g.:

```
TYPE daysofweek = (monday, tuesday, wednesday, thursday,
                   friday, saturday, sunday);

     colours   = (red, orange, yellow, green, blue, indigo, violet);
```

Here we see scalar types being used to identify the objects of interest (daysofweek), and to identify the attributes of an object (colours). Another important use of this kind of type is as a state indicator. For example, while searching a table we might wish to have a variable of type state, defined by

```
TYPE state = (looking, found, notpresent);
```

Such variables are often used in place of boolean variables. Even if there are only two states we get a clearer program if they are explicitly named than we do using a boolean variable. More importantly, using enumerated states makes it easy to add another state if the need should arise—remember the requirement that programs should be easily modifiable.

Having defined a scalar type we can also define subranges over it, e.g.:

```
TYPE workdays = monday .. friday;
```

There are three primitive operations available for any enumerated type. Suppose we have

```
TYPE t = (t1, t2, t3, .., tn);
...
...
VAR x: t;
```

then

    ord(x)   has a value in the range $0 .. (n - 1)$ which is the ordinal number of x in the enumeration,

    succ(x)   gives the successor of x in the enumeration, and

    pred(x)   gives the predecessor of x in the enumeration.

Note that succ(tn) and pred(t1) are undefined. Thus given the declaration of the type daysofweek and

    VAR today: daysofweek; ...
    ...
    today := tuesday;

then

    ord(today) = 1,
    succ(today) = wednesday,
    pred(today) = monday.

3. Sets

Given a scalar type as a base, we can define a set type whose range of values is the power set of the base type. For example, having defined daysofweek, we can declare

    VAR   today: daysofweek;
            sunnydays: set of daysofweek

sunnydays is a variable whose value is a set made up of any combination of the values defined in the enumeration daysofweek or an empty set. Thus we could write

    sunnydays := [ ];   {the empty set}

    sunnydays := sunnydays + [wednesday];   {set union}

We can also have set intersection (*), set difference (−), and most important, set membership, e.g.:

    today in sunnydays

has the value true if the current value of today is a member of the set which is the current value of sunnydays. We can also write explicit set constants, e.g.:

[monday, tuesday, sunday]
[monday .. friday]

These are very useful. For example, if c is a character variable we can test whether its value is a decimal digit by writing

(c in ['0' .. '9'])

4. Arrays

An array is an ordered aggregate of items all of the same type. A particular item is identified by its ordinal position or index, e.g.:

TYPE vector = array[1 .. 15] of integer;

Note that the bounds of the array, here specified by an integer subrange, can be of any enumeration type, e.g.:

TYPE timeworked = array[daysofweek] of smallinteger;

The primitive operation on an array is the selection of a component: once selected the component can be used in exactly the same way as a simple variable of the appropriate type.

5. Records

Like an array, a record is an aggregate of other data objects. It differs in that the components need not be all of the same type, and they are identified by name, not by ordinal position, e.g.:

```
TYPE date = record
                day,
              month,
                year: integer
            end;
```

Here the components are all of the same type, and the information could have been represented using an array type, e.g.:

TYPE date = array[1 .. 3] of integer;

Then the day and month could be referred to as date[1] and date[2]: fine, except that to an American reader the day and month would be date[2] and date[1] respectively. So even in this simple case, using names to identify the components is worth while. In practice one would prefer to use subranges to limit day, month and year to acceptable values, e.g.:

```
TYPE date = record
        day:    1 .. 31;
        month:  1 .. 12;
        year:   0 .. maxint
        end;
```

Note that we have used a shorthand to avoid having to invent names for the subrange type: this is acceptable for integer subranges, despite the earlier advice to use explicit type names. Since the year cannot be negative we have declared it accordingly. If we were catering for the non-numerate we might define the record as

```
TYPE months = (jan,feb,mar,apr,may,jun,jul,aug,sep,oct,nov,dec);

        date = record
        day:    1 .. 31;
        month:  months;
        year:   0 .. maxint
        end;
```

It is important to note that the components of a record can be of any type, including user-defined types, and in particular including records. Thus hierarchical record types are possible.

The primitive operation on a record is field selection (analagous to indexing an array. We use the notation *recordname . fieldname*, e.g. today.day.

Statements and Expressions

We have so far discussed variables and data types, and the way in which they can be defined. To specify the steps of an algorithm we use *statements* and *expressions*.

An expression is a specification of how to compute a value, e.g.:

```
(x + 2)/(y − 2)
succ(today)
today in sunnydays
```

It consists of a sequence of operands, which are variables or constants, and operators appropriate to the types of the operands. The operators may be primitive, e.g. +, −, succ, etc., or may be user-defined functions (see below).

Evaluation of an expression yields a value, but should have no other effect. (We shall see later that it is possible to write expressions whose evaluation has undesirable *side-effects*. This is bad programming practice.) In contrast, a statement is an imperative command which causes something to happen, e.g. an assignment statement changes the value of a variable, a control statement changes the sequence of the computation.

Control Structures

The control structure of an algorithm determines the flow of control through the steps of the algorithm. We use only three basic control structures, but obtain a surprising richness of expression using very general composition rules. The three methods of structuring simple statements into more complicated units are sequence, repetition, and selection.

Sequence   implies obeying statements in strict order.

Repetition   implies obeying statements either as long as a certain condition holds (non-deterministic repetition) or a number of times which is known before the repetition starts.

Selection   implies choosing one statement from a group of statements, the selection being determined by the value of a variable or expression.

A statement can be

> an assignment statement
>
> a procedure call
>
> a compound statement
>
> a repetition statement
>
> a selection statement

In what follows, let S stand for any of the above varieties of statement.

(i)   An assignment statement assigns a value, obtained by evaluating an expression, to a variable (which may be a component of a structure or an element of an array). The general form is

> *variable* := *expression;*

(ii)   Procedure calls are discussed later.

(iii)   A compound statement is a sequence of statements enclosed in statement brackets thus:

> **begin** $S;S;S;\ldots;S$ **end;**

(this is only useful as part of another statement).

(iv)   Repetition statements can take several forms, thus:

        while b **do** S;

                S is obeyed repeatedly as long as the condition b remains true. Note that this implies that S may not be obeyed at all if b is false when first tested.

        repeat $S;S; \ldots S$ **until** b;

                The statement sequence is obeyed repeatedly until the condition b becomes true. Note particularly that the sequence will always be obeyed at least once.

        for $v := e1$ **to** $e2$ **do** S;

                v is a variable of some scalar (enumerated) type: $e1$, $e2$ are variables, constants or expressions of the same type. S is obeyed repeatedly with the 'control variable' v taking the sequence of values $e1$, $succ(e1)$, $succ(succ(e1)) \ldots e2$. If $ord(e2) < ord(e1)$ the statement has no effect.

        for $v := e1$ **downto** $e2$ **do** S;

                as above except that the sequence of values is $e1$, $pred(e1)$, $pred(pred(e1)) \ldots e2$. If $ord(e1) < ord(e2)$ the statement has no effect.

Note that the thing repeated in the **for** and **while** statements is an S, i.e. *any* statement, often a compound statement, or possibly another repetition. Thus common constructs are

    for $v1 := e1$ **to** $e2$ **do**
      for $v2 := e3$ **to** $e4$ **do**
        begin ...
        end;

    while b **do begin**
       ...
    end;

Note also that constructs like

    for day := monday to friday do ...

are common.

    The choice of the correct form of repetition statement is important. We first decide whether the repetition is for a fixed, known number of times. If so the for statement is appropriate. If the repetition depends on a computed terminating condition we use the while or repeat construct, choosing repeat if we know that the body must be obeyed at least once, and while otherwise.

(v)   A selection statement can take one of three possible forms.

        if b **then** S;

                b is a boolean variable or boolean-value expression. S is obeyed if and only if b is true.

if *b* **then** *S*1 **else** *S*2;

   This statement selects *S*1 or *S*2 according as *b* is true or false.

case *p* **of**

   *p*1: *S*1;
   *p*2: *S*2;
   . . .
   pn: *Sn*

end; {*case*}

   p is a variable or expression of an enumerated type; *p*1 ... *pn* are possible values of that type. The statement corresponding to the value of *p* supplied is selected. If there is no such statement an error is signalled.

The case statement is the most general form of selection statement, and its use is often to be preferred to the use of the if statement. Even when there are only two possibilities for the selection, using a two-state enumerated variable and a case statement is more perspicuous than a boolean and an if statement. For example, compare

   VAR male: boolean;
   if male then . . . else . . .

with

   VAR sex: (male, female);
   . . .
   case sex of
            male: . . .
            female: . . .
   end;

Moreover, this latter construct is easily changed if the number of alternatives is increased (e.g. by the addition of dontcare to male and female).

   The completely general composition rules allow a variety of useful constructs to be created from these simple building bricks. One such construct is

   if *b1* **then** *S1*
   else if *b2* **then** *S2*
   else if *b3* **then** *S3*
   . . .
   else *Sn*;

The rules also allow a construct of the form

   if *b1* **then if** *b2* **then** . . .

but this kind of thing is confusing, and should be avoided wherever possible. A useful combination makes use of sets as a discriminant, e.g.:

```
for day := monday to sunday do
    if day in sunnydays
    then . . .
    else . . .;
```

or

```
if today in [monday . . wednesday]
then case today of
        monday: . . .;
        tuesday: . . .;
        wednesday: . . .;
    end {case}
else . . .;
```

Composition is useful, but the general rule is not to get carried away—elaborately nested constructs are rarely easy to understand, and consequently prone to error.

Procedures, Functions, and Programs

There is one further piece of structuring to consider: the grouping of a number of statements into a single entity identified by a name. The simplest form is the *parameterless procedure*. For example,

```
PROCEDURE initialize;
begin
    . . .
    . . .
    . . .
end;
```

Having declared this procedure, a subsequent statement in the program of the form

```
initialize;
```

will cause the statements between the begin and end of the procedure to be obeyed.

Named blocks of code are very useful. However, to exploit the full power of procedures we need two more things:

(i) Local variables. It is highly desirable that a procedure should be 'transparent' to the rest of the program. To achieve this it must have access to *local* variables that are private to the procedure, and cannot be 'seen' by the calling program. This ensures that accidental coincidences in the names of variables used in the procedure and elsewhere do not matter. Extending this idea, Pascal also provides local constants and types, thus making the procedure a 'black box' whose arbitrary internal complexity can be hidden from its users.

(ii) A well-defined interface with its environment, so that its inputs and outputs can be defined in a way that gives a complete functional specification of the procedure. This interface takes the form of *formal parameters* whose names and types are listed in the procedure heading. When the procedure is called, the call provides *actual parameters* that replace the formal parameters during the execution of the procedure body. This replacement can take two forms. For 'input' parameters we effectively substitute the value of the actual parameter, while for 'output' parameters (denoted in the procedure heading by var) the effect is as if the actual parameter identifier were substituted for the formal parameter.

A procedure is a named block of statements, and the procedure call is a form of statement. Closely allied is the *function*: this is a named group of statements that generate a value; thus a function call is a form of expression. If f is a function whose value is of type T, then a call of f can occur anywhere in an expression where a variable or constant of type T would be acceptable.

Procedure and function definitions can be nested. This allows us to hide the definitions of procedures which are 'building bricks' of a higher-level procedure. The importance of procedures and functions cannot be overemphasized: you should cultivate the habit of viewing a program as a collection of procedures and functions, each of which does a single well-defined job.

Finally, a *program* is a procedure that communicates with the outside world by means of *files*. The names of these files appear in the program heading as formal parameters.

1.3 Layout and Style

One of the most important, yet most elusive characteristics of a good program is *style*. It is easy to recognize good style when we see it, but much harder to set out the rules by which it can be achieved. A good programming style contributes immensely to the readability and comprehensibility of a program. It is an amalgam of things large and small: at one extreme good choice of control and data structures; at the other, felicitous choice of identifiers and well-judged layout. We shall not attempt to teach style: we will illustrate it in our examples, and we will occasionally point out what we believe to be particularly important points of style.

One area where we can offer specific guidelines is the question of program layout. Probably as a result of the constraints of punched-card technology, program layout has not in the past been regarded as important. However, modern VDUs and printers allow us considerable flexibility in the preparation of programs. Like books, programs on paper or VDU screen are meant to be read by humans, and in both cases the major concern is with readability and comprehensibility. Programs have more internal structure than English prose, and the purpose of good layout is to provide *visual clues* to the structure.

How are such visual clues generated? Among the possible methods are:

(i)   use of different typefaces
(ii) use of capital letters
(iii) underlining
(iv) layout on the page

We now look at these in more detail.

(i)   Typeface. This is a very common technique in printed material. Typesetting makes it easy to use a variety of type sizes and founts (e.g. bold face, italic). Pascal programs in textbooks are commonly printed in a mixture of bold and italic. However, we cannot usually employ different typefaces on a VDU or printer, and we certainly can't use them in handwriting. We feel that the reader will absorb the ideas of good program layout if the examples we give look something like the programs he produces himself on his local terminal equipment. Therefore, with one exception to be mentioned later, we shall stick to a single typeface for the program fragments that appear in the text, using a typeface that resembles (good quality) computer output.

(ii) Capital letters. In the bad old days programs were produced entirely in upper-case because that was the only form of input–output available. Some backward computing centres still have upper-case-only terminals, but even if you are afflicted with such monstrosities, there is no need to use only upper-case when you are writing programs on paper. Most modern VDUs and printers provide upper- and lower-case (but beware of nasty dot-matrix printers that don't use lower-case descenders, making letters like 'g' and 'p' illegible), and most Pascal compilers accept either case of letters indiscriminately. Our programming convention is to use lower-case almost all the time, with occasional capitals for special effect. Lower-case in bulk is readable, and when keying in a program it is easier if we stay in the same shift most of the time. Thus we use upper-case for the words like TYPE, CONST, PROCEDURE that introduce major sections of a program, but not much elsewhere.

(iii) Underlining. Most terminal devices make underlining difficult or impossible, so we do not use it. You may find it convenient to use underlining in manuscript in place of capitals to delimit major sections of program. This is a matter of personal taste.

(iv) Layout. This is a most powerful tool. Pascal programs are highly structured, and layout helps to convey the structure. In our convention, major sections of a program/procedure (constants, types, variables, procedures, body) are separated by blank lines so that their extent is clearly apparent. Within constant and type declarations we align the equals sign for greater clarity: in variable declarations we align the colons, as in the following example.

```
CONST           space = '   ';
                charmax = 100;
                linemax = 75;

TYPE            charrange = 1 .. charmax;
                linerange = 1 .. linemax;
                pagerange = 1 .. maxint;

VAR             position: charrange;
                line: linerange;
                pageno: pagerange;
```

Within the body of a procedure we use indentation to clarify nested constructs, e.g.:

```
PROCEDURE writeline(line:lines);

    VAR i: 0 .. linemax;

    BEGIN
      i := 1;
      while line[i] < > slash do begin
        write(line[i]);
        i := i + 1;
      end;
      writeln;
    END; {writeline}
```

The indentation shows clearly the extent of the while loop, since the end is aligned with the while. Note particularly that the begin is written on the same line as the do, to avoid an extra level of indentation. Note also that we have labelled and capitalized the END of the procedure. In a complex program with more deeply nested structures it is sometimes convenient to label other end's with a suitable comment, e.g.:

```
for i := 1 to linemax do begin
  . . .
  . . .
end; {actions for each line}
```

Labelling every end in this way is counter-productive: we only do it if it adds to the clarity of the program. (However, we almost invariably label the end of a case statement with end; {case}, since there is no matching begin.)

The essence of good style is not slavish adherence to rules, but judicious use of the tools available. For example, indentation usually helps, but too much indentation can positively hinder comprehension, as the following example illustrates.

```
while (i < count) do
    begin
        x := a[i];
        if x > a[i + 1]
            then
                begin
                    j := i;
                    k := i + 1;
                end
            else
                begin
                    j := i + 1;
                    k := i;
                end;
    end;
```

This can be made more readable as follows:

```
while (i < count) do begin
    x := a[i];
    if x > a[i + 1]
    then begin
        j := i;
        k := i + 1;
    end
    else begin
        j := i + 1;
        k := i
    end;
end;
```

It hardly needs adding that readability is greatly enhanced by the use of meaningful (and often long) identifiers.

When we design a program using the *top-down* technique, we often wish to indicate that a section has still to be inserted. It is helpful to provide a brief description in English and/or pseudo-Pascal to describe the missing section. In manuscript one usually circles this to draw attention to the fact that it is not part of the program proper. In this book we print such sections in italics, e.g.:

```
PROCEDURE readyear (var date: yearrange);
    VAR n: integer;
    BEGIN

        read a number into n
        If it is in the required range, copy it
            into date and mark it as in the set.
        Otherwise put out an error message
            and do not mark it as in the set

    END; {readyear}
```

We shall follow these precepts in all our examples. We repeat that they are not absolute rules but guidelines, and the reader should note particularly the occasions when we depart from the norm in the interests of clarity.

A program is punched as it is written, each order being followed by carriage return and linefeed symbols ... single spaces may be included, if desired, to improve the appearance of the printed page. Similarly, additional linefeeds may be included for the same purpose.

(From *Programming for EDSAC 2*, ca. 1955)

1.4 Assignment—An Excursion into Date Theory

The purpose of this assignment is to get you into the proper way of programming in Pascal. Working at a normal pace, the three exercises should take you two to three weeks, depending on whether you are new to Pascal or not.

Introduction

This sequence of exercises is centred around the manipulation of dates. An introduction and three questions explore the operations to

    swopdates
    readdates
    comparedates
    timebetweendates

The algorithms and procedures developed here will be used in the Family Tree Project (Section 6.5).

The exercises rely on some of the results of the previous ones, but the new programming in each should not exceed about 60 lines of well laid-out Pascal. Explanations of new concepts and hints are provided for guidance. The emphasis is on designing and writing correct, coherent procedures and each procedure should be carefully checked before it is tested on the computer. It is not easy to write good procedures, but this is what advanced programming is all about.

Dates as a Data Type

Dates can be written in various ways, e.g.

25/12/76   or   25 December 1976

Sometimes the order of the parts is different, e.g.

December 25, 1976

We shall define

```
TYPE dates = RECORD
                day : 1 . . 31;
                month : 1 . . 12;
                  year : 0 . . 2000
                END;
```

Typical variables might be

```
VAR birthday, christmas, today : dates;
```

and we can refer to

christmas.day or birthday.year.

Exercise 0 Write a short Pascal program to swop two dates held in

```
VAR d1, d2 : dates;
```

and print them out neatly. Do not read the dates in, but use assignments to set them up. For example,

```
dl.day:=7;
dl.month:=12;
dl.year:=1829;
WITH d2    do begin
   day:=29;
   month:=8;
   year:=1914;

end;
```

The WITH construct is a shorthand aid for factoring out the record name when one is only concerned with its fields.

This program need not be run on the computer.

Reading Dates

It is important to agree on the ordering of the date components for the purposes of reading them in. We shall use day, month, year. However, someone might get it wrong and by checking each component against its range, some of the errors can be caught. For example 2/17/76 is invalid in the British system, but means 17 February 1976 to an American.

Exercise 1 Write the body for

```
PROCEDURE readdate (VAR d:dates);
```

which reads three integers and checks that they are within range. If any of them is not, print the date and an explanatory error message and return 1, 1, 0 in d.

Hints 1. Pascal automatically checks ranges, but halts the program on an error. The reading will have to be done into a variable of a more accommodating type than date so that *you* can detect the error.
2. Checking is more complicated than you think! Remember 'Thirty days hath September, etc.' It might be useful to set up this rhyme in your procedure.
3. Ignore leap years initially.

Testing Write a short program to test your procedure with ten carefully chosen dates that will reveal if your error checks work. Run it on the computer and examine the results. Note that for your program to stop in an orderly fashion, it must be provided with either (1) a count of the number of data items or (2) a signal item at the end of the data.

Comparing Dates

Dates often need to be compared and it would be convenient to be able to say

```
if mybirthday < yourbirthday then iamolder := true;
```

However, concatenating day month year in that order means that algebraic relations will give incorrect results. e.g.:

As integers	10356 < 250256
But as dates	1/3/56 > 25/2/56

So we shall use a function called datecompare which will enable us to say

```
if datecompare (mybirthday, before, yourbirthday)
    then iamolder: = true;
```

Exercise 2 Using

```
TYPE daterelation = (before, beforeorequalto, equalto,
                     afterorequalto, after, notequalto);
```

write the body for

```
FUNCTION   datecompare (d1: date; relation: daterelation;
                        d2: date) : boolean;
```

Hints 1. Notice that there are actually only three distinct relations, because, for example,

before ≡ *not* afterorequalto.

2. Equalto is a stricter relation than before or after. The first comparison on years might establish equalto or notequalto. However, even with years and months equal, one date may be before another.

Challenge Try and write the function without using a single if-statement. (Boolean variables and boolean expressions are good substitutes for if)

Testing Write a short program to read several pairs of dates and call datecompare for each relation, printing out the dates, the relation and the answer (true or false). Remember to check if readdate rejected the data.

Time Between Dates

The next important operation is to find the time between two dates. This could be required in whole years, months or days. As a golden rule, the earlier date will be excluded in the calculations and the later one included. For example if *mybirthday* is 7/10/51 and *today* is 20/8/76 then *years between (mybirthday, today)* will be 25.

This rule gives sensible results and simplifies the formula somewhat. To give you a start, here is the first function:

```
FUNCTION yearsbetween (d1, d2: date): integer
BEGIN
        yearsbetween:= abs (d1. year − d2. year);
END;
```

Note that it should not matter which date is earlier and you may need comparedates to sort this out for the next two functions.

Exercise 3 Using yearsbetween as defined above, write the bodies for

FUNCTION monthsbetween (d1, d2: date): integer;
FUNCTION daysbetween (d1, d2: date) integer;

Hints 1. These functions have what are called *value* parameters. This means that even though the function may change parts or all of the dates, these changes will not be passed back to the calling program. However d1 and d2 can be passed to another procedure as *reference* parameters, in which case any changes made will be reflected back. It might be useful to declare swopdates as such a procedure, e.g.:

PROCEDURE swopdates (VAR d1, d2: date);

2. Ignore leap years initially.

Testing Write a short program to read a pair of dates and calculate the years, months, and days between them. e.g.:

7/10/51   18/8/76

YEARS = 25 OR MONTHS = 298 OR DAYS = 9082 (9075 if leap years ignored)

Use this pair to check your algorithms, and then try your program with at least ten carefully chosen pairs of dates that will illustrate whether the procedures work over all boundary cases (e.g. over December; within a month; from the first to the 30th or 31st; and so on).

Chapter 2

Algorithms (Part 1)—Fundamental Methods

A professional programmer, like a professional cook, has at his command certain standard procedures which he can call up during the preparation of something more elaborate. In this chapter we look at a few such algorithms, at the same time exercising some of the features of Pascal which are often skimmed over in an introductory course: symbolic enumerated scalars, procedure parameters, recursion, and set manipulation. Throughout, we reinforce the tenets of good programming—it must work, it must work well, and it must be robust, readable, and maintainable.

2.1 Picking and Choosing

A common requirement in programs is having to select certain items from a group. Formally, we have n items in a list a. The items are identified by position as in a_i and we wish to select m items at random, where $m \leqslant n$. Examples of this process can be found in selecting the winners of a Jackpot competition or in shuffling a pack of cards. In Jackpots, the questions are usually so easy that there are many thousands of entries with the correct answers, although only a few prizes. Typically, $n = 20\,000$ and $m = 300$. On the other hand, when shuffling a deck of cards, we have $m = n = 52$.

Given a formal specification of the solution such as above, we see that it reduces to repeated use of the sequence

Generate a random integer, j

Pick out a_j.

Random Numbers

The first step is to find a way of generating a random number. A computer cannot generate a sequence of truly random numbers, since it is a machine that operates according to deterministic rules. However, it is possible to generate the next best thing, which is a sequence of *pseudo-random* numbers. The numbers in such a sequence qualify as random in that they have no correlation with each other, but they are pseudo-random in the sense that:

(a)   the sequence is of finite length and eventually repeats
(b)   the sequence can be generated again by using the algorithm again.

The finite length of the sequence is of little consequence, since it is possible to generate sequences of about 10^9 items. The fact that the sequence can be regenerated is a positive advantage, otherwise we could not test a program under precisely replicated conditions.

Let us assume that we can generate fractions which are evenly distributed in the interval 0 to 1. If $0 \leqslant f < 1$ is such a random number, then it follows that $f*n$ lies in the range $0 \leqslant f*n < n$, and by setting $j = trunc(f*n)$ we ensure that $0 \leqslant j \leqslant (n-1)$. To get a number between 1 and n, we simply add 1:

$j := trunc\ (f*n) + 1$

A respectable sequence of such fractions can be generated by very simple means. The basic idea is to multiply the previous number by some constant, add another, and remove the integer part. This gives a new fraction which in itself bears no relation to the previous one. In random number theory, the starting point of the sequence is called the *seed*. The seed is regenerated over and over by the above method. For example, we could use

```
seed := seed* 27.182 813 + 31.415 917;
seed := seed − trunc(seed);
```

In incorporating this with the transformation to an integer between 1 and n, we notice that n might vary according to the application, and so we design a random number generator as a function with this limit as a parameter.

```
FUNCTION random (limit : integer) : integer;
   BEGIN
      seed := seed * 27.182 813 + 31.415 917;
      seed := seed − trunc (seed);
      random := trunc (seed * limit) + 1;
   END; {random}
```

Interlude—do we Mean Integer?

In the above function, both limit and random are declared to be integers, yet it is known from the statement of the problem that neither will ever be negative. What we should have done is first declare

```
TYPE natural = 0 .. maxint;
     cardinal = 1 .. maxint;
```

and then set out the function as

FUNCTION random (limit : cardinal) : natural;

This makes it clear that a limit of 0 is quite meaningless and that we are not dealing with the whole range of integers.

Unfortunately, laziness often makes us skip this distinction, but in a large program it is a valuable one and can be taken advantage of by making it a habit to declare these two types at the start of every new program.

The Selection Process

To set the selection in motion, we need two arrays—one for the things to be chosen and one for the chosen things. To keep track of where we are in these two lists, we need two indices. With these and a loop, the whole selection process can be specified.

```
VAR    thingstochoose : array [1 .. n] of thing;
       chosenthings   : array [1 .. m] of thing;
       from           : 1 .. n;
       into           : 1 .. m;
BEGIN
    for into := 1 to m do begin
       from := random(n);
       chosenthings[into] := thingstochoose[from];
    end;
END;
```

If this program is left to run, most of the time it will work to specification, but now and again we get m items that are not all different. This means that the random function is producing duplicate numbers. Why is this so? To see the reason, we need to think about the process whereby the random numbers were calculated.

The numbers called seed in the program were between 0 and 1 and guaranteed different until the sequence repeated itself. However, to get numbers between 0 and 100, say, effectively only the first two digits of each number were used. While no two numbers repeat in the original sequence, there is no guarantee that two successive digits won't repeat. Therefore it is possible (and probable) that a sequence of 100 numbers from the function random will contain repetitions.

Eliminating duplicates

How are we to ensure that we eliminate duplicates? An obvious way is to compare each item as we select it with all the others selected previously. Each time we do this, there will be one more item to consider, and the total number of comparisons involved will be

$$1 + 2 + 3 + \ldots + (m - 1) = \frac{m(m - 1)}{2}$$

This is going to slow the selection process down with time being proportional to m^2. It is also aesthetically unsatisfactory, particularly if the probability of duplication is fairly small, since a lot of time will be spent looking for something which doesn't usually happen.

A solution to the problem is found when we recall that the original group of items was not necessarily ordered: we imposed ordering by labelling the items from 1 to n, but that was for the convenience of the algorithm and not inherent in the problem. Once it is realized that the ordering is not important, we can eliminate duplicates by reordering the items each time, putting the selected items at the end as we go along and omitting them from the selection process in the future. The revised program is as follows:

```
VAR    thingstochoose : array [1 .. n] of thing;
       chosenthings   : array [1 .. m] of thing;
       from, limit    : 1 .. n;
       into           : 1 .. m;

BEGIN
    limit := n;
    for into := 1 to m do begin
        from := random(limit);
        chosenthings [into] := thingstochoose[from];
        exchange (thingstochoose[from], thingstochoose[limit]);
        limit := limit – 1;
    end;
END;
```

We have assumed the existence of a procedure called exchange, which does the obvious thing.

Picking Everything

If this algorithm is to be used for shuffling cards, we may wonder whether the fact that $m = n$ constitutes a special case. Here we have all the cards in any order and they have to be got into a different order. As the algorithm unfolds, we notice something important: the list of things chosen is duplicated at the end of the list of things to choose. Because both lists are the same size, we can do away with the list of things chosen and shuffle *in situ* with just one list.

Figure 2.1 shows a complete program to shuffle cards. The cards are represented by a suitable record, but the procedure to write out the pack has been suppressed so as not to confuse the issue. Because the fields of cards are enumerated scalars, the writing out will consist of extended case statements generating the appropriate string for each value.

UCSD Pascal Compiler at Wits University

```
 1   1  1    1  PROGRAM Shuffling (output);
 2   1  1    3
 3   1  1    3  TYPE
 4   1  1    3    cardrange = 1..52;
 5   1  1    3    cardindex = 0..52;
 6   1  1    3        faces = (two, three, four, five, six, seven,
 7   1  1    3                 eight, nine, ten, jack, queen, king, ace);
 8   1  1    3        suits = (clubs, diamonds, hearts, spades);
 9   1  1    3        cards = RECORD
10   1  1    3                    face : faces;
11   1  1    3                    suit : suits;
12   1  1    3                END;
13   1  1    3        packs = ARRAY [cardrange] of cards;
14   1  1    3
15   1  1    3  VAR  pack : packs;
16   1  1  107       seed : real;
17   1  1  109
18   1  2    3  FUNCTION random (limit : integer) : integer;
19   1  2    0    BEGIN
20   1  2    0      seed := seed * 27.182813 + 31.415917;
21   1  2   23      seed := seed - trunc(seed);
22   1  2   39      random := trunc(seed*limit) + 1;
23   1  2   52    END; {random}
24   1  2   64
25   1  3    1  PROCEDURE bringoutthepack;
26   1  3    1    var i : cardindex;
27   1  3    2        s : suits;
28   1  3    3        f : faces;
29   1  3    0    BEGIN
30   1  3    0      i := 0;
31   1  3    6      for s := clubs to spades do
32   1  3   17        for f := two to ace do begin
33   1  3   28          i := i+1;
34   1  3   36          pack[i].suit := s;
35   1  3   50          pack[i].face := f;
36   1  3   62        end;
37   1  3   76    END; {bringoutthepack}
38   1  3   92
39   1  4    1  PROCEDURE exchange (var x,y : cards);
40   1  4    3    var temp : cards;
41   1  4    0    BEGIN
42   1  4    0      temp := x;
43   1  4    5      x := y;
44   1  4    9      y := temp;
45   1  4   14    END; {exchange}
46   1  4   26
47   1  5    1  PROCEDURE shuffle;
48   1  5    1    var into, from : cardrange;
49   1  5    3        limit      : cardindex;
50   1  5    0    BEGIN
51   1  5    0      limit := 52;
52   1  5    6      for into := 1 to 52 do begin
53   1  5   23        from := random(limit);
54   1  5   33        exchange (pack[from], pack[limit]);
55   1  5   55        limit := limit-1;
56   1  5   63      end;
57   1  5   70    END; {shuffle}
58   1  5   84
81   1  6  416    {$L+}
82   1  1    0  BEGIN {Main program Shuffling}
83   1  1    0    seed := 1.23456789;
84   1  1   12    bringoutthepack;
85   1  1   14    printpack;
86   1  1   16    shuffle;
```

```
87  1  1  18      printpack;
88  1  1  20      shuffle;
89  1  1  22      printpack;
90  1  1  24   END.
```

2C	3C	4C	5C	6C	7C	8C	9C	10C	JC	QC	KC	AC
2D	3D	4D	5D	6D	7D	8D	9D	10D	JD	QD	KD	AD
2H	3H	4H	5H	6H	7H	8H	9H	10H	JH	QH	KH	AH
2S	3S	4S	5S	6S	7S	8S	9S	10S	JS	QS	KS	AS

8C	7S	AC	4C	4H	3D	9D	4D	6C	3S	10H	5C	2D
QH	6H	2C	AD	JS	10S	KC	2S	JD	KH	2H	7C	QS
8H	6D	6S	3H	3C	8S	10D	5D	9C	JH	10C	7H	4S
KD	JC	AS	AH	5H	QD	5S	9H	8D	QC	7D	9S	KS

7S	8C	JH	KS	6S	KD	2C	QD	7D	4C	10D	9D	9H
4D	4H	3C	2S	7C	4S	AH	AD	8S	6C	8H	KH	9S
JS	3S	9C	KC	JD	10S	7H	QH	AS	10H	JC	10C	2D
5S	3H	5H	QC	8D	6D	3D	AC	5C	6H	2H	5D	QS

Figure 2.1   The shuffling program

2.2   Finding and Keeping—Formal Procedures

Another common requirement is that of finding a given item in a table. In formal terms, we have a table a consisting of n items and we wish to find the index i such that $a_i = x$, where x is the required value. Using the same terminology, the appropriate declarations for such a search are:

```
TYPE range = 1 .. n;
     index  = 0 .. n;

VAR a    : array [range] of thing;
    j    : index;
    x    : thing;
```

The algorithm can be stated as:

```
BEGIN
   i := 0;
   repeat
     i := i + 1;
   until a[i] = x;
END;
```

Notice that the array subscripts range from 1 to the maximum n, but that the index needs to start off outside this range.

32

Interlude—What's in a Name?

In this algorithm we seem not to have adhered to the recommended style of using meaningful variable names. 'Meaningful' is usually taken to mean English words, which would disqualify x, n, and i. However, these are perfectly good names for anyone with even a slight acquaintance with mathematics: x is the unknown, n is the number of things, and i is the index. Because these terms are so common, it would be clumsy to replace them by English phrases just for the sake of it. Often the brevity of the way in which an algorithm is expressed adds to its understanding.

Note, however, that in the picking and choosing algorithm, we have more than one list and several indices. In this case, the mathematical notation must be abandoned because calling things a and b or i, j, and k only leads to confusion. Would a have been the things to choose or the things chosen?

The moral is that, unlike Humpty Dumpty, we cannot use words and have them mean what we want them to mean: the meaning must be clear and unambiguous to everyone.

Dummy Value Terminators

Studying the algorithm, we find that it is fine, provided we are assured that the required thing is definitely in the table. If it is not, the index will eventually exceed n and an execution error will result. One way of ensuring that the algogithm terminates, is to add on a dummy item at the end of the table and to set it to the value that is being searched for. Since it is inconvenient to start talking of $n + 1$ now, we shall add the dummy item on at the zeroth position and scan the table backwards. We now have

```
VAR    a: array [index] of thing;
       i : index;
       x: thing;
```

The algorithm can be stated as:

```
BEGIN
    a[0] := x;
    i := n;
    while a[i] < > x do
        i : = i − 1;
END;
```

While this addition of a dummy item will ensure that the loop terminates, we must consider the consequences for the user of the algorithm. Presumably, having found the item, he will wish to do something with it, update it in some way maybe. It is certainly not meaningful to manipulate an item which was deliberately inserted outside the boundary of the real table, so he would have to make a check to see whether the item was genuinely found or not, i.e.

if i = 0 then . . . .

Loop State Indicators

Although effective, this reliance on a zeroth element is aesthetically unpleasing. It would be much better if the check for the not-found case was obvious, rather than being expressed as an numerical comparison. In other words, we would like the above question to be replaced by

if result = notthere then . . .

The dummy item as a terminator can be replaced by a state indicator which works in parallel with the loop, keeping track as to whether the item is still expected or has been found or the list is exhausted without finding it. For such a state indicator, we use an *enumerated scalar*

VAR state = (searching, found, notthere);

The loop is written thus:

```
i := 1;
state := searching;
repeat
   if x = a[i] then state  := found else
   if i = n   then state    := notthere else
                         i := i + 1;
until state < > searching;
```

Does this loop work on the boundaries? When the table is full and x is the last item, it does, because the actions have been carefully arranged as

Look at the current item
Check imminent overflow.
Move on

In other words, the last item is considered before the check for being on it. However, there is a problem if the table is empty because then the 'current item' does not exist and we certainly can't look at it! One solution would be to phrase the loop

> *Check for empty*
> *Look at current item*
> *Check imminent overflow.*
> *Move on*

It would be inefficient to make a check for empty every time around the loop, since this condition only applies once. Such a check should be put outside the loop, as in

```
i := 1;
state := searching;
if i > n then state := notthere else
repeat
    if x = a[i] then state := found else
    if i = n then state     := notthere else
                    i := i + 1;
until state < > searching;
```

This loop can be regarded as the prototype for a large category of searches. In fact, the only differences that may occur are in the stepping on to the next item (it won't always be a simple $i := i + 1$, as we shall see in the next chapter) and in the order of the conditions. Although neat and powerful, these loops can go wrong on the boundaries if not carefully thought out, and it is best to minimize the chance of an error by sticking to a single pattern. Notice that this pattern avoids increment-ing i beyond its range. As a result, we no longer need the index type as well as the range.

All in all, this solution to the search is twice as long (in lines) as the original attempt but it does not require additional elements for either the list or the index and has the advantage of providing readable information at the end. When the loop is finished, we can ask

```
case state of
    found        : . . . . .
    notthere     : . . . .
end;
```

There are two approaches to the action to be taken when the item is not there. Depending on the reason for searching, notthere could be the successful or the unsuccessful outcome. For example, a computer system always checks your user identifier against a list it has of those who have registered, and if it is not found, then your job fails. On the other hand, when you first register as a user, your chosen identifier is checked against the existing list and only if it is not there is it added. In this case, finding is very closely associated with keeping.

Finally, we give the complete prototype searching algorithm:

```
CONST n = ...;
TYPE range = 1 .. n;

VAR   a       : array [range] of thing;
      i       : range;
      x       : thing;
      state   : (searching, found, notthere);

BEGIN
    Obtain a value for x.
    i := 1;
    state := searching;
    if i > n then state := notthere else
    repeat
       if x = a[i] then state    : = found else
       if i = n    then state    := notthere else
                           i      := i + 1;
    until state < > searching;
    case state of
       found    : ....
       notthere : ....
    end;
END;
```

Counting Frequencies

As an example of this algorithm, let us suppose we wish to count the frequency of words (reserved or otherwise) in a program. Figure 2.2 gives a program to do this, with the procedure to read words omitted for brevity's sake. It starts off with an empty table. As each word is encountered, a search is done. If the word is not there, it is added to the table with a frequency of 1, and n is increased. If the word is found, its corresponding frequency is incremented. So in this example, neither approach is erroneous—they just have different actions.

Looking at such a program, one is immediately tempted to improve it in order to gain more information from the output. Improvements which spring to mind are:

> making upper and lower case the same
> omitting words in strings or comments
> sorting the words into alphabetical or frequency order.

These topics are the subject of future chapters. One important aspect of this program, though, is how it would be adapted to count the frequency of individual letters. Although a searching algorithm could be used for counting letters, a far

36

```
 1   1  1    1 PROGRAM Frequency (input, output);
 2   1  1    3
 3   1  1    3   CONST tablemax   = 100;
 4   1  1    3   TYPE  tablerange = 1..tablemax;
 5   1  1    3         tableindex = 0..tablemax;
 6   1  1    3         natural    = 0..maxint;
 7   1  1    3         alfa       = packed array [1..8] of char;
 8   1  1    3
 9   1  1    3   VAR   words   : array [tablerange] of alfa;
10   1  1  403         counts  : array [tablerange] of natural;
11   1  1  503         n       : tableindex;
12   1  1  504         i       : tablerange;
13   1  1  505         w       : alfa;
14   1  1  509         state   : (searching, found, notthere);
15   1  1  510
33   1  2  196   {$L+}
34   1  1    0   BEGIN {Main Program Frequency}
35   1  1    0     n := 0;
36   1  1    9     WHlLE not eof(input) do begin
37   1  1   20       readword(w);
38   1  1   25       i := 1;
39   1  1   32       state := searching;
40   1  1   36       if i > n then state := notthere else
41   1  1   51
42   1  1   51       repeat
43   1  1   51         if w = words[i] then state := found else
44   1  1   77         if i = n         then state := notthere else
45   1  1   92                          i := i+1;
46   1  1  103       until state <> searching;
47   1  1  110
48   1  1  110       case state of
49   1  1  115         found    : counts[i] := counts[i] + 1;
50   1  1  152         notthere: begin
51   1  1  152                     n := n + 1;
52   1  1  163                     words[n] := w;
53   1  1  180                     counts[n] := 1;
54   1  1  200                   end;
55   1  1  202       end; {case}
56   1  1  214     END; {while}
57   1  1  216
58   1  1  216     writeln('FREQUENCY COUNTS FOR ', n:1, ' WORDS');
59   1  1  287     writeln;
60   1  1  295     i := 1;
61   1  1  302     repeat
62   1  1  302       write(words[i], counts[i]:4,' ':6);
63   1  1  357       if i mod 3 = 0 then writeln;
64   1  1  374       i := i+1;
65   1  1  385     until i > n;
66   1  1  394   END.
```

FREQUENCY COUNTS FOR 51 WORDS

PROGRAM	1	Frequenc	3	input	2
output	1	CONST	1	tablemax	3
TYPE	1	tableran	4	tableind	2
natural	2	maxint	1	alfa	3

packed	1	array	3	of	4
char	1	VAR	1	words	4
counts	5	n	10	i	16
w	4	state	7	searchin	3
found	3	notthere	4	BEGIN	1
Main	2	Program	2	WHILE	1
not	1	eof	1	do	1
begin	2	readword	1	if	4
then	4	else	3	repeat	2
until	2	case	2	end	2
END	2	while	1	writeln	3
FREQUENC	1	COUNTS	1	FOR	1

Figure 2.2   The frequency program

more efficient method is one which recognises that, in Pascal, characters can be used directly as indices for an array. Thus instead of maintaining and searching a table, we go straight to the count we require by indexing the array. The only complication is that we have to be sure as to the exact ordering of the letters, i.e. do the capitals precede the smalls? Assuming that this is the case, we define

TYPE letters = 'A' .. 'z';   {assumes uppers before lowers}

VAR lettercounts : array [letters] of natural;

and the counting process becomes

> *Set all counts to zero*
> **while** *not eof* **do begin**
>   *Get next letter*
>   *lettercounts*[*letter*] := *lettercounts*[*letter*] + 1;
> **end;**

This discussion has only touched on the issue of searching. In Chapter 5, the matter is taken up again and more general and efficient algorithms are developed.

Procedure Parameters

Given a prototype searching algorithm, it is reasonable to investigate whether it could be usefully turned into a procedure. Since the kind of array being searched will have to be the same every time, having a procedure would only be useful if the basis of the search is going to vary. If the array is composed of records containing several different fields, then the simple condition we had of $a[i] = x$ could become more varied and complex. If there are going to be different searches, it would be nice to phrase them thus:

> **if** *thereexists* ({*an*} *i*, {*in*} *a*, {*for*} *n*, {*suchthat*} $a[i] = x$)
> **then** ...
> **else**

Or, as another example,

> **if** *thereis* (*{a} user, {in the} usertable, {of} n {users},*
> *{such that} usertable[user].id = inputcode*)
> **then** *runthejobfor* (*usertable[user]*)
> **else** *writeln* ('*You are not a registered user.*');

Notice how the use of comments to amplify the parameters is very effective.

However, there is a problem. Inside these functions the condition has to be repeatedly evaluated to reflect the new values of the index each time. How can this re-evaluation be requested from a procedure call? The answer is to make the 'such that' parameter into a function. Then whenever the loop encounters the condition, it will call the function and obtain the present state based on the new values of the index. The above examples are therefore properly phrased as

```
FUNCTION match (i : range) : boolean;
   BEGIN
      match := a[i] = x;
   END; {match}

if thereexists ({an} i, {in} a, {for} n,
                {such that there is a} match)
   then . . .
   else . . .
```

and

```
FUNCTION idsmatch (user : userrange) : boolean;
   BEGIN
      idsmatch := usertable[user].id = inputcode;
   END; {idsmatch}

if thereis ({a} user, {in the} usertable, {of} n {users},
            {such that the} idsmatch)
   then runthejobfor (usertable[user])
   else writeln ('You are not a registered user.');
```

(Note that thereexists and hereis are different functions with different parameters, and therefore they have different names.)

To show how these search functions can be used to great advantage, suppose we wish to go through the table of users, blocking any user who has exceeded his budget. To do this, we add another parameter to thereis so that the search can start where it left off, rather than from 1 every time.

```
FUNCTION overbudget (user : userrange) : boolean;
   BEGIN
      with usertable[user] do
      overbudget := usage > budget;
   END; {overbudget}

here := 0;
REPEAT
   if thereis ({another} user, {in the} usertable, {of} n {users},
                  {starting from} here, {who is} overbudget)
   then block (usertable[user])
UNTIL here = n;
```

Here would be a var parameter, which is updated by the search.

Interlude—The Lost Parameter-Passing Mechanism

Although neat enough, it does seem a bit clumsy to have to give these conditions a name and put them in functions which may end up being quite far away from where the search is actually called. It is therefore of historical interest to note that in older programming languages (starting with Algol 60) there was a third kind of parameter-passing mechanism called *call-by-name*. Generalizing over the various languages of the time, the three methods most common were:

call-by-value	a single value enters the procedure.
call-by-reference	a reference enters the procedure, enabling variables outside it to be altered.
call-by-name	an expression enters the procedure and is evaluated each time it is named.

For reasons chiefly connected with efficiency, call-by-name fell into disrepute and was omitted from languages from Pascal onwards. However, the mechanism of repeated evaluation was deemed necessary, and most languages provide for it by means of procedure and function parameters instead.

To complete the picture, Figure 2.3 gives a definition of thereexists which also includes the parameter to start the index from a given point. Notice that because the array is a parameter, it has to be given a type name. Although some Pascal systems permit array types to be defined in parameter lists, this is not correct according to original or standard Pascal.

Notice how packaging the loop up in this function relieves the user of having to refer to the words found or notthere, which after all were part of the searching mechanism and not really part of the problem we were trying to solve.

Before leaving this section, we note that procedure or function parameters have

```
{Definitions needed outside the function thereexists}
CONST n = . . .;
TYPE range = 1. .n;
     index = 0. .n;
     table = array [range] of thing;

FUNCTION thereexists (var i    : range;
                          a     : table;
                          n     : index; {table may be empty}
                          start: range;
                          function condition (i : index) : boolean)
              : boolean;
     VAR state : (searching, found, notthere);
     BEGIN
         i := start;
         state := searching;
         if i > n then state := notthere else
         repeat
             if condition(i) then state := found else
             if i = n        then state := notthere else
                                  i := i + 1;
         until state < > searching;
         case state of
             found    : thereexists := true;
             notthere : thereexists := false;
         end; {case}
     END; {thereexists}
```

Figure 2.3   The general searching function

other uses than that of obtaining repeated evaluation of a parameter. Often they
are used when specifically different actions have to be taken at different calls of a
procedure, examples of which occur later in the book.

2.3   Round and Round—Recursion

Recursion is a means for defining things in terms of themselves. This is not quite
as silly as it sounds, because we arrange that there is always a stopping point. Let
us first look as a simple application of recursion.

The Party Problem

A list of guests is being drawn up for a party and we wish to determine the
number of people who might come as well as the number of invitations to print.
We only need to send one invitation to families or couples, so the two numbers

will be different. Suppose the list looks like this:

    Tom & Pat
    Daphne & Richard
    Allan
    David & Anne & Kathryn
    Matthew
    Lucy
    Nicholas & Valerie

Then the routine to count invitations could be written as

```
PROCEDURE countinvitations;
    VAR people, invitations : integer;
    BEGIN
        people := 0;
        invitations := 0;
        while not endoflist do
            countperson;
            invitations := invitations + 1;
        end;
    END;
```

The routine to count a person is different, because as we have already remarked, it may have to count a family. The way it does this is to add one to the number of people, then to check whether an & follows. If one does, it simply calls itself again. So we have

```
PROCEDURE countperson;
    BEGIN
        people := people + 1;
        if ampersandfollows
            then countperson;
    END;
```

(countperson is, of course, defined inside countinvitations, as it makes use of the people variable.) If we work through the routines together, we see that we need 7 invitations and a possible 12 people might come to the party.

Last-line Recursion

This solution to the party problem is an example of last-line recursion, i.e. the recursive call is on the last line of the procedure. When we come back from such a call, there is nothing more to do, so we 'bubble' right out to the original outside call. If we want to skip one or more spaces when reading into a variable ch, we could write

```
PROCEDURE spaceskipper;
   BEGIN
      if ch = space then begin
         read(ch);
         spaceskipper;
      end;
   END;
```

It is not hard to see that last-line recursion has the property that it can be rewritten iteratively. In other words, instead of the recursive calls, we could have used a common-or-garden loop. Then we would have:

```
PROCEDURE countperson;
   BEGIN
      repeat
         people := people + 1;
      until not ampersandfollowing;
   END;
```

and

```
PROCEDURE spaceskipper;
   BEGIN
      while ch = space do read(ch);
   END;
```

Both versions are perfectly valid and it is really a matter of taste as to which you use.

Last-line recursion with parameters

A slightly more interesting version of last-line recursion includes parameters and uses a function instead of a procedure. Suppose we wish to sum the series:

$$1 + 2 + 3 + \ldots + n$$

Looking at it as

$$n + [(n-1) + [(n-2) + [\ldots [\mp 1] \ldots]]]$$

we see that the sum can be expressed as

either 1
  or *number plus the sum of (number − 1)*

We can write this as a recursive function, i.e.

```
FUNCTION sum (i : integer) : integer;
BEGIN
    if i = 1 then sum := 1
             else sum := i + sum(i - 1);
END;
```

which we could call with, for example, write (sum(10)) or x := sum(n);.

Although sum qualifies as last-line recursion, we notice that there is work to be done on return from a call: the result of the call must be added to i and become the result of the function. If we express sum as an iterative function, then we see that an extra variable is needed. In effect, the recursion was taking care of these subtotals in the background:

```
FUNCTION sum (i : integer) : integer;
    var s : integer;
BEGIN
    s := 0;
    while i > 0 do begin
        s := s + i;
        i := i - 1;
    end;
    sum := s;
END;
```

Once again, both solutions are neat, but the astute reader will know that neither recursion or iteration is necessary to get the answer: Gauss at the age of 6 realized that

$$1 + 2 + 3 + \ldots + n = \frac{n \times (n - 1)}{2}$$

But it was a good example!

Recursion for Real

So recursion is interesting, but is it actually very useful? It certainly is. Once the number of recursive calls written in a procedure or the number of parameters involved increases beyond 1, the recursive solution will be shorter, more elegant, and more easily readable. The difference lies in the information retained by a procedure at the time that it calls itself. When it comes back from the call, that information must be available to it again; in other words, it must resume operation in its original environment.

In the sum routine, the environment consisted of the parameter i and the function value itself. At the first call to sum, i has the value n. Subsequent calls create new values for *i*, but do not destroy previous ones, which must remain in waiting for each addition. Suppose we call sum(4), then after four recursive calls, *i* will be 1 and its previous values will be waiting in the wings like this:

sum	*	*	*	1
i	4	3	2	1

As *i* is 1, sum, does not call itself again but returns a value of 1 to the previous call, giving:

sum	*	*	3
i	4	3	2

Sum and *i* are added and the value returned to the previous incarnation of sum Finally, we have:

sum	6
i	4

and we compute sum = 10 and exit.

The point is that a language that provides recursion does all the work of maintaining the various versions of the environment and correctly reinstating the current values of the variables on each return. To illustrate this power, we consider the following class of problems.

Evaluating All Possibilities

As we saw in Section 2.1, picking and choosing can be done on a random basis. Another requirement might be to choose the next item on the basis of a calculated suitability rating. For example, we can calculate in advance the effect of various feeds on the milk yield of various breeds of cows, and thereby decide which to use at what stage. Here each calculation is independent of the others. A far more complex choosing operation must be undertaken when a calculation proceeds in several steps, and at each stage there may be a response from somewhere that affects the next step. A real example of this process is the simulation of war manoeuvres. It would be very advantageous if one could calculate every possible deployment of the forces available, and for each deployment every possible response by the enemy. Then one could simply look at the final results, choose the best and follow that plan.

Unfortunately, the power of combinatorics prevents us winning a war for sure, even if we could detail every possible response by the enemy. But the idea is sound, and so we follow it up in a more formal field: that of two-person games. Of these, the real classic is chess. Why not get a computer to calculate every move after every move and store this as a blueprint for winning? Once again the sheer number of possibilities is too great: it has been estimated that even on the fastest computer available, a complete chess 'plan' would take thousands of millions of years! So we turn our attention to a more modest game, such as noughts-and-crosses (tic-tac-toe).

Noughts-and-crosses is a simple two-person game with a three-by-three board:

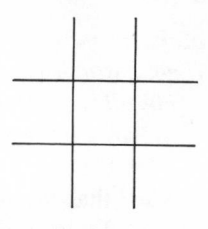

The object is to get three pieces in a row in any direction. After the first move being made in the middle (as is clearly sensible), there are only eight other possible moves, and after that, seven. So the number of possible board configurations is 8! = 40320. Although a large number, this is not impossible for a computer to generate in reasonable time (a matter of minutes, perhaps). Having generated them, we can see which sequence of 9 moves results in a win for X or for O or a draw.

Although noughts-and-crosses serves as an example, we shall proceed to investigate the generation process in general. Going back to the other two more exciting examples—war manoeuvres and chess—we note that similar processes can be used to generate the possibilities down to a certain level. At that point, guesswork or some other calculation based on the human's idea of what is a 'good' configuration take over. Such systems have been designed to great effect and can be studied in books on computer wargames, computer chess, or artificial intelligence.

The States of a Game

A game consists of a board, two players, and the moves that are made in sequence. There is also an outcome: win, lose, or draw. Playing the game can be expressed recursively, as

Play a move for a player:
> *Make the move*
> *Play a move for the other player.*

A recursive algorithm must have a stopping point, and in this case, it is a check for a win straight after making a move, giving

> *Play a move for a player*:
> > *Make the move*
> > *If not a win*
> > > *then Play a move for the other player.*

Now we wanted to play all possible moves at each stage, so the call to play in response must involve a loop. This gives

> *Play a move for a player*:
> > *Make the move*
> > *If not a win then*
> > > *For all possible moves*
> > > *Play a move for the other player.*

Formulating this in Pascal, we see that the move and the player vary and therefore must be parameters. A third parameter is a picture of the board itself, since after completing a game we want to go back to a previous configuration and try out another possible move. Without committing ourselves to the kind of game (and therefore to the actual details of the board or the moves), we get

```
TYPE
      boards = ...      {some representation of the board}
      moves = ...       {appropriate specification of a move}
      players = (A, B);


FUNCTION other(player : players) : players;
   BEGIN
      if player = A then other := B else other := A;
   END;

PROCEDURE play (move : moves; player : players;
                   board : boards);
   BEGIN
      Make the move
      if won
      then
      Record the winning board
      else begin
         player := other(player);
         Find all possible moves;
         For all possible moves
            play (move, player, board);
      end;
   END;
```

The power of recursion is now evident: we can make a move, then go down a particular path, coming back automatically once it is over and picking up from where we left off, only to start down another path. Although this procedure has the essentials, it is usually necessary to add refinements. Certainly one addition would be a check for a draw: without it, a drawn game would cause the procedure to recurse infinitely, each player calling the other and neither having a move to make. This check depends on the game and the board, but would be inserted after the check for a win.

Another improvement is based on the fact that no game is completely exhaustive: even the simple ones have elements of 'good play' which can be used to trim the configurations. For example, if someone is about to win, then the other player must try to block a winning move. In this case, the number of possible moves reduces to one. The improved procedure is

```
PROCEDURE play (move : moves, player : players;
                      board : boards);
    BEGIN
        Make the move {changing the board}
        if won
        then
            Record the winning board
        else
        if stalemate
        then
            Record the stalemate board
        else begin
            player := other(player);
            Find all possible moves;
            Amend possible moves for good play
            For all possible moves
            play (move, player, board);
        end;
    END;
```

To see an example of this procedure in action, we shall first have to consider ways of representing boards. This is the subject of a later section.

Other Recursive Problems

The play procedure was designed to be a general solution to a class of problems. In *Algorithms + Data Structures = Programs*, Wirth develops a similar general solution for finding all possible positions that a moving piece can occupy on a board. He then applies the algorithm to two famous chess problems: the Knight's Tour (find a path for a knight such that it visits every square once and only once) and the Eight Queens (put eight queens on a board so that none can capture any other). Both his solution and ours are unusual in their generality—most examples of recursion choose very specific examples. These examples form part of our folklore and if you have not encountered recursion before, you should study some of them. The classics are the Towers of Hanoi and the Calculator.

Our first example, the party problem, introduced recursion nicely because the data we were dealing with was recursive. In Chapter 6, more examples of recursive data are covered, and the appropriate algorithms developed.

2.4   In and Out—Set Manipulation

Since the introduction of 'new maths' in the 1960s, the function and operation of sets has become commonplace. Pascal is the only high-level language which directly provides for sets and set operations. The basics of sets were given in Section 1.2, but a more detailed study is warranted.

Sets and Set Membership

By far and away the most common use of sets is establishing whether an element is a member of a set. Without any preceding declarations, we can use *anonymous sets* very effectively for this purpose, as in:

```
if month in [sept, april, june, nov] then days := 30;

borderlinecase := mark in [49, 59, 69, 74];

isadigit := ch in ['0' . . '9'];
```

If the sets are to be used more often, or manipulated in any way, then we should define the set type and set variables of that type. Following through, this becomes a four-stage process.

1. Define the base type

```
TYPE months = (jan, feb, march, april, may, june, july,
                    aug, sept, oct, nov, dec);
       marks = 0. .100;
   {char is predefined}
```

2. Define the set type

```
TYPE    monthset = set of months;
        markset = set of marks;
        charset = set of char;
```

3. Declare set variables

```
VAR    allmonths, months30 : monthset;
       classes, borders     : markset;
       digits, letters      : charset;
```

4. Initialize the sets

```
    allmonths := [jan. .dec];
    months30 := [sept, april, june, nov];
      classes := [50, 60, 70, 75];
      borders := [49, 59, 69, 74];
       digits := ['0'. .'9'];
      letters := ['a'. .'z', 'A'. .'Z'];
```

An easy (and frequent) mistake is to assume that once a set has been declared, it then has all possible elements in it, or has no elements at all. This is definitely not the case: a set only has the potential for all elements. As with any other kind of variable, it is a golden rule that:

> Any set variable
> must be initialized.

Set Manipulation

The four set operations can be listed dryly as

- `+`   set union
- `*`   set intersection
- `−`   set difference
- `<=`   set inclusion

Here we show how they are actually used in typical cases.

1. Creating sets from sets

Frequently, a large set has disjoint subsets, which can be formed by set difference. For example, we can declare and initialize.

```
    VAR    months31 : monthset;

    months31 := allmonths − months30 − [feb];
```

(This is exactly what the traditional rhyme does, i.e. '. . . All the rest have thirty-one, excepting February alone . . .'). Notice that the set operations work on sets and it would have been incorrect to say −feb instead of −[feb].

2. Creating sets from data

The elements of a set cannot always be fixed as constants in the program. For example, not all schools and universities have the class borders for marks as given earlier. To create the set dynamically, we initialize it to the empty set and use set union:

```
classes := [ ]; borders := [ ];

for i := 1 to 4 do begin
   read (mark);
   classes ; classes + [mark];
   borders := borders + [mark–1];
end;
```

3. Printing a set

A set is not a simple type; it is a structure created from simple types. As such, it cannot be printed using the Pascal write statement. To print all the elements present in a set, we have to loop through the whole base type and use set membership. For example,

```
for mark := 0 to 100 do if mark in classes then
   write (mark);
```

(We deliberately put the if on the same line as the for because they form one construct in this case.) In fact, to perform any operation on all elements of the set, we need a for-and-if loop.

4. Cardinality of a set

Sometimes it is useful to know how many elements are in a set, i.e. its cardinality. To find this, we have to loop once again through all possible elements and use set membership. In general, such a function is defined as

```
FUNCTION cardinality (s : someset) : somerange;
   VAR i, count : somerange;
   BEGIN
      count := 0;
      for i := 0 to somemax do if i in s then
         count := count + 1;
      cardinality := count;
   END;
```

(In some Pascal systems, this function is predefined and is called *card*.)

Noughts and Crosses

To see how sets can be used to great effect, we return to the noughts-and-crosses problem. To actually implement the algorithm for playing all games, we have to set up the representation of the board and the moves. First we note that the positions on the board can be numbered as:

1	2	3
8	9	4
7	6	5

A move can therefore be defined as a number:

```
TYPE moves = 1..9;
```

Each position can have one of three states: empty, nought, or cross. So we define

```
status = (nought,cross,empty);
```

and the players are a subrange of this type, i.e.

```
players = nought..cross;
```

Now for the board. One is tempted to immediately choose an array such as

```
VAR board : array[moves] of status;
```

and indeed this would adequately describe any configuration. However, we should first look more closely at the functions that will use the board. The most complex will be deciding on a win, and calculating whether it is necessary to block an imminent win by the other player. Both operations require a knowledge of the position of each player's pieces distinct from the other's and the empties. We could keep three more boards for this purpose, but instead we define a board configuration as a set, and then keep only the three distinct boards. The complete board can be obtained from their union. This gives

```
TYPE    configuration = set of moves;
        boards        = array [status] of configuration.
```

The initial board is

```
VAR initialboard : boards;

initialboard[empty] := [1..9];
initialboard[cross] := [ ];
initialboard[nought] := [ ];
```

With these definitions, we can declare the header of the play procedure as

```
PROCEDURE play (player : players;
                board  : boards;
                move   : moves);
```

and set up the initial call with X moving first into the centre as

```
play (cross, initialboard, 9);
```

The routines that have to be written are

making a move
checking for a win
adjusting the possible moves for good play.

The first uses simple set union and difference:

```
PROCEDURE placeit;
  BEGIN
    board[player] := board[player] + [move];
    board[empty] := board[empty] – [move];
  END;
```

Deciding on a win needs more thought. It is necessary to know what a win is, and this can either be done by programming a check for three-in-a-row, or by setting up beforehand a list of all possible winning configurations. As there are only eight of these, a list will be the simplest and most efficient. This gives

```
lines : array[winrange] of configurations;
```

and the appropriate set assignments can be made. Now the winning function can search through each of these, seeing whether it is included in the set of moves already made by a player. The nub of the routine uses set inclusion:

```
if lines[w] ⇐ board[player] then state := found
```

The routine which decides whether to block an imminent win uses a more complex set expression. For each winning line, we need to know if two positions have already been occupied by the player and if the third one is empty. (This last is important, because as the game progresses, there may be several two-in-a-row patterns with the third already blocked by the other player.) This is expressed as

```
VAR inline, needed : configurations;
```

```
inline := lines[w] * board[other(player)];
needed := lines[w] – inline;
if (card(inline) = 2) and ((needed * board[empty]) < > [ ])
then state := mustblock
```

To illustrate the process described in these four lines, consider the board

O	X	X
1	2	3
8	X 9	4
7	O 6	5

when nought has to move. When we get to the line [3, 7, 9] we have

$$inline = [3, 7, 9] * [2, 3, 9] = [3, 9]$$
$$needed = [3, 7, 9] - [3, 9] = [7]$$

$card(inline) = 2$ and [7] is in [4, 5, 7, 8].

Therefore, nought must block in position 7. At each round, the set of playable positions starts off as *board[empty]*, i.e. all the empty places. If a block is necessary, then we set

$$playable := needed;$$

Symmetry

One further modification is necessary before we can run the complete program for all games of noughts and crosses. We calculated earlier that there would be 40 320 different games. Yet many of these will be identical because of symmetry. For example, given the board

1	O 2	3
8	X 9	4
7	6	5

moves into squares 4 or 8 will produce boards that are the same, reflected on the horizontal axis. Similarly, 1 and 3 will give vertically reflected boards. Rotation is another form of symmetry, so that in

```
 1 | 2 | 3
   | X |
 8 | 9 | 4
   |   |
 7 | 6 | 5
```

we can detect that only 1 and 2 are unique moves. We can also check for rotation in an anti-clockwise direction, which would establish that in

```
 O
 1 | 2 | 3
   | X |
 8 | 9 | 4
   |   |
 7 | 6 | 5
```

moves into 2 and 8 will produce equivalent boards.

In order to check for these symmetries, we have to compare a board with its 'tilted' equivalent. This means that we need to access each position on the board and know whether it is empty, a nought, or a cross. We now realize that we cannot do this with sets. Sets are unordered structures: the elements are simply *in* them, and we cannot find the value of a given position. This is the function of an array. Therefore, for the symmetry procedures, we create an array representation of the board.

Calculating the tilt for a position depends on the kind of symmetry. For the reflections, there is no relationship between the position numbers, and so the only way is to program in each reflection using a case statement. The rotations, however, are based on adding 2, 4, or 6 to the position, and then taking the modulus of 8. Expressed in Pascal, we have

```
t := (m* kind) mod 8;
if t = 0 then tilt := 8
         else tilt := t;
```

(Verify for yourself that the if–then–else is necessary to get the correct result.)

The procedure to determine symmetries is given in the full listing of noughts-and-crosses in Figure 2.4. The reader should study it carefully and understand how it works. There is a full Comprehension on it later.

Restrictions on Sets

We have already mentioned that sets can only contain scalar elements. The reason for this is that sets are seen at the machine level as strings of bits, each bit representing the ordinal value of an element. Thus the set

[sept, april, june, nov]

would be the bit string

0	1	2	3	4	5	6	7	8	9	10	11
0	0	0	1	0	1	0	0	1	0	1	0

Because each scalar value has an ordinal value, this suffices to locate the associated bit. However, there is no ordinal ordering for reals or strings and so a set of, say,

'*Update*', '*Save*', '*Receive*'

cannot be implemented in the same way. To achieve the effect of a set and of set membership, we will have to store the strings in an array and use a search (such as the procedure thereexists) to find an item.

The above restriction is a fairly reasonable one, and is a rule of the language. There is another restriction on sets which is not part of the language but which is introduced by the implementors of each compiler. Each implementation has an upper limit on the ordinal value that a set can handle. On some systems, this is large enough not to feature as a limitation (4095 is a popular choice) but on many of the older systems, the limit is quite small. Specifically, it could be 64 or even 48. In both these cases the real problem is that a set of characters cannot be declared. More seriously, one cannot even create a set of letters. Even though there are only 52 (or 26) possible letters, their ordinal values depend on the underlying character-collating sequence which will be ASCII or EBCDIC or some derived code. In all of these, the ordinal value of '*Z*' exceeds 64.

Mapped Characters

If one is faced with a restrictive set limit, it is worth considering the technique of mapped characters. We set up an enumerated scalar to contain the names of all the characters that the program really needs to use: these will surely number fewer than 64. Then for input, we use a special readch routine which transforms a normal character into a mapped one. Thereafter the program deals only with mapped characters, and sets are possible. On output, the mapped characters are 'unmapped' back to the real-world versions. For example, typical declarations and mapping function might be:

```
TYPE mappedchars = (null, space, stop, comma, quote, exclamation,
                    question, dash, left, right,
                    ach, bch, cch, dch, ech, . . ., zch);
```

```
FUNCTION map (ch : char) : mappedchars;
  BEGIN
     if ch in ['A' .. 'Z'] then
        map := map(chr(ord(ch) – ord ('A') + ord('a')));
     case ch of
        ' ' : map := space; '.' : map := stop;
        ',' : map := comma; '!' : map := exclamation;
        ',,' : map := quote; '?' : map := question;
        '–' : map := dash; '(' : map := left;
        ')' : map := right;
        'a' : map := ach; 'b' : map := bch;
        . . . . . . .
        'y' : map := ych; 'z' : map := zch;
     end;
  END;
```

Notice the nice and natural use of recursion in handling the upper-case letters via the lower-case ones!

That ends our chapter on the more advanced features of Pascal. We hope that readers will be encouraged to recognize places where they can be used and to enrich their programs thereby.

2.5   Comprehension—Enumerating all States

An attempt at a program to calculate all different noughts-and-crosses games is listed in Figure 2.4. The 240 lines are well written and should do the job, but there are problems: the answers do not seem quite right and the output is very difficult to read. The purpose of this comprehension is to correct and improve the program, thereby enhancing your knowledge of recursion and sets.

Read the program through once, marking (in coloured pen) the important procedures and actions. Work through the first game generated by the program, taking care to understand the workings of the adjust and removesymmetries procedures. Now answer the questions.

Mistakes

The output does not look right. Intuitively we feel that 413 different games is too many. Moreover, the twelve listed have duplicates (2 and 5, 4 and 7).

1. Do you feel these two problems are connected? If so, how?
2. Errors can creep in on two levels—minor mistakes and incorrect logic. Check the various constants and preset data for correctness. (There is one such blatant mistake.)
3. The adjusting for good play looks at whether the other player might win, and blocks. Is this sufficient?

UCSD Pascal Compiler at Wits University

```
 1   1  1    1 PROGRAM noughtsandcrossses;
 2   1  1    3   CONST centre = 9;
 3   1  1    3   TYPE
 4   1  1    3       moves         = 1..9;
 5   1  1    3       moveindex     = 0..9;
 6   1  1    3       status        = (nought,cross,empty);
 7   1  1    3       players       = nought..cross;
 8   1  1    3       winrange      = 1..8;
 9   1  1    3       configurations = set of moves;
10   1  1    3       boards        = array [status] of configurations;
11   1  1    3       counts        = 0..maxint;
12   1  1    3
13   1  1    3   VAR lines         : array [winrange] of configurations;
14   1  1   11       initialboard  : boards;
15   1  1   14       wins          : array[status] of counts;
16   1  1   17
17   1  2    3 FUNCTION other(player : players) : players;
18   1  2    0   BEGIN
19   1  2    0     if player = nought then other := cross
20   1  2    5                        else other := nought;
21   1  2   19   END;
22   1  2   32
23   1  3    1 PROCEDURE play (player : players;
24   1  3    2                 board  : boards;
25   1  3    3                 move : moves);
26   1  3    7
27   1  3    7   VAR playable : configurations;
28   1  3    8
29   1  4    3   FUNCTION card (aset : configuration) : moveindex;
30   1  4    4     var m : moves;
31   1  4    5         c : moveindex;
32   1  4    0     BEGIN
33   1  4    0       c := 0;
34   1  4    6       for m := 1 to 9 do
35   1  4   23         if m in aset then c := c+1;
36   1  4   44       card := c;
37   1  4   50     END;
38   1  4   64
39   1  5    1   PROCEDURE placeit;
40   1  5    0     BEGIN
41   1  5    0       board[player] := board[player] + [move];
42   1  5   32       board[empty] := board[empty] - [move];
43   1  5   60     END;
44   1  5   72
45   1  6    3   FUNCTION won  : boolean;
46   1  6    3   VAR w : winrange;
47   1  6    4       state : (searching, found, notyet);
48   1  6    0     BEGIN
49   1  6    0       w:=1;
50   1  6    6       state := searching;
51   1  6    9       repeat
52   1  6    9         if lines[w] <= board[player] then state := found else
53   1  6   43         if w=8                       then state := notyet else
54   1  6   53         w := w+1;
55   1  6   61       until state <> searching;
56   1  6   66       won := state = found;
57   1  6   71     END;
58   1  6   86
59   1  7    1   PROCEDURE adjust;
60   1  7    1     var w : winrange;
61   1  7    2         inline, needed : configurations;
62   1  7    4         state : (searching, mustblock, clear);
63   1  7    0     BEGIN
64   1  7    0       w := 1;
65   1  7    6       state := searching;
66   1  7    9       repeat
```

```
 67   1   7    9       inline := lines[w] * board[other(player)];
 68   1   7   46       needed := lines[w] - inline;
 69   1   7   65       if (card(inline) = 2) and ((needed * board[empty]) <> [])
 70   1   7   92       then state := mustblock else
 71   1   7  100       if w = 8 then state := clear else
 72   1   7  110       w := w+1;
 73   1   7  118     until state <> searching;
 74   1   7  123     if state = mustblock then
 75   1   7  128       playable := needed;
 76   1   7  135   END;
 77   1   7  150

 78   1   8    1   PROCEDURE removesymmetries;
 79   1   8    1     CONST symmmax = 6;
 80   1   8    1     TYPE symmetries = 1..symmmax;
 81   1   8    1     VAR symm : symmetries;
 82   1   8    2         trial, m, i : moves;
 83   1   8    5         tryboard, flatboard : array[moves] of status;
 84   1   8   23         canimprove : boolean;
 85   1   8   24

 86   1   9    3     FUNCTION tilt (m : moves; kind : symmetries) : moves;
 87   1   9    5       VAR t : moveindex;
 88   1   9    0       BEGIN
 89   1   9    0         case kind of
 90   1   9    3         1,2,3 : begin {rotations}
 91   1   9    3                   t := (m + kind*2) mod 8;
 92   1   9   15                   if t = 0 then tilt := 8
 93   1   9   20                              else tilt := t;
 94   1   9   34                 end;
 95   1   9   36         4     : {vertical reflection}
 96   1   9   36                 case m of
 97   1   9   39                 1 : tilt := 3;   3 : tilt := 1;
 98   1   9   55                 8 : tilt := 4;   4 : tilt := 8;
 99   1   9   71                 7 : tilt := 5;   5 : tilt := 7;
100   1   9   87                 2,6 : tilt := m;
101   1   9   95                 end;
102   1   9  120         5     : {horizontal reflections}
103   1   9  120                 case m of
104   1   9  123                 1 : tilt := 7;   7 : tilt := 1;
105   1   9  139                 2 : tilt := 6;   6 : tilt := 2;
106   1   9  155                 3 : tilt := 5;   5 : tilt := 3;
107   1   9  171                 8,4 : tilt := m;
108   1   9  179                 end;
109   1   9  204         6     : begin {reverse}
110   1   9  204                   t := 10-m;
111   1   9  212                   if t = 9 then tilt := 1
112   1   9  217                              else tilt := t;
113   1   9  231                 end;
114   1   9  233         end;
115   1   9  252       END;
116   1   9  268

117   1   8    0     BEGIN
118   1   8    0       if card(playable)>1 then begin
119   1   8   14         for i:= 1 to 9 do
120   1   8   32           if i in board[cross] then flatboard[i] := cross else
121   1   8   61           if i in board[nought] then flatboard[i] := nought
122   1   8   86                              else flatboard[i] := empty;
123   1   8  109         for m := 1 to 8 do if m in playable then begin
124   1   8  135           tryboard := flatboard;
125   1   8  141           flatboard[m] := player;
126   1   8  155           for symm := 1 to symmmax do begin
127   1   8  173             trial := tilt(m,symm);
128   1   8  190             if trial in (playable-[m]) then begin
129   1   8  201               tryboard[trial] := player;
130   1   8  215               canimprove := true;
131   1   8  218               for i := 1 to 8 do
132   1   8  236                 if flatboard[i] <> tryboard[tilt(i,symm)]
133   1   8  268                 then canimprove := false;
134   1   8  282               if canimprove then
135   1   8  286                 playable := playable - [trial];
```

```
136   1   8   298            tryboard[trial] := empty;
137   1   8   310          end;
138   1   8   310        end;
139   1   8   317        flatboard[m] := empty;
140   1   8   329      end;
141   1   8   336    end;
142   1   8   336    END;
143   1   8   364

144   1  10     1    PROCEDURE printboard;
145   1  10     1    VAR m : moves;
146   1  10     0    BEGIN
147   1  10     0      for m := 1 to 9 do
148   1  10    17        if m in board[nought] then write(´  O  ´) else
149   1  10    50        if m in board[cross]  then write(´  X  ´) else
150   1  10    83                                    write(´     ´);
151   1  10   106    END;
152   1  10   120

153   1   3     0    BEGIN
154   1   3     0      placeit;
155   1   3     7      if won then begin
156   1   3    13        printboard;
157   1   3    15        writeln(´ win at ´,move:1);
158   1   3    53        wins[player] := wins[player] + 1;
159   1   3    78      end else
160   1   3    80      if board[empty] = [] then begin
161   1   3    95        wins[empty] := wins[empty] + 1
162   1   3   112      end else begin
163   1   3   122        player := other(player);
164   1   3   135        playable := board[empty];
165   1   3   149        adjust;
166   1   3   151        removesymmetries;
167   1   3   153        for move := 1 to 9 do if move in playable then
168   1   3   176          play (player, board, move);
169   1   3   195      end;
170   1   3   195    END;
171   1   3   210

172   1   1     0    BEGIN
173   1   1     0      lines[1] := [1,2,3];   lines[2] := [3,4,5];
174   1   1    33      lines[3] := [5,6,7];   lines[4] := [7,8,1];
175   1   1    67      lines[5] := [2,9,6];   lines[6] := [8,9,4];
176   1   1   101      lines[7] := [1,9,5];   lines[8] := [5,4,3];
177   1   1   133

178   1   1   133      initialboard[nought] := [];  initialboard[cross] := [];
179   1   1   157      initialboard[empty] := [1,2,3,4,5,6,7,8,9];
180   1   1   172

181   1   1   172      wins[nought] := 0;  wins[cross] := 0; wins[empty] := 0;
182   1   1   217      play (cross, initialboard, centre);
183   1   1   229      writeln(´Nought wins ´,wins[nought]:1,
184   1   1   271              ´  Cross wins ´,wins[cross]:1,
185   1   1   314              ´  Draws ´,wins[empty]:1);
186   1   1   360
187   1   1   360    END.
```

```
0   0   X   X   0           X   X   win at 8
0   0   X   X   0   0   X   X   X   win at 8
0   0   X   0   X   X   X   0   X   win at 6
0   X   X   0   0   X   X   0   X   win at 2
0   0   X   0   0   X   X   X   X   win at 8
0   0   X   0   X   X   X   0   X   win at 6
0   X   X   0   0   X   X   0   X   win at 2
X   0   0   X   X           0   X   win at 1
X   0   X   X   0   X   0   0   X   win at 1
X   0   X   0   X   X   0   0   X   win at 1
X   0           0   X   X   0           win at 1
X   0   0   0   X   X   0   X   X   win at 5
Nought wins 0  Cross wins 12  Draws 401
```

Figure 2.4   The noughts-and-crosses program

Make any changes to the program to correct the errors, and run the program if possible.

Improvements

1. Is it actually possible to eliminate all duplicate games by means of good play and removing symmetries? If not, how would you keep a list of all games that could be checked at each final move? At what level must the list be defined? Will the recursion cause difficulties?
2. The output of each game does not give an indication of the sequence of moves—it may even be that two identical outcomes result from a different sequence of moves. Devise a means of recording and printing the move sequence for each game. Would sets or arrays be more appropriate, and why? At what level must the moves be recorded? How will the recursion affect your choice?
3. The purpose of this program was to provide a blueprint of how to play the game optimally. Does this justify a proper printing of the board at each move? If you think so, alter printboard accordingly.
4. It is still possible that not all the 'good play' factors have been incorporated. Examine the output of the revised program and determine whether adjust needs to be augmented.

Chapter 3

Data Structures (Part 1)—Linear Lists

In our first examples, we concentrated on getting the algorithm right and were not too concerned about how we stored the data. Arrays seemed to be the natural choice, but why was this so? The answer is partly historical—all languages since the 1950s have had arrays and therefore people were most at home with them. In this chapter we look at other more flexible data structures and examine the properties that will help us decide on the right tool for the job.

3.1 Dynamic Variables

We shall introduce the new data structures by presenting two posers.

Poser 1. Caesar's Speeches

Computers are not only used for scientific and commercial uses; the arts get a look in, too. It did not take language scholars long to discover how useful a computer could be in reducing the drudgery associated with analysing great works of literature. The use of computers in comparative linguistics, as it is called, was initially confined to counting the frequencies of words and constructing concordances—the huge indices used by preachers and biblical scholars for finding every occurrence of every word in the Bible. These days, computer programs are being written which can analyse phraseology and style and can make comparisons of passages, from which scholars can deduce the date of a work, or even the author.

Taking Shakespeare, how would we represent a single speech by, say, Julius Caesar? Since a speech is composed of lines, we could try

    TYPE   speeches = array [1. .n1] of lines.

This looks fine, and we could even extend it to

    scenes = array [1. .n2] of speeches;
    acts = array [1. .n3] of scenes.

But what are the values of n1, n2, and n3? Speeches can vary from one line to sixty or more. We cannot choose an average $n1$, because this will not be big enough for the exceptionally long speeches, yet by making $n1$ large enough for these, an enormous amount of space will be wasted with short speeches such as occur in dialogue. Similarly, scenes and acts vary greatly in length and the average will seldom be correct.

> A man with his head in the oven
> and his feet in the fridge
> is, on average, perfectly comfortable.

We need a way of storing variable-sized speeches and the array is not good enough.

Poser 2. The Poet's Friend

Every computer system these days has a text editor which is used for making changes to programs that have been stored in files. Such editors are also being used increasingly for preparing text such as reports, theses, write-ups, letters, and even poetry. Picture a poet at a terminal with the following immortal lines typed in:

1 On either side the river lie
2 Long fields of oats that meet the sky
3 And through the fields a road runs by
4 To many-towered Camelot.

It's not quite right is it? Suppose we had represented the poem as an array of lines. Replacing the line by two others means moving the rest of the lines down. This would give:

(was 1) 1 On either side the river lie
          2 Long fields of barley and of rye
          3 That clothe the world and meet the sky
(was 3) 4 And through the field a road runs by
(was 4) 5 To many-towered Camelot.

Apart from the inefficiency of all the moving, this method disturbs the position of the lines; line 4 is no longer at position 4 and if we ask to delete it, we would have to distinguish between the old and new. And, of course, we might run into the first problem, that the array might not be big enough for all the lines.

> 'Neither do men put new wine into old bottles; else the bottles break, and the wine runneth out, and the bottles perish.'
>
> (Matt 9: 17)

Finally, this shifting around is not at all what the poet would have done in the old days—he would probably make liberal use of arrows and lines as follows:

> On either side the river lie
> Long fields of ~~oats that meet the sky~~   barley and of rye
> And through the fields a road runs by   { That clothe the world
> To many-towered Camelot.   { and meet the sky

This time the array has failed us because it is not elastic.

Properties of Data Structures

Let us summarize the properties of an array, as we have discussed them in the above two posers.

> An array is of fixed size
> New items can only replace existing ones
> Unwanted items must be blanked out.

What we need is an alternative data structure with more flexible properties. We shall call it a *list* and specify its properties as follows:

> A list is of variable size
> New items can be squeezed in anywhere
> Unwanted items can be removed and the list contracts

We can see immediately that to achieve such elasticity, the items in a list must be free and independent, yet connected in some way. This is achieved by means of nodes and links.

Nodes and Links

A *node* is an item in a list which carries a *link* around with it. This link indicates the next node in the list.

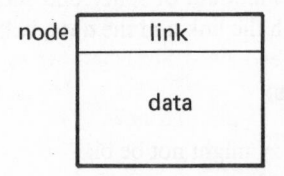

The first node in a list is pointed to by a link which stands alone; let us call it *front*. At the other end, the value of the last link, which points nowhere, is called *nil*.

front

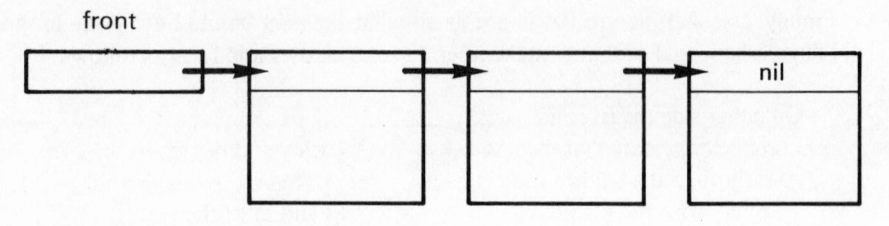

In Pascal, a node is defined as

```
TYPE    nodes = record
                   link : tonodes;
                   data : whatever;
                end;
```

where

```
tonodes = ↑nodes.
```

The arrow sign (which is sometimes written as a 'hat' (^) or 'at' (@)) is the pointer symbol and indicates that variables of type tonodes are pointers to nodes.

To create a list, we first declare a front pointer:

```
VAR front : tonodes.
```

Then each node is created on demand. The full creation of a node involves three steps:

1. Get space for a node.
2. Put the data into it.
3. Forge a link with the list.

The first two steps are common to all lists; the last depends on exactly where in the list the new node is to go. So we shall clear up 1 and 2 here and then discuss variations for 3 in the following sections.

Space for a node is obtained by sending a pointer to the standard procedure *new*. New looks at the type of the pointer and from this deduces the size of the node required. It supplies this amount of space and sets the pointer to point to it. The contents of the node, both the link and the data, will be undefined:

```
VAR    temp : tonodes;

new (temp);
```

We immediately follow the new with step 2, which copies data into the node and initializes the link to nil. (The link may be immediately set to something else in step 3, but it's best to be safe.)

```
read (temp↑.data);
temp↑.link := nil.
```

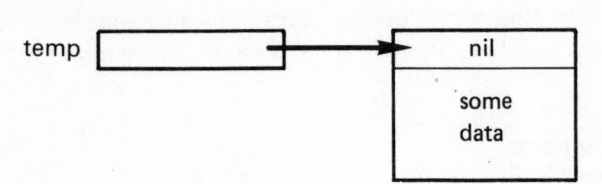

Notice that the expression temp↑.data (or temp↑.link) mirrors exactly what happens: go to temp, follow the arrow to the node it is pointing to, and then find the data field.

3.2 Stacks—The Simplest Lists

Adding a Node

Having created a node, we need to add it to the list. This is going to involve referring to existing links by name and so far there is only one that has a name—front. All the other links are named after front as in front↑.link (the link in the first node) and front↑.link↑.link (the link in the second node). So the simplest position for adding on is going to be at the front of the list.

Interlude—Names of links and nodes

It is best to get this idea of names absolutely clear. This diagram shows the *names of the links* in the list, i.e. the name of the topmost field of each node.

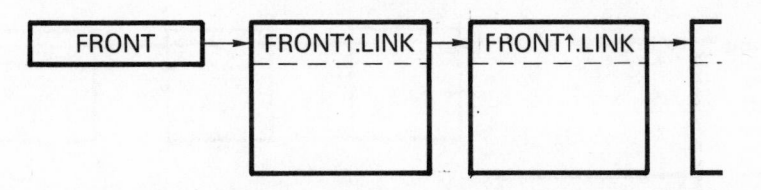

On the other hand, each link points to a node and as such is the name of that node. This diagram gives the names of the *nodes* in the list.

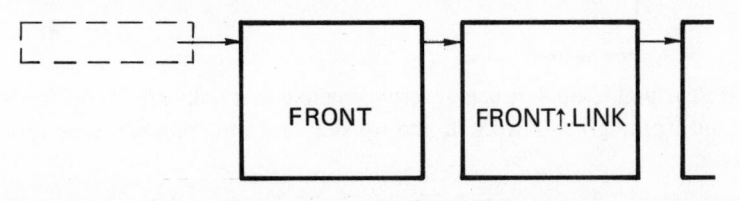

The distinction is worth making and we shall use it to explain the more complicated link-forging algorithms that occur in later sections.

Pictorially, we see that the link from front to the first node has to be broken in two and replaced by two new links from front to the new node and from the new node to the first node. Now we see that the name of the first node is front, and so we construct the link to it first, before altering its name. The sequence to forge the link is therefore

    temp↑.link := front;
    front := temp.

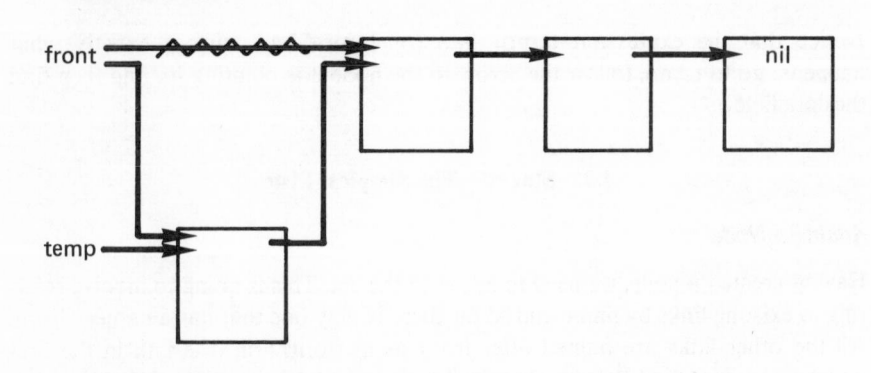

If we had instead said

    front := temp;
    temp↑.link := front

we would have landed up with

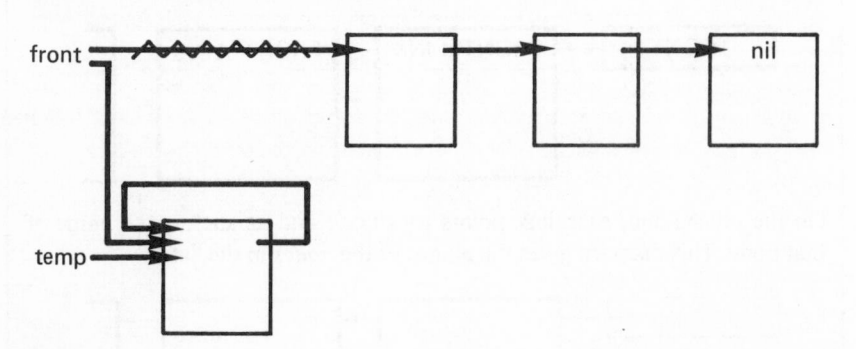

which is clearly nonsense. It is a general principle that links are forged starting at the list and working away from it, and we shall have to continue to be careful to get this right.

Boundary Conditions

A second point of concern is the boundaries of the list. What happens when front or front↑.link or any other link mentioned in a sequence is nil? Well, there is no problem if we are assigning it to something else, nor if it is being replaced by something else. Thus in the case where there is no list and front starts off as nil, the add on sequence still works:

    temp↑.link {which was nil} := front {still nil};
    front   {which was nil} := temp {starting the list}.

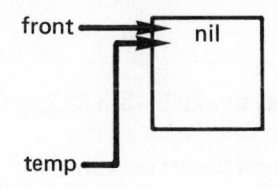

Removing a Node

To remove the node at the front and give it back to temp, we have to reverse the process and replace two links by one:

    temp := front;
    front := temp↑.link;

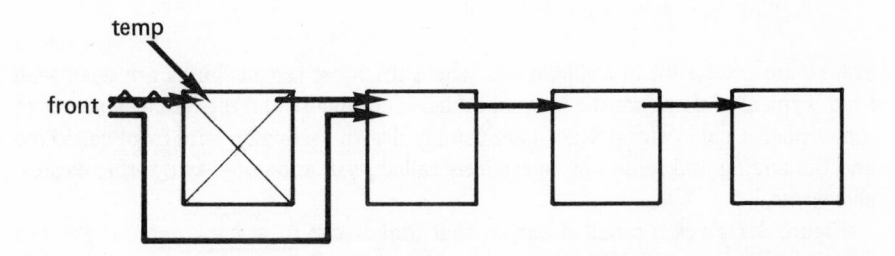

The question arises as to what we want to do with the node once it has been removed. In some cases, it will contain information which will be handled elsewhere in the program, but in others it will simply be thrown away. To do this, we give it to a system procedure called *dispose* which will enable the space to be re-used. (Other possibilities for re-using nodes are explored later in Section 3.5.) The sequence in full is therefore

    temp := front;
    front := temp↑.link;
    dispose (temp);   {if required}

Checking the boundaries again, we see that the kind of expression that can cause trouble is a relative name when the 'head of the family' does not exist. If front itself is nil, then the name front↑.link is meaningless and will have to be avoided. Clearly an attempt to remove a node from an empty list should be an error. In computing, this is called an *underflow* error. The sequence therefore becomes

```
if front = nil then Signal an underflow error
else begin
    temp := front;
    front := front↑.link;
    dispose (front);
end;
```

In summary, the two points to watch when forging links are:

Order. Always work from the list outwards.
Nil. Protect any $p↑.f$ accesses where p could be *nil*.

Properties of a Stack

The kind of list we've developed here is the very simplest example and is called a *stack*. The properties of a stack are:

One named pointer, the front
Adding and removing at the front.

Stacks are used a lot in applications where the most recent things are dealt with first. Typical of these are the symbol tables in compilers and the memory stacks of many pocket calculators. Stacks are usually drawn vertically, with front called *top* and the adding and removing operations called *push* and *pop*—two rather expressive terms.

Figure 3.1 gives a small program that makes use of a stack such as the one found in pocket calculators. The input is in postfix notation with single-digit operands and the four usual operators. The important point to note is that all the details of the stack are kept within the three stack operations, push, pop, and startstack. The main program is then quite simple. Also note that the main program knows nothing of nodes or links and has only to send the data to the stack operations.

The program in Figure 3.1 is, of course, not a real program, but it is a typical example of the test programs one writes when checking that a new idea is well understood. Such test programs perform a useful function and should not be despised. The trick is not to clutter them up with extraneous detail, and we can see that this was neatly done by making fairly severe restrictions on input.

3.3   Queues—Caesar's Speeches

Having established a means by which we can get as many or as few nodes as required, we can now reconsider the problem of storing Caesar's speeches. The

UCSD Pascal Compiler at Wits University

```
 1   1  1    1 PROGRAM Teststacks (input, output);
 2   1  1    3
 3   1  1    3 TYPE tonodes = ^nodes;
 4   1  1    3      nodes   = record
 5   1  1    3                     link : tonodes;
 6   1  1    3                     data : integer;
 7   1  1    3                  end;
 8   1  1    3
 9   1  1    3 VAR  top     : tonodes;
10   1  1    4      value, answer,
11   1  1    4      lhs, rhs: integer;
12   1  1    8      ch      : char;
13   1  1    9
14   1  2    1 PROCEDURE startstack;
15   1  2    0   BEGIN
16   1  2    0     top := nil;
17   1  2    3   END; {startstack}
18   1  2   16
19   1  3    1 PROCEDURE push (thisvalue : integer);
20   1  3    2   VAR temp : tonodes;
21   1  3    0   BEGIN
22   1  3    0     new(temp);
23   1  3    5     temp^.data := thisvalue;
24   1  3   10     temp^.link := top;
25   1  3   13           top := temp;
26   1  3   16   END; {push}
27   1  3   28
28   1  4    1 PROCEDURE pop (var thisvalue : integer);
29   1  4    2   VAR temp : tonodes;
30   1  4    0   BEGIN
31   1  4    0     if top = nil then begin
32   1  4    5       thisvalue := 0;
33   1  4    8       write ('[underflow]');
34   1  4   31     end else begin
35   1  4   33       temp := top;
36   1  4   36       top := top^.link;
37   1  4   40       thisvalue := temp^.data;
38   1  4   44       {dispose (temp);}
39   1  4   44     end;
40   1  4   44   END; {pop}
41   1  4   56
42   1  1    0 BEGIN {Main program Teststacks}
43   1  1    0   while not eof do begin
44   1  1   13     startstack;
45   1  1   15     repeat
46   1  1   15       read(ch);  write(' ',ch);
47   1  1   45       if ch <> '=' then
48   1  1   50
49   1  1   50         if ch in ['0'..'9'] then
50   1  1   66           push (ord(ch)-ord('0'))
51   1  1   69
52   1  1   69         else begin
53   1  1   73           pop (rhs);
54   1  1   77           pop (lhs);
55   1  1   81           case ch of
56   1  1   84             '+' : value := lhs + rhs;
57   1  1   91             '-' : value := lhs - rhs;
58   1  1   98             '*' : value := lhs * rhs;
```

UCSD Pascal Compiler at Wits University

```
59  1  1  105              ´/´ : value := lhs div rhs;
60  1  1  112            end; {of possible operators}
61  1  1  132            push (value);
62  1  1  135          end; {a calculation}
63  1  1  135        until ch = ´=´;
64  1  1  140
65  1  1  140        pop(answer);
66  1  1  144        writeln(answer:1);
67  1  1  162      end; {of all input}
68  1  1  164    END.
```

```
3 4 - 5 6 * + = 29
3 -[underflow] 4 5 6 * + = 34
3 4 5 6 - * + = -1
3 4 5 - * 6 + = 3
```

Figure 3.1   The test stacks program

stack mechanism creates a list which grows from the front, giving

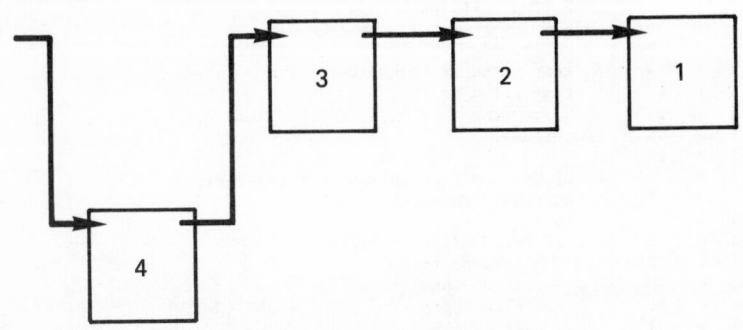

which is inappropriate for a speech because the lines will be in reverse order. To add a node onto the end of a list, we shall have to either

(a)   scan the list from the front each time

or

(b)   set up a permanent pointer to the last node.

The second alternative is cheaper and gives a double-ended list.

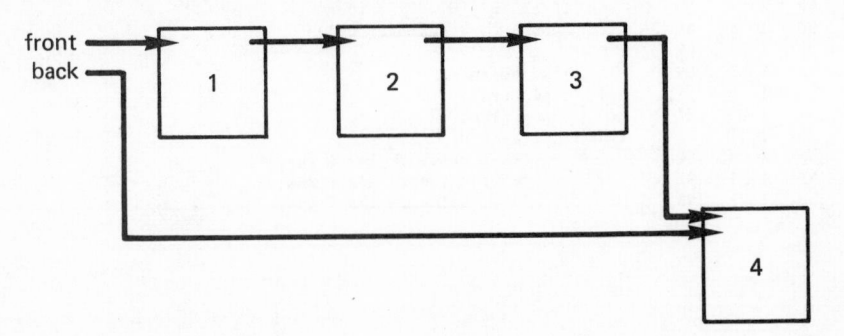

Properties of a Queue

Because there are now two names, we can potentially make alterations to either end at any time. However, it is useful to restrict the possibilities to those which we shall really need, i.e.

Additions are made at the end
Removals are made from the front.

In real life, this kind of list is a very common phenomenon (especially in the British Isles) known as a *queue*.

> Where two or three Englishmen
> are gathered together, there
> will be a queue.

If the rules are relaxed a bit to allow 'pushing in' (nodes can be added to the front) and 'reneging' (people at the back get fed up with waiting and leave), then the list is called a double-ended queue or *dequeue*. Although theoretically interesting, there are not many applications for a dequeue, and it would certainly be frowned upon in real life.

To return to Caesar's speeches, we notice that the front and back pointers define and control the list (or queue). We therefore define:

```
TYPE    speeches = record
                        firstline,
                        lastline : tolines
                   end;
```

and

```
            tolines = ↑lines;
            lines = record
                        link : tolines;
                        text : lotsofcharacters
                   end;
```

A speech is declared as

```
    VAR    speech : speeches;
```

Interlude—Names of types and variables

By now the reader will have noticed that there is a certain consistency in the choice of names given to types, variables, and in particular pointers. This is all in the cause of readability and is worth summarizing:

1. Type names are plurals. This helps when a variable and type need almost identical names. For example, we declared speech of type speeches.
2. Pointer types start with the prefix 'to'. This distinguishes them from their associated base type and pointer variables.
3. Link is used in list nodes of any kind. Another possible name for this pointer is next. It is best to stick to one or the other term.

Creating a Queue

In the context of storing Caesar's speeches, the basic operation is going to be reading in a list of lines and making them into a speech, using the queue mechanism. A procedure to read a whole speech, for a first try, would be:

```
PROCEDURE readspeech (var speech : speeches);
   VAR temp : tolines;
   BEGIN
      WITH speech do begin
         firstline := nil;
         while not end of speech do begin
            new(temp);
            read(temp↑.text);
            temp↑.link := nil;
            Link temp to the end of the speech
         end; {while}
      end; {with}
   END; {readspeech}
```

Because we are adding to the end of the list, only one link needs to be set up, but lastline must also be moved on, giving:

```
lastline↑.link := temp
lastline := temp;
```

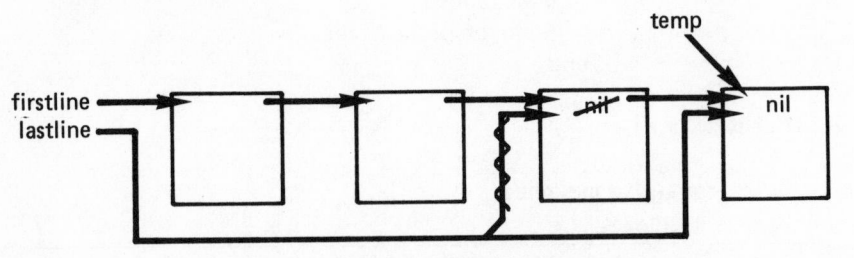

Notice that we followed the guideline of working from the list outwards and thereby did things in the right order. Our second guideline must be followed too since if lastline is nil, then lastline↑.link does not exist. This is not an error—it simply means that if temp is the first node then firstline is used in forging the link instead. This is done by:

```
if firstline = nil then firstline := temp
                  else lastline↑.link := temp;
lastline := temp;
```

This sequence suffers from a disadvantage that we have mentioned earlier: there is a one-off test inside a loop. The then-part of the test will only be done once, at the start of the list, and so it makes sense to put it and the test outside the loop. Remember the maxim:

> There is always
> a better way.

We start by taking a careful look at what new does. When the space is created, the temp pointer points to the start of it. The next statement sets lastline↑.link to point to temp. Since lastline↑.link is a pointer too, why not use it in the call to new? In the normal case, this would give

```
new (lastline↑.link);
lastline := lastline↑.link;
```

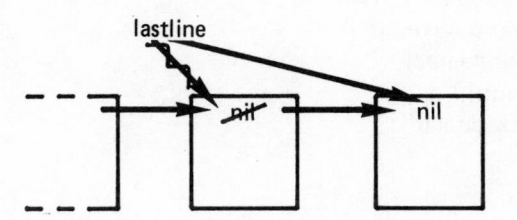

Because lastline↑.link does not exist when a list is started, the first line is handled separately outside the loop, giving

```
PROCEDURE readspeech (var speech : speeches);
  BEGIN
    WITH speech do begin
      new(firstline);
      read(firstline↑.text);
      firstline↑.link := nil;
      lastline := firstline;
      while not end of speech do begin
        new (lastline↑.link);
        lastline := lastline↑.link;
```

```
                read (lastline↑.text);
                lastline↑.link := nil;
            end; {while}
        end; {with}
    END; {readspeech}
```

This improved version has one drawback: it needs at least one line per speech. It is not unreasonable to expect that readspeech would not have been called otherwise. However, the previous algorithm will work in the general case.

Scanning a Queue

Since removing lines is not actually required by this problem, we shall leave the preparation of the algorithm for queues to the reader. However, one operation that will be needed is the writing out of a speech, which is equivalent to scanning a queue from front to end. This involves a scan of the queue from start to finish, giving

```
    PROCEDURE writespeech (speech : speeches);
        VAR temp : tolines;
        BEGIN
            with speech do begin
                temp := firstline;
                while temp < > nil do begin
                    writeln(temp↑.text);
                    temp := temp↑.link
                end; {of lines}
            end; {with}
        END; {writespeech}
```

Lists versus Arrays

Readspeech creates a structure such as the following:

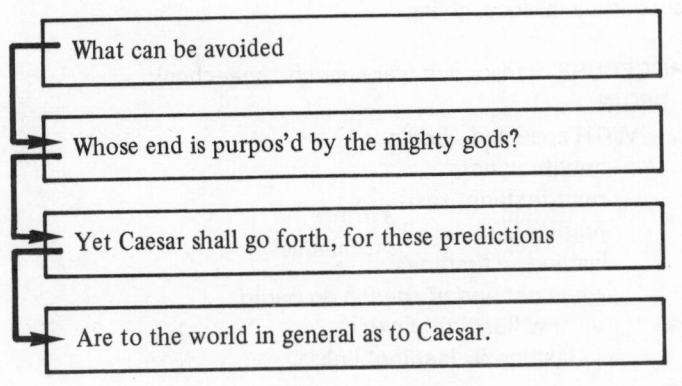

At this point we notice that the lines of the speech vary considerably in length as well. Should they also be represented as a linked list of words? The answer is no. An array of characters wastes the space at the end of shorter lines, but we can establish that the maximum line is 60 characters and most lines exceed 40. On the other hand, a list of words will incur an overhead of four characters (say) for a pointer for every word. Doing the sums we have:

$$\text{characters used: array} = \text{max}L$$
$$\text{list} = L + 4W$$

where L is the number of characters in the line and W is the number of words. Taking various values for L and W we get

characters used: array = 60

	L	W	Total space
list =	60	12	108
	40	8	72
	20	4	36

If we assume that about forty characters is the most common case (an assumption which can be verified by a brief inspection) then lists require consistently more space than arrays. This leads us to the principle that

A good solution is not universally applicable

3.4 Linked Lists—The Poet's Friend

The second poser concerned how to set up a list of lines so that *ad hoc* changes could be made easily. The problem is made easier by reducing it to two steps:

1. Find a node whose link can act as front.
2. Use a mixture of stack and queue techniques.

Leaving aside the finding, let us establish what exactly is going to happen in the general cases for adding and removing in the middle of a list.

Adding

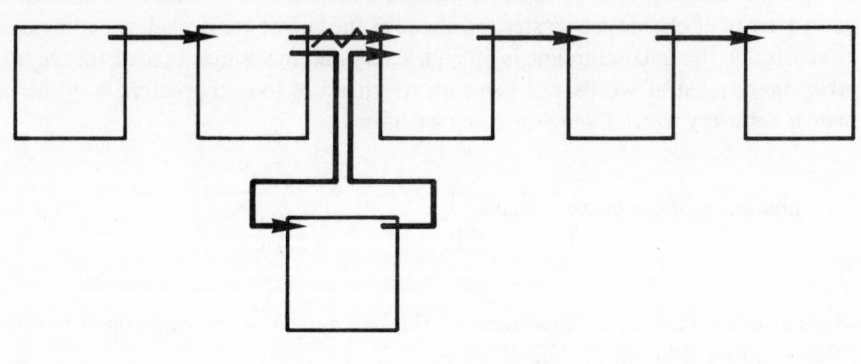

Removing

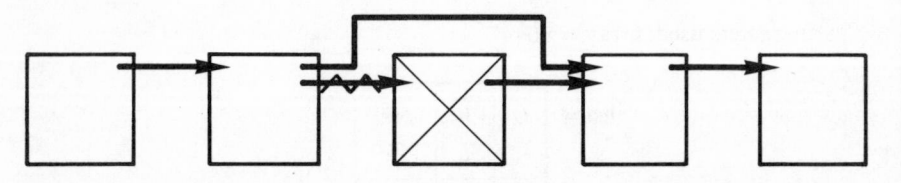

For both operations we see that the important point is that we have the name of the link to the front of the sub-list to be altered, rather than the name of the first node itself. But as we have already found, nodes in the middle of lists do not have names. In discussing queues, we postulated two alternatives, that is, make names for the nodes that could be involved in alterations, or scan from the front each time. Clearly, the first is not feasible here, and scanning will have to be done. We return therefore to the first part of the problem and work out how to get from a name we know (firstline) to the node that precedes our sub-list. If we declare

    VAR   current : tolines;

and set

    current := firstline;

then we can move down the list with

    current := current↑.link

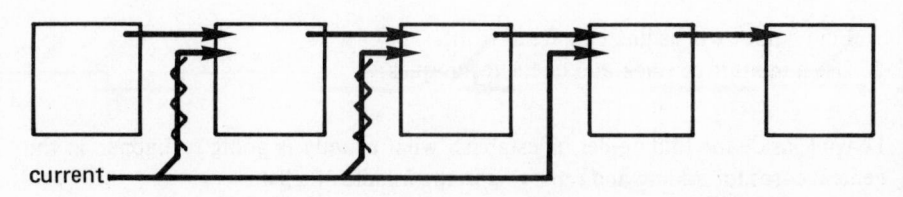

current

The question is where to stop. This is a problem in its own right: the poet could have said something like 'Skip 6 lines' or 'Find the line with "lea" in it' or, with a cursor editor, he could have simply pressed a down-arrow key until he saw he was at the right line. All of these are possible and pose the questions that when we stop, do we

- add a node *before* or *after* where we are?
- remove the node *at* or *after* where we are?

Oddly enough, there is no consensus among text editors as to which combination to choose. As far as designing our adding and removing algorithms is concerned, we can see that the 'after' case is going to be the most convenient because current will act as the front of the sub-list which we wish to alter. The sequences are then:

Add after

```
temp↑.link := current↑.link;
current↑.link := temp;
```

Remove after

```
temp := current↑.link;
current↑.link := temp↑.link;
dispose (temp);
```

The astute reader will see that these are the same as the stack operations, with current↑.link standing in for front. Consequently, the various special cases are handled accordingly.

A More Difficult Case

In the case of *adding before* or *removing at* the node, we find there are problems because the link of the *previous* node is affected. Thus we shall have to keep track of this node as well. With three named nodes, the number of special cases is going to increase considerably and we are prompted to find a way of simplifying things. The worst special case is going to be when current is at the front of the list and previous does not point anywhere—it hasn't yet come into play. To remedy this particular situation, we create a dummy node for previous to point to. We then extend the use of the dummy node by letting it act as a header to the list, giving

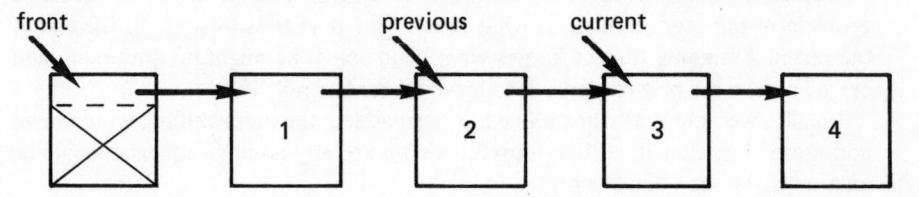

Now notice that every real list node has a relative name, as compared with previously when the first one had a direct name. (See the Interlude above on Names of links and nodes.) Adding before current and removing current is now easy, with no special cases that involve front.

Add before current

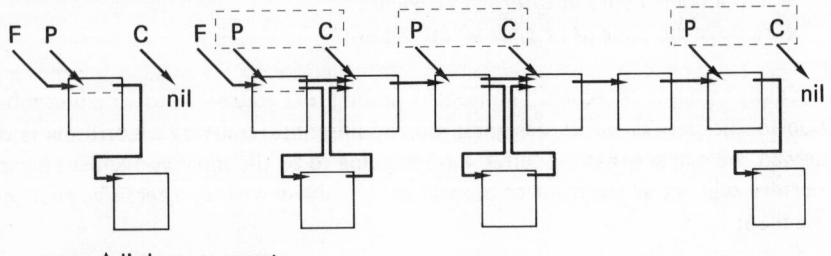

```
temp↑.link := current;
previous↑.link := temp;
previous := temp;
```

Remove current

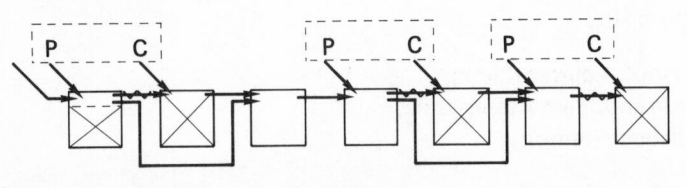

```
if current = nil then Signal underflow error
else begin
    previous↑.link := current↑.link;
    dispose (current);
    current := previous↑.link;
end;
```

The reader should verify from the pictures that all the boundary conditions are covered by these sequences.

Scanning a List

As we have seen, a scan of a list can stop for a variety of reasons and the particular scanning procedure will have to choose one or other of these. A problem of the scan, though, is what to do if the poet tries to scan off the end of the poem. Assuming that he knows what he is doing, he might be wanting to add extra lines, so the best response is to leave current as nil.

Finally, we note that when a line has been added, the natural thing would be to add more lines after it, so that a useful addition to any adding sequence would be an automatic 'scan one line on'.

Doubly Linked Lists

If the poet is going to be able to treat his computerized poem just as easily as one scribbled on paper, he will probably need to go backwards as well as forwards through the stanzas. With the operations developed above, going backwards involves jumping to the front and then scanning forwards. While this additional work can be hidden from the poet, it may be better to spend space on an extra pointer per line, giving a *doubly linked list*.

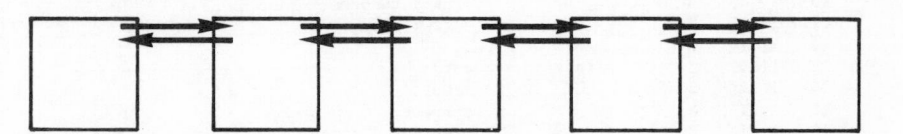

The decision as to whether to add the backward pointers will depend on the length of the poems being handled, the speed at which scanning can be done, and the amount of space available. It is not an easy decision to make, and the reader should perhaps 'do the sums' to get a better idea of when the balance tilts in favour of the extra link.

The routines to add and delete nodes with two links are slightly more complicated than the single-link operations, but follow the general pattern described above.

A Linked List Example

Figure 3.2 is another test program which exercises list operations. Once again it is organized so that the main program does not know the internal structure of the lists, except that it may inspect the value of current↑.data. In order to establish this degree of separation, the three operations so far—add, remove, and scan—were augmented by five others. The full eight operations are:

startlist	sets up the header
endlist	disposes any nodes and the header
startof	sets current to the front of the list
next	moves current on one
eol	tests if current has reached the end
addto	adds a node before current
removefrom	removes and disposes the current node
find	finds the node with a given data value

These form a fairly complete set of list-handling operations and could easily be used in other circumstances with other types of data in the nodes.

Common Mistakes with Pointers

If one sticks to the guidelines for forging links, lists and pointers should not cause

80

```
 1   1  1    1  PROGRAM Testlists (input, output);
 2   1  1    3
 3   1  1    3  {The program reads in characters and constructs two lists -
 4   1  1    3   one with unique letters and one with repeated letters.  The
 5   1  1    3   method deliberately involves a lot of work in order to
 6   1  1    3   exercise the list operations fully.}
 7   1  1    3
 8   1  1    3  TYPE tonodes  = ^nodes;
 9   1  1    3       nodes    = record
10   1  1    3                     link : tonodes;
11   1  1    3                     data : char;
12   1  1    3                   end;
13   1  1    3       lists    = record
14   1  1    3                    front,
15   1  1    3                    current,
16   1  1    3                    previous : tonodes
17   1  1    3                  end;
18   1  1    3       nodepositions
19   1  1    3              = (on, before);
20   1  1    3
21   1  1    3  VAR   singles,
22   1  1    3        multiples : lists;
23   1  1    9        ch        : char;
24   1  1   10        position  : nodepositions;
25   1  1   11
26   1  1   11  {********** The List Operations ************}
27   1  1   11
28   1  2    1  PROCEDURE startlist (var list : lists);
29   1  2    2  {-----------------}
30   1  2    0    BEGIN
31   1  2    0      new (list.front);
32   1  2    6      list.front^.link := nil;
33   1  2   10      list.previous := list.front;
34   1  2   14      list.current := nil;
35   1  2   19    END; {startlist}
36   1  2   32
37   1  3    1  PROCEDURE startof (var list : lists);
38   1  3    2  {---------------}
39   1  3    0    BEGIN
40   1  3    0      list.previous := list.front;
41   1  3    4      list.current := list.front^.link;
42   1  3   11    END; {startof}
43   1  3   24
44   1  4    3  FUNCTION eol (list : lists) : boolean;
45   1  4    7  {----------}
46   1  4    0    BEGIN
47   1  4    0      eol := list.current = nil
48   1  4    6    END; {eol}
49   1  4   22
50   1  5    1  PROCEDURE endlist (var list : lists);
51   1  5    2  {---------------}
52   1  5    2  VAR temp : tonodes;
53   1  5    0  BEGIN
54   1  5    0    startof (list);
55   1  5    3    while not eol(list) do begin
56   1  5   11      temp := list.current;
57   1  5   15      list.current := list.current^.link;
58   1  5   22      {dispose(temp);}
59   1  5   22    end; {while}
60   1  5   24    {dispose(list.front);}
61   1  5   24  END; {endlist}
62   1  5   38
```

```
63   1  6    1    PROCEDURE next (var list : lists);
64   1  6    2    {------------}
65   1  6    0      BEGIN
66   1  6    0        list.previous := list.current;
67   1  6    4        list.current := list.current^.link;
68   1  6   11      END; {next}
69   1  6   24
70   1  7    1    PROCEDURE addto (var list : lists; thisvalue : char);
71   1  7    3    {------------}
72   1  7    3      VAR temp : tonodes;
73   1  7    0      BEGIN
74   1  7    0        new(temp);
75   1  7    5        temp^.data := thisvalue;
76   1  7   10        temp^.link := list.current;
77   1  7   14        list.previous^.link := temp;
78   1  7   18        list.previous :=temp;
79   1  7   21      END; {addto}
80   1  7   34
81   1  8    1    PROCEDURE removefrom (var list : lists);
82   1  8    2    {------------------}
83   1  8    0      BEGIN
84   1  8    0        if eol(list)
85   1  8    1        then write ('[remove error]')
86   1  8   33        else with list do begin
87   1  8   38          previous^.link := current^.link;
88   1  8   44          {dispose(current);}
89   1  8   44          current := previous^.link;
90   1  8   51        end;
91   1  8   51      END; {removefrom}
92   1  8   64
93   1  9    1    PROCEDURE find (thisvalue : char; var list : lists;
94   1  9    3    {------------}  var result : nodepositions);
95   1  9    4      VAR state : (scanning, found, notthere);
96   1  9    0      BEGIN
97   1  9    0        state := scanning;
98   1  9    3        startof(list);
99   1  9    6        repeat
100  1  9    6          if eol(list)          then state :=notthere else
101  1  9   18          with list.current^ do
102  1  9   22          if data = thisvalue then state := found else
103  1  9   33          if data > thisvalue then state := notthere else
104  1  9   44                                          next(list);
105  1  9   47        until state <> scanning;
106  1  9   52        case state of
107  1  9   55          found    : result := on;
108  1  9   60          notthere : result := before;
109  1  9   65        end;
110  1  9   76      END; {find}
111  1  9   90
112  1  9   90    {*********** The Test Program *****************}
113  1  9   90
114  1 10    1    PROCEDURE print (list : lists);
115  1 10    0      BEGIN
116  1 10    0        startof(list);
117  1 10    9        while not eol(list) do begin
118  1 10   18          write(' ',list.current^.data);
119  1 10   39          next(list);
120  1 10   43        end; {while}
121  1 10   45      END; {print}
122  1 10   60
123  1  1    0    BEGIN {Test Lists}
124  1  1    0      WHILE not eof do begin
125  1  1   13        startlist (singles); startlist (multiples);
126  1  1   21        write('DATA:      ');
```

```
127  1  1   43      repeat
128  1  1   43        read(ch);  write(' ',ch);
129  1  1   73        find (ch, {in} singles, {giving} position);
130  1  1   80        case position of
131  1  1   83          on : begin
132  1  1   83                 removefrom (singles);
133  1  1   87                 find (ch, {in} multiples, {giving} position);
134  1  1   94                 case position of
135  1  1   97                   on    : { Do nothing};
136  1  1   99                   before : addto (multiples, ch);
137  1  1  106                 end; {case}
138  1  1  118               end;
139  1  1  120          before : addto (singles, ch);
140  1  1  127        end; {case}
141  1  1  138      until eoln(input);
142  1  1  148
143  1  1  148      startof (multiples);
144  1  1  152      while not eol(multiples) do with multiples do begin
145  1  1  161        find (current^.data, {in} singles, {giving} position);
146  1  1  169        if position = on then removefrom (singles);
147  1  1  178        next(multiples);
148  1  1  182      end; {while}
149  1  1  184
150  1  1  184      readln; writeln;
151  1  1  200      write('SINGLES:   '); print(singles); writeln;
152  1  1  234      write('MULTIPLES:'); print(multiples); writeln; writeln;
153  1  1  276      endlist(singles); endlist(multiples);
154  1  1  284    END; {while}
155  1  1  286  END.
```

```
DATA:       W I L L I A M
SINGLES:    A M W
MULTIPLES:  I L

DATA:       W I L L I A M S H A K E S P E A R E
SINGLES:    H K M P R W
MULTIPLES:  A E I L S

DATA:       J U D Y B I S H O P
SINGLES:    B D H I J O P S U Y
MULTIPLES:

DATA:       N I G E L B I S H O P
SINGLES:    B E G H L N O P S
MULTIPLES:  I

DATA:       K O K O
SINGLES:
MULTIPLES:  K O

DATA:       K O K O Y O Y
SINGLES:
MULTIPLES:  K O Y
```

Figure 3.2   The test lists program

too many errors in programming. However, if things do go wrong, here are two common mistakes to watch for. Both could have occurred in the little print procedure in testlists.

The first concerns the use of with as a shorthand aid. If print had been written as

```
PROCEDURE print (list : lists)
   BEGIN
      startof (list);
      with list do {source of error}
      while not eol(list) do begin
         write (' ',current↑.data);
         next (list);
      end; {while}
   END; {print}
```

then current would always refer to the same node: that is, the one to which it
pointed when the with statement was executed. Calls to next, while changing the
real current pointer, would not alter the shorthand reference established by the
with. The golden rule is:

> Don't use a with outside
> a list-scanning loop.

Putting the with inside the loop gives quite a different effect, as it is evaluated each
time round and sets up the correct values of the list pointers for use in shorthand
references.

The second common mistake concerns var parameters. If print is declared as

```
PROCEDURE print (var list : lists);
```

then the values of the list pointers will be updated to point to the end of the list.
Such alteration is both unnecessary and potentially dangerous. Print is an
example of a useful procedure which could be called at various stages of the
program to show the current status of the list. It is therefore not desirable that
print should alter the status of the list in any way. Making the list a value
parameter gives print local copies of the list pointers which it can then alter,
without affecting the originals.

> Only use var parameters
> when absolutely necessary.

3.5 Garbage Collection

In some computer systems, a procedure such as dispose is a standard utility and
serves a useful purpose: any disposed items are put back into the pool of available
storage from which the procedure new can create new nodes. Other systems do
not have such a mechanism. Why is this so? The reason is the same as that which
discourages wine merchants from recycling wine bottles—they don't come in
standard sizes. A line as defined above may occupy some 21 words of memory

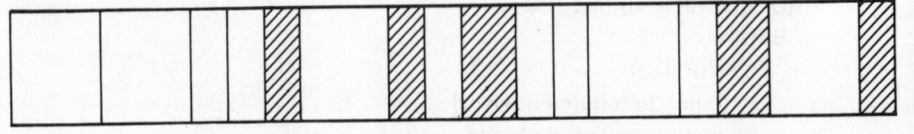

Figure 3.3   Storage with large and small nodes and free space

whereas a node to hold all the information on one student in a records system could use up to 200 words. If only lines have been disposed and then a student node is required, there may not be enough *contiguous* words available, although in total there are more than 200 free. This is called *memory fragmentation* and is illustrated in Figure 3.3.

At this point the system could just give up, or it could try to reclaim the unused areas and then see if the request can be handled. This technique is called *garbage collection*. One way of reclaiming nodes is to move every thing up and reset all the links. The algorithms to consolidate nodes in this way are extensive and well researched, but beyond the scope of this book. Another remedy is to minimize the chance of fragmentation occurring by ensuring that an item is created in an area just big enough for it so that no space is wasted.

The Second-hand Store

Let us postulate

TYPE sizes = (big, medium, small)

to describe the kinds of nodes that will be created. We will let the system control the pool of space initially, with each request for a new node going straight through to it. As soon as a *dispose* occurs, we step in and capture the unwanted node. If

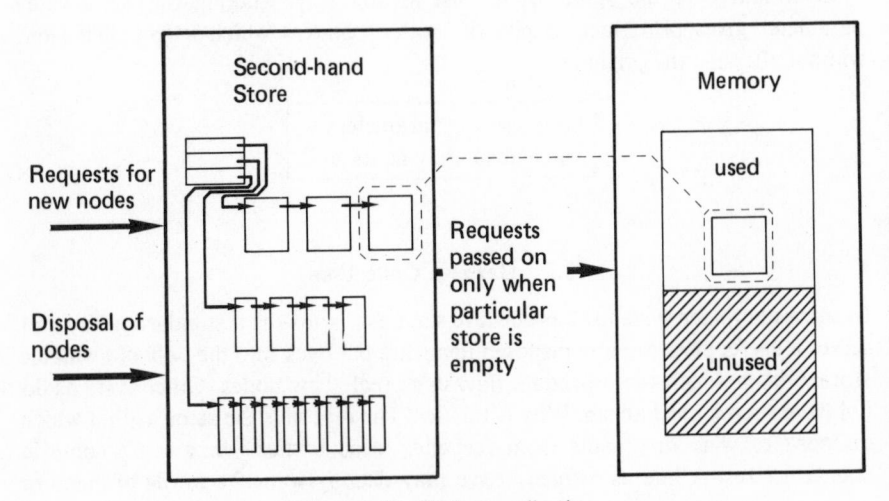

Figure 3.4   Garbage collection

more nodes of the same type are disposed, these will be linked up to form a chain of re-usable nodes. Now, when a request for a new node is made, we can supply it from our 'second-hand' store. If that particular item is 'out' (the list is empty) then the request has to be passed on to the system.

The result of this is that there will, from the system's point of view, be no 'garbage' in memory. There will be only a used area (which includes nodes currently 'live' as well as those waiting to be re-used) and an unused area. Of course, the second-hand nodes do exist in memory, but not in the messy way they did before. They are now all tidily linked up in lists of the same size.

Multiple Stacks

The particular type of list chosen is a stack because it is the easiest to use and the order in which the nodes are supplied is immaterial. To head each stack, we need a front pointer. Since the stacks will be identified by size, why not have an array of front pointers, as implied in the diagram in Figure 3.3? This is a fine idea, but unfortunately is not possible at the level at which we have to program. The elements of a Pascal array must be all of the same type and, while the fronts are all pointers sure enough, they are pointers to different sized nodes. This makes their types different. Each front pointer will have to be explicitly declared.

```
TYPE    tobignodes     : ↑bignodes;
        tomediumnodes : ↑mediumnodes;
        tosmallnodes   : ↑ smallnodes;

VAR     bigstack       : tobignodes;
        mediumstack : tomediumnodes;
        smallstack     : tosmallnodes;
```

and we set

```
bigstack       := nil;
mediumstack := nil;
smallstack     := nil;
```

The procedure to add to the lists is called when a node is to be disposed. But how can a procedure work for three different types? The dispose procedure we proposed earlier would have been a system procedure which could ignore types. In ordinary Pascal, we cannot do this. So we are left with two choices: make a different procedure for each type or supply three pointers each time to a general procedure, with two of them dummies. We are now beginning to see that

> The dirtiest job is
> cleaning up.

The choice is between

 disposebig (thisnode)

or

 disposeany (thisnode, dummymedium, dummysmall, big);

where the last parameter in disposeany indicates which of the other three is the real one. Since disposeany would still have to have separate sections for each case, the first alternative seems neater.

```
PROCEDURE disposebig (thisnode : tobignodes);
BEGIN
    thisnode↑.link := bigstack;
    bigstack := thisnode;
END; {disposebig}
```

Requests for new nodes are handled by three procedures, one for each size. Each first checks if there are any second-hand nodes, and only if there are not, does it ask the system for more storage.

```
PROCEDURE bignew (var thisnode : bignode);
BEGIN
    if bigstack = nil
    then {pass the request on}
        new (thisnode)
        else begin
        thisnode := bigstack;
        bigstack := bigstack↑.link;
    end;
END; {bignew}
```

The procedures for the other sizes will follow the same pattern.

3.6 Sequential Storage

At the start of this chapter we posed two problems that required extensible and elastic data structures. We went on to show how controlling space through new and dispose provided the extensibility, and forging links with pointers achieved the desired elasticity. But what if new, dispose, and pointers are not available, as is the case when programming in FORTRAN, BASIC, or assembly language? Do the algorithms developed for

- controlling space
  and
- forging links

still apply? The answer is yes: with the one proviso that the maximum expected number of nodes must be predefined, an array of elements can actually be manipulated just as deftly as a pointer-controlled list of nodes.

Array–Pointer Equivalents

Pointers give access to a large mass of free space known as the *heap*. The heap could be simulated by an array:

```
TYPE    heaprange = 1..heapmax;
        heapindex = 0..heapmax;
VAR     heap : array [heaprange] of nodes;
```

in which case, pointers become indices of type heapindex. Since the heap itself runs over heaprange, the extra value in heapindex, namely zero, can be used for nil. What is the type of nodes? As we saw before, nodes obtained by new can vary in type and size. But with an array, all the nodes must be the same. So to simulate the heap, we must first split it up into several arrays, one for each type. For example, we could have

```
VAR     listofsmalls   : array [smallrange] of smalls;
        listoflines    : array [pagerange] of lines;
        listofnumbers : array [tablerange] of real;
```

The next problem is the links. With pointers, each node was a record and one of its fields was a link. Mapping straight across to arrays, we might have

```
TYPE    nodes = record
                    link : heapindex;
                    data : anytype;
                end;
```

However, if a language does not have pointers, it is unlikely to have records either. Once again, we split the structure into separate arrays, one for each field, giving

```
VAR     heaplink  : array [heaprange] of heapindex;
        heapdata : array [heaprange] of anytype;
```

To access the equivalent of current↑.data, say, we would then use

```
heapdata [current]
```

and current↑.link := nil would be translated into

```
heaplink [current] := 0;
```

Array Lists

Given this straightforward correspondence between pointer-nodes and arrays, we can set about specifying all the list operations in array form. We note that the header node, pointed to by front, can be represented neatly by the zeroth element of the array. In order to distinguish zero (meaning front from the other use of zero (meaning nil), we define a constant

CONST nul = 0

	Pointers	Arrays
Declare	TYPE tonodes = ↑nodes; 　　nodes = record 　　　　link : tonodes; 　　　　data : anytype; 　　　　end; VAR front, previous, 　　current : tonodes;	CONST nul = 0; TYPE listrange = 1. .listmax; 　　listindex = 0. .listmax; VAR　link : array [listrange] 　　　　of listindex; 　　data : array [listrange] 　　　　of anytype; front, previous, current : listindex;

Initially	new (front);
	front↑.link\ := nil;
	previous　:= front;
	current　　:= nil;
		front := 0;
		link[front] := nul;
		previous　:= front;
		current　　:= nul;

Add before	new (temp);
	read (temp↑.data);
	temp↑.link　　:= current;
	previous↑.link　:= temp;
	previous　　　:= temp;
		getnode (temp);
		if temp=nul then *overflow*
		else begin
		　read (data[temp]);
		　link[temp]　　:= current;
		　link[previous] := temp;
		　previous　　　:= temp;
		end;

Remove at	if current = nil then underflow
	
	else begin
	　previous↑.link
	　　　　:= current↑.link;
	　dispose (current);
	　current := previous↑.link;
	end;
		if current = nul then
		　　　　underflow
		else begin
		　link[previous]
		　　　　:= link[current];
		　returnnode (current);
		　current := link[previous];
		end;

Figure 3.5　List operations using pointers and arrays

(We use nul so as not to lose the use of nil itself.) Figure 3.5 gives the complete mapping from pointers to arrays for lists.

Figure 3.6 shows the diagrams used for array lists. The example begs the question as to how getnode and returnnode operate. Returnnode is simple and closely resembles the disposebig of the previous section, i.e.

```
VAR    avail : listindex    {initially nul}

PROCEDURE returnnode (temp : listindex);
   BEGIN
      link[temp] := avail;
      avail      := temp;
   END; {returnnode}
```

Getnode has more to do. Like bignew, it first checks the avail stack and will re-use a node if possible. Failing that, it has to get the next element in the array. To mark

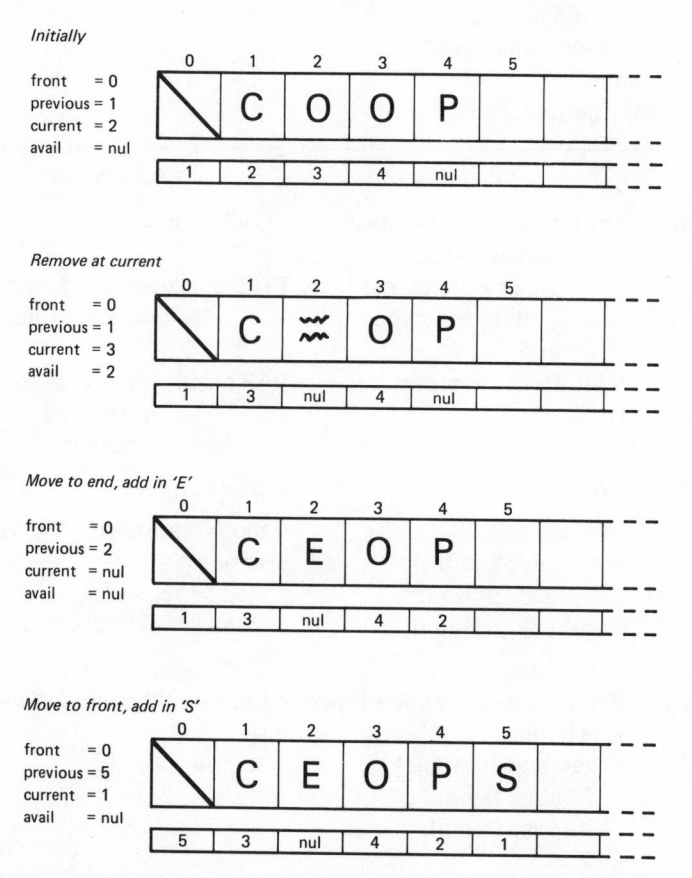

Figure 3.6   Example of array lists COOP → COP → COPE → SCOPE

the highest used index so far, a variable called the *tide mark* is kept. When the avail stack is empty, getnode increases the tide mark and occupies the next element. Naturally, a check is made to see whether the new tide mark will overflow the bounds of the array. Getnode is therefore

```
VAR    tide : listindex; {initially set to front i.e. 0}

PROCEDURE getnode (VAR temp : listindex);
  BEGIN
      temp := nul;
      if avail = nul then
          if tide = listmax then overflow
          else begin
              tide := tide + 1;
              temp := tide;
          end
      else begin
          temp := avail;
          avail := link[avail];
      end;
  END; {getnode}
```

	Pointers	Arrays

Declare	TYPE tonodes = ↑.nodes;
	    nodes = record
	        link : tonodes;
	        data : anytype;
	        end;
	VAR front : tonodes;
		CONST nul = 0;
		
		TYPE stackrange = 1. .stackmax;
		    stackindex = 0. .stackmax;
		
		VAR stack : array [stackrange]
		           of anytype;
		    top : stackindex;

Initially	front := nil;	top := nul;

Add	new (temp);
	read (temp↑.data);
	temp↑.link := front;
	front↑.link := temp;
		if top = stackmax then overflow
		else begin
		    top := top + 1;
		    read (stack[top]);
		end;

Remove	if front = nil then underflow
	else begin
	    temp := front↑.link;
	    front := temp;
	    dispose (temp);
	end;
		if top = nul then *underflow*
		else
		    top := top − 1;

Figure 3.7 Pointers and array operations for stacks

As a check, the reader should verify that the tide mark at each of the four steps in the example of Figure 3.6 has values 4, 4, 4, 5 respectively. Also check that getnode will successfully start off a new list when called for the first time.

Stacks and Queues

It is not difficult to see that stacks and queues could be represented on arrays in exactly the same way. However, if we simulate several operations on an array-stack, we see that the avail stack is unnecessary because nodes are always returned at the end of the stack, and reassigned from there too. In fact, it seems as if the links are also unnecessary, since the nodes do not move around, but stay in their original order—the numerical order of the array indices. In other words, a stack gets its nodes sequentially, which is just the way the array provides them. Both the abstract notion of a stack, and the concrete structure of an array, use what is known as *sequential allocation*.

The getnode and returnnode operations also fall away, being replaced by adding 1 and subtracting 1 from the front index. Figure 3.7 gives the array equivalents for stack operations. The development of similar routines for queues is left to the reader.

3.7   Project—Play Structure

Introduction

Pascal belongs to the latest generation of high-level programming languages designed in the 1970s. One of the main advances over the languages of the 1960s (FORTRAN, ALGOL 60, BASIC) is the provision for data structures other than sequential arrays. Record definitions with named fields were used in Cobol for business data processing, but their true worth shows in the area of linked-list processing. Not only can a record consist of items of several different types, but it can also point to other records.

This project is concerned with the creation and manipulation of a data structure containing the text of a Shakespeare play. We are going to look at the structure of the play—its divisions into acts, scenes, and events, the entries, exits, stage directions, and so on—rather than the meaning of the words in the speeches. The idea is to read in scenes or acts and hold them in the computer in a manageable form that can be used by other people wishing to examine aspects of a play such as the length of time actors are on the stage, or esoteric details of Shakespeare's use of English.

Looked at from this point of view, a play consists of a sequence of events, some of them with associated text. For example:

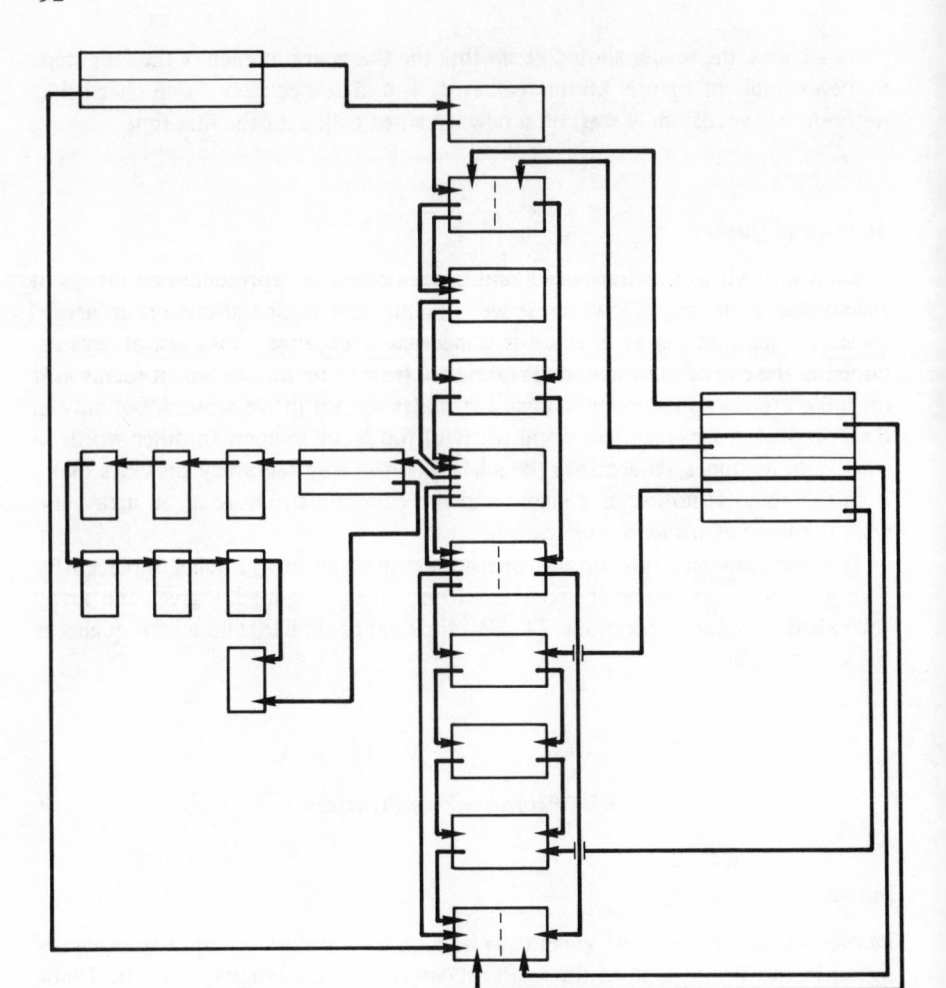

Figure 3.8   Example of a data structure for a play

EVENT	TEXT
Enter	*Antony and Scarus with Force, Marching.*
Speech	*Ant. Their preparation is to-day by sea,/We please them not by land.*
Stage Direction	*Alarum afar off, as at a sea-fight.*
Exit	*Cleopatra*
Exeunt	

Exeunt means that all actors currently on the stage exit, but who they are must be deduced from previous events.

An important part of the project will be printing out scenes or speeches and here we must follow the standard format for Shakespeare as shown overleaf. Books can make use of different typefaces (capitals and italics) to emphasize events, but on a line-printer the only means of achieving this is by suitable spacing. In common with the book, we can centre entry events and right-justify exits and stage directions. A good way of making a speech stand out is to indent all lines except the first, which has the actor's name.

By the end of seven weeks, you should have developed a suite of procedures which will:

1. Read a scene and print it out correctly.
2. Link the speeches for each actor and print them out.
3. Link the events for each actor and print out his (her) part, complete with cues.
4. Condense the text in various ways so that several scenes can be analysed concurrently.

0. A Scene Structure

A scene is composed of events with associated speeches. For our purposes, an entry or exit is considered as an unspoken 'speech' and stage directions are speeches belonging to the Stage Manager. A speech itself is composed of lines. As described in Section 3.3, we have a header and each line consists of its text and a pointer to the next line. As was also described in Section 3.3, we use a list header for the speech itself, keeping pointers to the first and last lines, and each line consists of actual text and a link to the next line. Thus we have the types

> *speeches*—a record with two pointers
> *lines*—a record with some text and a link.

and the associated pointer types, prefixed with to-, i.e. tolines and tospeeches.

The next two levels up the hierarchy—events and scenes—follow a similar pattern. Events look the same as lines, having a next field and a text field. The text field is not an array, but a pointer to a speech. In addition to these two fields, there should be a field indicating the kind of event, e.g. speech, enter, exeunt. At the last level that we are concerned with, a scene, has the same structure as a speech, in that it is a list header pointing to the first and last events. This gives us the following types:

> *scenes*—a record with two pointers
> *events*—a record with the kind, a pointer to a speech, and a link

Exercise 0. Putting this all together, define the types for scenes, events, speeches, and lines. The types should describe a structure which could grow to look like that in Figure 3.8. This figure shows the first ten events of the given data, i.e. up to the re-entry of Antony and Scarus.

ANTONY AND CLEOPATRA

SCENE X.—*Between the two Camps.*

Enter ANTONY *and* SCARUS, *with Forces,*
marching.

Ant. Their preparation is to-day by sea;
We please them not by land.
    Scar.   For both, my lord.
    Ant. I would they'd fight i'the fire or i'the air;
We'd fight there too. But this it is; our foot 4
Upon the hills adjoining to the city
Shall stay with us; order for sea is given,
They have put forth the haven,
Where their appointment we may best discover
And look on their endeavour.   [*Exeunt.*

Enter CAESAR, *and his Forces, marching.*
    Caes. But being charg'd, we will be still by
    land,
Which, as I take't, we shall; for his best force
Is forth to man his galleys. To the vales,   12
And hold our best advantage!   [*Exeunt.*

Re-enter ANTONY *and* SCARUS.
    Ant. Yet they are not join'd. Where yond
    pine does stand
I shall discover all; I'll bring thee word
Straight how 'tis like to go.   [*Exit.*
    Scar.   Swallows have built 16
In Cleopatra's sails their nests; the augurers
Say they know not, they cannot tell; look grimly,
And dare not speak their knowledge. Antony
Is valiant, and dejected; and, by starts,   20
His fretted fortunes give him hope and fear
Of what he has and has not.
        [*Alarum afar off, as at a sea-fight.*

Re-enter ANTONY.
    Ant.   All is lost!
This foul Egyptian hath betrayed me;
My fleet hath yielded to the foe, and yonder 24
They cast their caps up and carouse together
Like friends long lost. Triple-turn'd whore!
'tis thou
Hast sold me to this novice, and my heart
Makes only wars on thee. Bid them all fly; 28
For when I am reveng'd upon my charm,
I have done all. Bid them all fly; be gone.
        [*Exit* SCARUS.
O sun! thy uprise shall I see no more;
Fortune and Antony part here; even here   32
Do we shake hands. All come to this? The
    hearts

That spaniel'd me at heels, to whom I gave
Their wishes, do discandy, melt their sweets
On blossoming Caesar; and this pine is bark'd,
That overtopp'd them all. Betray'd I am.   37
O this false soul of Egypt! this grave charm,
Whose eyes beck'd forth my wars, and call'd
    them home,
Whose bosom was my crownet, my chief end, 40
Like a right gipsy, hath, at fast and loose,
Beguil'd me to the very heart of loss.
What Eros! Eros!

               Enter CLEOPATRA.
                    Ah! thou spell. Avaunt!
  Cleo. Why is my lord enrag'd against his
love?
  Ant. Vanish, or I shall give thee thy de-
serving,
And blemish Caesar's triumph. Let him take
    thee.
And hoist thee up to the shouting plebeians;
Follow his chariot, like the greatest spot   48
Of all thy sex; most monster-like, be shown
For poor'st diminutives, for doits; and let
Patient Octavia plough thy visage up
With her prepared nails.   [*Exit* CLEOPATRA.
                 'Tis well thou'rt gone, 52
If it be well to live; but better 'twere
Thou fell'st into my fury, for one death
Might have prevented many. Eros, ho!
The shirt of Nessus is upon me; teach me, 56
Alcides, thou mine ancestor, thy rage;
Let me lodge Lichas on the horns o' the moon;
And with those hands, that grasp'd the heaviest
    club,
Subdue my worthiest self. The witch shall die:
To the young Roman boy she hath sold me, and
    I fall   61
Under this plot; she dies for't. Eros, ho!   [*Exit.*

Figure 3.9   Example of Shakespeare layout

1. Readscene and Writescene

Just as there is a hierarchical structure to the data, so we have a corresponding
hierarchy of procedures to read in and write out each component.

Exercise 1

(a) Write the body for

    PROCEDURE readscene (var thisscene : toscenes);

which will accept data in the form described by the interlude below. The other procedures are nested inside readscene as follows:

```
PROCEDURE readscene (var thisscene : toscenes);
  PROCEDURE getevent (var anevent : toevents);
    PROCEDURE readspeech (var thisline : tospeeches);
      PROCEDURE readline (var thissline : tolines);
        BEGIN
        END; {readline}
      BEGIN {readspeech}
      END; {readspeech}
    BEGIN {getevent}
    END; {getevent}
  BEGIN }readscene}
  END; {readscene}
```

Hint: The work of the next chapter will help with the proper formulation of readline.

(b) Write the body for

PROCEDURE writescene (thisscene : toscenes);

In this case, we can foresee that in later programs, writespeech and writeline might be needed in contexts other than the writing of an entire scene, so that the accompanying procedures are not nested.

```
PROCEDURE writeline (thisline : tolines);
  BEGIN

  END; {writeline}
PROCEDURE writespeech (thisspeech : tospeeches);
  BEGIN

  END; {writespeech}
PROCEDURE writescene (thisscene : toscenes);
  BEGIN

  END; {writescene}
```

(c) Write a program to read in a scene from Shakespeare and print it out in the accepted form in Figure 3.9. Use the data from *Antony and Cleopatra* provided.

Interlude—Shakespeare data format

1. The end of a line has no meaning.
2. Each event is typed as it comes and identified by a marker.
3. A marker consists of a star followed by a letter.
4. This letter indicates the kind of the event and therefore some initial words (e.g. enter) are omitted.
5. The marker is followed by the relevant text.
6. Lines in a speech are separated by slashes. There is no slash after the last line in a speech.
7. The last exit (or exeunt) is followed by a dollar.

MARKER	EVENT
*C	*scene*
*E	*enter*
*S	*speech*
*X	*exit*
*R	*reenter*
*U	*exeunt*
*G	*stage direction*
*M	*more speech*

A 'more speech' marker is used when a speech resumes after an interruption (e.g. an exit) without the actor's name being repeated.

Example

*CX.—Between the two camps.*EAntony and Scarus, with Forces, marching.*SAnt. Their preparation is today by sea;/We please them not by land.*SScar. For both, my lord.*SAnt. I would they'd fight i' the fire or i' the air;/We'd fight there too. But this it is; our foot/Upon the hills adjoining the city/Shall stay with us; order for sea is given,/They have put forth the haven,/Where their appointment we may best discover/And look on their endeavour.*U.*ECaesar, and his Forces, marching.*SCaes. But being charg'd, we will be still by land,/Which, as I tak't, we shall; for his best force/Is forth to man his galleys. To the vales,/And hold our best advantage! *U. *RAntony and Scarus.*SAnt. Yet they are not join'd. Where yond pine does stand/I shall discover all; I'll bring thee word/Straight how 'tis like to go.*X.*SScar. Swallows have built/In Cleopatra's sails their nests; the augurers/Say they know not, they cannot tell; look grimly,/And dare not speak their knowledge. Antony/Is valiant, and dejected; and, by starts,/His fretted fortunes give him hope and fear/ Of what he has and has not.*GAlarum afar off, as at a seafight. *RAntony.*SAnt. All is lost!/This foul Egyptian hath betrayed me;/My fleet hath yielded to the foe, and yonder/They cast their caps up and carouse together/Like friends long lost. Triple-turn'd whore! 'tis . . .

2. Actors

Another way of looking at a play is from the actor's point of view. As far as (s)he is concerned, the main events are her (his) first and last speeches. Therefore we define

```
TYPE actorrecord = record
            name : word;
            firstspeech, lastspeech : evententry
        end;
        cast = 1. .noofactors;
```

and

```
VAR actortable : array [cast] of actorrecord.
```

Given our basic scene structure, we can now superimpose on it a list running through all the speeches for a single actor. This will enable individual parts to be printed out.

Actor names

At the front of a play is a list of Dramatis Personae. For our purposes, a short list would be

```
    ANTONY
    SCARUS
    CAESAR
    EROS
    CLEOPATRA
    FORCES
```

However, to identify a speech, an abbreviation is used in most texts. In order to match a speech to an actor, we need to:

1. Read in the cast list (using a readword procedure).
2. Pick off the abbreviation from the first line of the speech (using an adapted readword).
3. Compare the abbreviation to a shortened form of each word in the actor table (using a function to compare words).

Events are already linked in order of appearance. To run other lists through them, we need an extra field called, say,

```
nextforactor : evententry.
```

The list controller will, of course, be the appropriate actortable record.

Exercise 2 Write the procedures which are needed in the following main program:

```
begin
    readscene (testscene);
    writescene(testscene); (* just to check *)
    readcastlist;
    linkspeechesin (testscene);
    for actor := 1 to noofactors do writeallspeechesfor(actor);
end.
```

Interlude—What is expected

The last exercise marked the end of the carefully guided classwork. The statement of Parts 3 and 4 will be more general and open-ended. It will be up to you to decide on how far to take the solutions, what procedures you will need, and what output to produce. It will therefore be necessary for you to explain to the examiner in a document accompanying your listings exactly what your programs do, as well as how they do it, although the latter may not amount to much if your Pascal is sufficiently readable.

Obviously higher marks will be given for a greater amount of work. However, it is more important to understand the whole problem and select a portion of it which can be realistically completed in the time available, than to hand in ambitious systems which only half work. As has been emphasized all along, marks will be given for initiative, clear style, layout, and readability.

---

3. Cues

For learning a part, a list of speeches is sufficient, but when one comes to act it, cues are necessary. A cue is the last line of the event preceding the current one. However, there are problems with this definition.

Technically, the cue for Caesar to enter is the exeunt of Antony and Scarus. In practice, it is more helpful to have the last line of Antony's speech as the cue, i.e.

'. . . and look to their endeavour.'

Another problem is the occurrence of multiple events such as

Re-enter Antony and Scarus.

In order to link all events for an actor (not just speeches), ones like this will have to be analysed and split up into two event entries, as the nextofactor link can only occur in one list. Now, should the cue for Scarus to enter be Antony's entry or Caesar's exit, or the last line of Caesar's speech? The latter is probably preferable, but it requires some thought.

In addition to the analysis of these entries, we need to keep semantic information about who is on stage at any one time in order to connect an exeunt or implied exit with the appropriate actors' event list. Sets should be useful here.

Don't forget that walk-on parts count too. You should be able to print out something like this:

FORCES' PART

CUE: Start of Scene X

Enter with Antony and Scarus

CUE: . . . and look to their endeavour.

Exit

CUE: Exit of Antony and Scarus

Enter with Caesar

CUE: . . . and hold our best advantage.

Exit

Unfortunately (unlike Caesar) we cannot distinguish between the two forces (they probably do a quick change backstage anyway.) The stage manager also has a part which should not be ignored—he handles all the alarums and so forth.

4. Space Conservation

So far we have not considered any more than a fairly short scene of about 75 lines. At a rough estimate, this occupies 1500 words of store. The entire play will probably require 100 000 words. While this may be possible on a large computer, an English Department likely to be interested in using these programs will probably only have a minicomputer with an upper limit of about 32 000 words. It is therefore worth investigating whether it is possible to reduce the size of a stored scene without prejudicing the ease with which the information can be manipulated. Two avenues are possible.

Firstly, not all lines require 64 characters. By reducing this to, say, 40, space is saved for most lines, but an overflow mechanism must be included for the longer ones. Alternatively, the list structure could be carried to a deeper level by dividing a line into chunks of 8 characters and linking these together. This increases the overhead of space required for pointers, though. A study must be made of the relationship between the length of lines and various chunk sizes to achieve the best balance. This means gathering statistics on the average, mean, and median number of characters in a line. It would also be worth testing a scene with more dialogue and less blank verse (one from a comedy would do) to see if a different strategy would be needed.

The second approach is to abbreviate commonly used words. Thus, 'the' could be replaced internally by *1 where 1 is the index to a dictionary. This only saves one character but greater savings are possible for longer words. As before, the first thing to do is to gather statistics on the most commonly used words. Then a decision must be made as to whether to 'escape-code' the most common words, regardless of meaning, or to select only those that are not significant to the context, such as pronouns, adverbs, etc. The answer will depend upon the ease with which procedures such as wordcompare and any others that you might imagine the English Department would require, can handle these escape-coded words.

With both approaches, you will need to present evidence of the improvement obtained. The program itself should monitor and report on the amount of store it uses.

Chapter 4

Input–Output (Part 1)—Verifying and Formatting

We now come to the third side of the programming triangle—input–output. To the outside world, it is this aspect that decides the quality of a program. The way in which a program demands its input to be arranged and the clarity with which it presents the results are as important as the elegance or efficiency of the algorithms and data structures. Too often, the process of learning how to program rushes past input–output in an effort to get to the inner principles. This was probably so in your introductory programming course. For example, how often did your programs verify that the data was correct? Never (or hardly ever) would probably be an honest answer.

In this course on advanced programming we have the time to sit back and quietly consider the effect of input and output design on users of our programs. Hand in hand with this comes data verification: from now on, you should resolve that no program of yours will ever crash on account of ill-formed or idiotic input. Like a pharmacist reading a doctor's prescription, a program should study the input, try and make sense of it based on prior experience, and only if this is impossible, leave it aside pending clarification and go on to the next one.

4.1 Line Input Done Well

During the discussion of Caesar's speeches, we avoided the question of how each line was read in. This is true to our top-down design strategy and we can appreciate the benefit we reaped by ignoring this question. However, it is now time to move down a level of detail and define the procedures to read a line and write a line. If we were still concerned solely with algorithms, we would at this point dive straight in and start writing the statements to do this. With our input–output hat on, we have to take a step back and consider first what the input looks like.

The Form of the Input

There are several steps to defining the form of the input:

1. What is the original layman's form of the input?
2. Does it need to be transformed at all for computer input?

3. What information (if any) inherent in the input should be collected as it is read in?
4. How is the data to be stored by the program?
5. In what form is the output required?
6. What test data will exercise the program properly?

For a quotation from a speech or poem, there are two possibilities for the first step: line-by-line form, or concatenated by slashes. For example:

> *'So that's what I make,*
> *When the day's all wet.*
> *It's a good sort of brake*
> *But it hasn't worked yet.'*

or

> *'So that's what I make/When the day's all wet./It's a good sort of brake/But it hasn't worked yet.'*

Moreover, we notice that a quotation always starts and ends with quotes. Our task is to write:

- a procedure to read a line and store it
- a procedure to write out a line neatly
- a program to test these for a quotation of several lines.

For step 2 above, could we be bold and devise a program that will work for either input format? Not easily. We have to consider how the readline procedure is going to stop. With the line-by-line format, it must stop when it reaches the end of an input-line, whereas the concatenated form implies that ends-of-line will be ignored. There are dodges one can employ to handle these two seemingly contradictory cases. The most common one is to require the line-by-line form to start a few spaces in from the margin, thus extending its end-of-line condition to be 'the end of an input-line followed by a few spaces'. (We need more than one space, because in concatenated form a word could coincide with the end of an input-line, in which case the next input-line will start with a space.)

However, this is not going to teach us much about programming—it is just a complication—so we will not take the dual input idea any further. In the back of our minds is the idea that these read and write line procedures might be useful in a Caesar's speeches-type problem, and we will adopt the data format most suited to that. Bearing in mind that there could be thousands of lines involved, the concatenated method is definitely going to save space, and so step 2 involves ensuring that the input is in this form. At this stage, we cannot see any 'hidden information' that should be gathered about each line as it is read in (step 3), and the data structure in which a line should be stored is a simple array (step 4). (We rejected a list structure for this purpose in the previous chapter.) Finally, the output (step 5) is going to be the line-by-line form and the test data (step 6) will be designed at the end.

Storing the Input

The lines are going to be stored in arrays defined by

```
TYPE    linerange = 1. .linemax;
        lineindex = 0. .linemax;
        lines = packed array [linerange] of char;
```

so the first attempt at a readline procedure is:

```
PROCEDURE readline (var line : lines);
  var i : lineindex;
  BEGIN
    i : = 0;
    repeat
      i := i + 1;
      read(line[i]);
    until line[i] = '/';
  END; {readline}
```

As a first attempt, this is not bad, but the boundary cases are going to complicate it a lot.

Interlude—The over-used line

Before the reader gets too confused, we must define all the nuances of the over-used term 'line'. With the prefixes that we have already started using, they are

poetry-line: the meaningful collection of characters that forms a line of the poem or speech (step 1)

input-line: the list of characters that forms one line of data of varying length (step 2)

stored-line: the array of characters in which a poetry-line is stored by the program (steps 3 and 4)

Ends-of-lines

The first boundary case starts off as being quite easy and relates to the nature of *input-lines* in Pascal. As the last character of an input-line is read, a flag called *eoln* is set. Reading the next character does not give the first of the following line, as one might expect, but a special end-of-line marker which appears to the program as a space. If we do not wish this to appear in our stored-lines we could insert a check after each read to ensure that we move over this marker, i.e.

```
if eoln then readln;
```

However, we might need this space. Consider whether the data is typed:

(a) in fixed-length input-lines with words possibly split over two lines, or
(b) in jagged ended lines, depending on how whole words fit within a given maximum input-line.

(a) is definitely not user-friendly. It looks ugly and also has the disadvantage that making corrections to the input could mean that the entire data from that point on will have to be retyped. Such regimentation will not endear our program to a user! (b) is a much better solution. The only problem is that there may be extra spaces trailing on the end of each input-line. These spaces may have been typed in or added on by systems that like to have all input-lines a fixed length. Whatever the reason, whenever we find the end of an input-line, it will be a simple matter to scan back along what has been read in and remove the superfluous spaces, if they exist.

Having removed all the spaces, the end-of-line's space need not be discarded, but can be used to separate the words on two input-lines. However, a final complication is that if a slash ends an input-line then we don't want any spaces at all. This condition is detected when the removal of the spaces from a stored-line leaves it empty. The handling of the eoln condition is therefore, in full:

```
if eoln then begin
    remove trailing spaces in the stored line
    If stored-line now empty, omit the eoln space
end;
```

Line separators and terminators

The second boundary case relates to the nature of the *poetry-lines*. Annoyingly, the last line of the poem does not end with a slash. Instead it has a quote, usually ', but in other uses to which readline will be put, it may be something else. Therefore we define a variable called endquote and use it in an extended until-condition. Further, this endquote may be missing by mistake, in which case the only stopping point is the end of the file. Checking for end-of-file is a natural precaution in any read routine. We now have

```
repeat
    Deal with eoln
    i := i + 1;
    read(line[i]);
until (line[i] = slash) or (line[i] = endquote) or eof;
```

Notice that in this routine, the final slash or quote will be copied into the stored-line. This seems a good idea, because it will give writeline a signal to stop writing. If the loop ended because of an eof, though, we shall have to insert the signal character.

Stored-line overflow

The third and final boundary effect concerns the *stored-lines* and is more disruptive than the other two. What happens if an exceptionally long line appears (perhaps caused by a forgotten slash) and the array is about to overflow? The eventuality will have to be checked for, and the loop terminated. This gives us a variation of the classic three-way loop of Section 2.2. This loop will continue until

> *either* the end of a poetry-line (slash or quote)
> *or* the end of the file
> *or* the end of a stored-line ($i >$ linemax)

In the latter case, we shall endeavour to set the program back on the rails by skipping on until one of the other conditions occurs. We must also print out a message saying we are doing this, even if it will appear in the middle of other legitimate printing.

> An error condition justifies
> messing up the output.

At least the error will be noticed!

Readline

Readline in comment form is therefore

```
PROCEDURE readline (var line : lines);
    VAR    state : (reading, ended, overflowed, noquote);
    BEGIN
        state:=reading;
        repeat
            {Check for an end of input-line and if so
                        adjust input-line and stored-line}
            {Read and store a character}
            {Check for end of poetry-line and if so set state to ended}
            {Check for end of stored-line and if so set state to overflowed}
            {Check for end of data        and if so set state to noquote}
        until state < > reading;
```

if state = overflowed then
{Continue reading, but output the characters directly,
instead of storing them, until one of the other end
conditions occurs i.e. end of poetry-line or end of data.}

{Ensure that the last character in the stored-line is slash}

END; {readline}

The Pascal version of readline is given in the program in Figure 4.1. Notice that we had to introduce the global variable ch which holds the character just read for all to see. The main program can interrogate ch to establish whether readline ended with a quote—the signal for it to end.

Interlude—Sequential conjunction

The reader may be a bit surprised that the loop for stripping spaces off the end of a line is preceded and followed by if statements. From Figure 4.1 we have:

if i>0 then begin
    while (i>1) and (line[i]=space) do i := i − 1;
    if (i=1) and (line[i]=space then i:=0;
end;

instead of the simple-minded

while (i>0) and (line[i]=space) do i := i−1;

The reason is that, in Pascal, the first condition of an 'and' does not necessarily guard the second from being evaluated. Therefore in the simple loop, i will become 0 and the final test will attempt to evaluate line[0], which does not exist. The while enclosed in two if statements protects line[i] if i is initially zero and also handles the final case when i is one and brings it down to zero.

Writeline has a much easier task, especially since readline has ensured that there will definitely be a slash to signify the end of a line.

Test Data

Having written the procedures, the test program to call them consists simply of a loop based on the two final end conditions—an endquote or an eof. What is more important is the design of the test data (step 6). Clearly, this must include all the cases that we have so carefully programmed for. These are:

● an input-line with trailing blanks
● a missing slash causing a stored-line to overflow
● a missing end quote causing an eof.

The last will have to be run as two tests—one to test that the ordinary case works, and one to test the eof. Other interesting cases might be:

● a poetry-line ending at the end of an input-line
● a poetry-line exactly as long as a stored-line
● a poetry-line one character longer than a stored-line
● a blank poetry-line

Suitable test data would be (with some lines having trailing spaces):

'Let it rain! / Who cares? / I've a train / Upstairs, / With a brake / Which I make / From a string sort of thing, / Which works / In jerks, / 'Cos it drops / In the string, / And the wheels / All stick / So quick / That it feels / Like a thing / That you make / With a brake, / Not string. . . . // So that's what I make / When the day's all wet. / It's a good sort of brake / But it hasn't worked yet.

The output from the program is shown in Figure 4.1.

```
UCSD Pascal Compiler at Wits University

 1   1  1    1   PROGRAM quotation (input, output);
 2   1  1    3      CONST space   = ' ';
 3   1  1    3            lineend = '/';
 4   1  1    3            linemax = 27;
 5   1  1    3
 6   1  1    3      TYPE  linerange = 1..linemax;
 7   1  1    3            lineindex = 0..linemax;
 8   1  1    3            lines     = packed array [linerange] of char;
 9   1  1    3
10   1  1    3      VAR   line      : lines;
11   1  1   17            endquote,
12   1  1   17            ch        : char;
13   1  1   19
14   1  2    1   PROCEDURE readline (var line : lines);
15   1  2    2      VAR  i     : lineindex;
16   1  2    3           state : (reading, endofline, overflow, noquote);
17   1  2    4
18   1  2    0   BEGIN
19   1  2    0      i := 0;
20   1  2    6      state := reading;
21   1  2    9      repeat
22   1  2    9         if eoln(input) then begin
23   1  2   19            if i>0 then begin
24   1  2   24               while (i>1) and (line[i]=space) do i:=i-1;
25   1  2   50               if (i=1) and (line[i]=space) then i:=0;
26   1  2   72            end;
27   1  2   72            if i=0 then readln;
28   1  2   85         end;
29   1  2   85         i := i + 1;
30   1  2   93         read(ch);  line[i]:=ch;
```

```
31  1 2  113        if ch = lineend   then state := endofline else
32  1 2  124        if ch = endquote  then state := endofline else
33  1 2  136        if i = linemax    then state := overflow else
34  1 2  146        if eof(input)     then state := noquote;
35  1 2  159      until state <> reading;
36  1 2  164
37  1 2  164      if state = overflow then begin
38  1 2  169        line[i] := space;
39  1 2  178        write(space:10,'***** Next line too long. Skipped :');
40  1 2  235        repeat
41  1 2  235          write(ch); read(ch);
42  1 2  256          if (ch=lineend) or (ch=endquote) or eof(input)
43  1 2  274          then state := endofline;
44  1 2  280        until state <> overflow;
45  1 2  285        writeln;
46  1 2  293      end;
47  1 2  293      line[i]:= lineend;
48  1 2  302    END; {readline}
49  1 2  320
50  1 3    1    PROCEDURE writeline (line : lines);
51  1 3   16      var i : lineindex;
52  1 3    0      BEGIN
53  1 3    0        i := 1;
54  1 3   11        while line[i] <> lineend do begin
55  1 3   24          write (line[i]);  i := i+1;
56  1 3   50        end;
57  1 3   52        writeln;
58  1 3   60      END; (* writeline *)
59  1 3   74
60  1 1    0    BEGIN  (* quotation *)
61  1 1    0      if not eof(input) then begin
62  1 1   13        read(endquote);
63  1 1   23        repeat
64  1 1   23          readline (line);
65  1 1   27          writeline (line)
66  1 1   29        until eof(input) or (ch=endquote);
67  1 1   47      end;
68  1 1   47      if ch <> endquote then
69  1 1   54        writeln(space:10,'***** The ending quote mark was missing.');
70  1 1  124    END.
```

```
Let it rain!
Who cares?
I've a train
Upstairs,
With a brake
Which I make
          ***** Next line too long. Skipped :g,
From a string sort of thin
Which works
In jerks,
'Cos it drops
In the spring,
And the wheels
All stick
So quick
That it feels
Like a thing
That you make
With a brake,
Not string....

So that's what I make
When the day's all wet.
It's a good sort of brake
But it hasn't worked yet.
```

Figure 4.1   The quotation program

4.2   Designing an Input Format

In the last example, we saw how the input format for a line had to be tightened up before it could be accepted by a program. This process is even more important as the data becomes more varied. Let us take an example from real life.

A certain young publisher wishes to set up a catalogue of all the books that are currently in print for children. (The term 'in print' means that the books have been printed and that stocks are available.) In common with other such catalogues, which are much used by libraries and bookshops, he wishes to arrange entries something like this:

> *Grass for the unicorn*
>   *P. Adams*
>   *Juta   100p*   6.30
>   *ISBN 0 7021 0662 3*
>
> *Adventures of scamp (The)*
>   *Newman Art*   95c
>
> *Stories South African*
>   *A. Lennox-Short &*
>   *R. E. Leighton eds.*   1978
>   *Perskor   241p   ill.*   3.95
>   *ISBN 0 628 01344 2 (Pbd) 2nd ed*

The entries will be updated annually as new books are printed or prices change and so on. Here is a clear case for computer assistance. If we store all the entries for this year on the computer, then next year only the changes and additions need be typed in. The value of the computer, however, is more in the interpretation of the entries and the additional information that can be gained thereby. Thus we can envisage the computer producing lists of all books by a certain publisher, or all books under a certain price, or even the average price of books over a range of page lengths. This means that we need to pay attention to step 3—gathering information from the input. One can see immediately that inputting the entries exactly as given above will not enable us to pinpoint the publisher, say, for each title. In these three examples, chosen at random, the publisher is on the third, second, and fourth lines respectively. These variations are caused by lack of information, such as the author of the second book. This is typical of many problems: real data is seldom complete and is always subject to updating.

An Input Scheme

How, then, are we to recognize each item of the entry? Either each item must be in a fixed place where it can be found, or it must be prefixed by some identifying mark. This leads to five distinct approaches to input schemes, each of which has advantages and disadvantages. The value of each scheme should be judged against the following three criteria:

1. Accuracy with which data can be entered
2. Flexibility to change the size of items or add new ones
3. Amount of wasted space for missing or short items.

The approaches are:

1. Fixed format

Each item is assigned a position within a line of input. The number of lines per entry and the number of characters per item are fixed. The specific space assigned to each item is known as a field, and a blank field can signify that the item is unknown. For the book entries described above, a suitable scheme would be

Title — 80								
Author — 20	Other authors — 20 each							
Pub. — 20	date 4	page 4	price 5	i 1	ed 2	bi 2	ISBN 13	////////

This method is much favoured in commercial business data processing, and is well-suited to programs written in languages that have formatted input facilities, such as FORTRAN and COBOL. However, schemes such as this do not match up to the criteria well. Positioning items in exact columns is error-prone, but can be assisted by having an input device (a card punch or programmable terminal) that can be programmed to accept tabs. A good deal of space is wasted when items are missing or are of average length. Most of all, it is impossible to lengthen a field without disrupting all the subsequent fields. Adding a new field on the end is, of course, quite simple.

2. Positional

One way of overcoming the wastage and inflexibility of a fixed-format scheme is to have the items occurring directly after each other, separated by some unusual character such as a slash. The items in the entry must come in a specified order and missing items are indicated by putting another slash immediately. If we assume that the specified order is the same as that for the previous method, then an example of a book entered with this scheme would be:

Grass for the Unicorn / P. Adams //// Juta // 100/6.30 / i ///0 7021 0662 3

This method is incapable of dealing with variable numbers of things, such as co-authors: here we assumed that there would be a maximum of three, and had to give empty fields for each. It is fairly easy to enter the data accurately, but difficult to check it visually, since a given field and a missing one could so easily have been interchanged. If an item that was previously missing has not been ascertained, then the whole entry has to be retyped so that the item can go in its correct position. However, the advantage is that there is complete flexibility in the length of each item and in the number of items—new ones can simply be given new positions at the end. And, of course, there is no space wasted.

3. Keywords

The previous method took advantage of an almost natural ordering of items in the data. If no such ordering exists, then it becomes much more difficult to enter and check data that relies on position for meaning. In this method, position is irrelevant and instead each item is prefixed by a keyword which indicates its kind. A problem is that the keywords must not be confused with the items themselves. If the items are strings, as in the above example, then either the string items must be enclosed in quotes or the keywords must be identified by some additional special symbol. Such a scheme makes entries easy to type and read, changes are simple, and there is little wasted space. However, for large amounts of data, the keywords do become cumbersome and one is then tempted to abbreviate them, thus losing the value of readability. As a result, this method is now used only in cases where there are not many entries and the items are generally numeric. An excellent example is the job control language required by many computers.

4. Marker driven

This method is a variation on keywords. Instead of using words—which can then be confused with valid text—each item is prefixed by a special symbol. The symbols are chosen so as not to coincide with anything that may appear in the data, and also to have some mnemonic significance. For example, a price may be prefixed by \$ or a number by #. As with abbreviated keywords, there is the disadvantage that the symbols, or markers, may sometimes be obscure, but the effect of this can be minimized if, by convention, the input is entered in a natural order, thus giving additional information to the reader. There is complete flexibility in omitting items and adding new ones, and no space is wasted.

5. Prompt driven

The above four methods are essentially 'batch' schemes, designed for input which is prepared in advance and then submitted to a program. An alternative is to type the input directly into the program as it is running. The program requests each item in order by typing a suitable message on the screen, and the typist responds by supplying the value of the item, or by typing RETURN (say) if the value is unknown. This method has the great advantage that input can be checked as entered. If an invalid value is detected, the program can request a retype immediately. There is complete flexibility in the size of items, and in adding new ones. The criterion of space does not apply, since the data is not stored anywhere prior to the program running. Other advantages and disadvantages of this 'interactive' approach are discussed in Chapter 7.

The choice of method depends on the relative importance of the criteria listed above. In the case of the books-in-print data, we know that items are frequently missing, so a fixed-format scheme would definitely be wasteful. A positional scheme would make the data difficult to read and check. A keyword scheme would be awkward because several of the fields are strings, and some are very small—it starts becoming ridiculous if the keywords are longer than the items! We shall therefore choose a marker scheme, which has the added advantage of being a fairly new idea and one which should enhance your programming repertoire.

In detail, the advantages of such a scheme for books-in-print are:

- the meaning of the item is established

- the type of data following can be deduced (i.e. numeric or alphabetic)

- only items that exist need be mentioned

- items may be mentioned in any order

- different items can appear on a single line because each is delimited by the marker of the next item

- common portions of items can be omitted or abbreviated

- new kinds of items can be easily added.

Making a start on the books-in-print entries, we can set up a scheme as follows:

MARKER	ITEM	TYPE OF VALUE
none	*title*	*string*
@	*author(s)*	*string*
%	*publisher*	*string*
*	*date*	*year*
/	*pages*	*integer*
$	*price*	*real*
!	*illustrated*	*boolean*
#	*ISBN number*	*string*

We also need some way of indicating the end of each entry. There are several ways in which this can be done. The simplest is actually to give the first item, the title, a marker as well. Alternatively, a stand-alone marker can be used at the end of every entry. A third option takes into account the way in which the data is stored and updated. Presumably, the entries will be stored in some text file and updated by means of a text editor. The person doing the updating is going to be the publisher himself, or an assistant. Therefore it is quite important that the data is easy to read on the screen. One way of achieving this is to separate each entry by a blank line. Although in the olden days, blank lines meant wasted cards, on today's terminal systems, a blank line will probably occupy no more than a character.

The blank line method therefore seems a good one, but will present some problems in the implementation of the reading routines; more of that later. Using this scheme, the three examples above would be presented to the program as

Grass for the Unicorn @*P. Adams* %*Juta* /100 $6.3 #7021 0662 3

Adventures of Scamp (The) %*Newman Art* $95c

Stories South African @*A. Lennox-Short* & *R. E. Leighton eds.* *1978 %*Perskor* /241 ! $3.95 #628 01344 2

The last two items of *Stories South African* (the binding and the edition) are left out until markers can be assigned to them. Notice that the first part of an ISBN number can be omitted since the seven characters 'ISBN 0' are common for all books produced in Europe and Africa, which is the scope of this catalogue.

Choosing Markers

Markers are chosen from among the special symbols that are available on computer input devices, but which do not usually occur in the items themselves. Of course, there are bound to be exceptional cases, such as a title *Europe on $10 a day*. In this case, we have to employ a technique known as *escape coding*. Whenever a marker appears normally in a field, it is doubled. Thus we would have *Europe on* $$10 *a day*. Another way of overcoming the ambiguity is to choose a really obscure symbol such as | and use this as a preface to each marker. This method is usually preferred where the markers are going to be letters, as in the Play Structure Project (Chapter 3). A third option is to have a second escape character which indicates that the next symbol has its real meaning, and is not to be interpreted as a marker. If | is such an escape character, then we would have $10 but *Europe on* |$10 *a Day*. Notice how the marker symbols should be chosen with some connection to the actual items (*percent* for publisher, *dollar* for price).

The Command Module

The design of the input routine now proceeds at two levels:

1. The command module which detects valid markers and passes control to the read modules.
2. The read modules. These each handle a specific type of item, e.g. a string or a number of a particular kind.

The design of a command module turns out to be remarkably simple, and sets a pattern that can be followed in similar circumstances. The m_i are the markers, with m_n being the one for the end of an entry.

```
{Initialize all fields}
repeat
    {Find a marker}
    case marker of
        m₁ : {Call to read routine for m₁}
        m₂ : {Call to read routine for m₂}
          .
          .
        mₙ : {Do nothing};
    end;
until marker = mₙ;
```

The marker m_n is assumed to be the one indicating the end of the entry. Since we have agreed not to have a marker *per se* but to use a blank line, the command module will have to rely on a rather clever nextch routine which will read a single character and in addition convert the occurrence of a blank line into a character which can serve as m_n. Let us suppose that ']' is the chosen character, and leave the design of the nextch routine to later.

In the scheme for books in print, we find that a title does not have a marker: it is always the first field and always exists. Therefore, it would be read in and stored before the general loop for all the other fields. Translating the skeleton command module into a working version for books in print, we get:

```
Initialize all fields
readstring (title);
repeat
    getoneof (markerset);
    marker := ch; nextch;
    case marker of
        '%' : readstring(publisher);
        '@' : readstring(author);
        '*' : readyear(date);
        '/' : readpages(pages);
        '$' : readprice(price);
        '!' : illustrated:=true;
        '#' : readstring (ISBN);
        ']' : ;
    end;
until marker = ']';
```

Here, markerset is defined as a set of characters and initialized to include the special marker characters as follows

```
TYPE charset : set of char;
VAR  markerset : charset;

markerset := ['@', '%', '*', '/', '$', '!', '#', ']'];
```

WARNING! Remember that not all systems allow sets of characters. The way to get around such a restriction was discussed in Section 2.4.

Low-level Reading Routines

The getoneof procedure proposed above may skip over blanks, but if anything else is found, then it is clearly in the wrong place. Getoneof must report such a mistake and recover by continuing to search for one of the markers. Actually, this is a useful process which could operate on any given set of characters, such as letters or digits, as well. In order to make the skipping message appropriate for each set, we include a description of the set as an alfa parameter. Therefore we have:

```
PROCEDURE getoneof (these : charset; description : alfa);
  BEGIN
    while ch = space do nextch;
    if not (ch in these) then begin
      write ('**** Invalid ',description,'. Skipping :');
      while not eof(input) and not (ch in these) do begin
        write(ch); nextch;
      end;
      writeln;
    end;
  END; {getoneof}
```

Getoneof makes use of nextch, and also mentions the possibility of an end-of-file occurring unexpectedly. It is now time to define nextch and to show how end-of-file and the special ends-of-line are catered for. The full nextch is:

```
PROCEDURE nextch;
  BEGIN
    if eof(input)
    then begin
      error ('data eof');
      ch := endofentry;
    end
    else
    if eoln(input)
    then begin
      readln(input);
      if not eoln(input) {and therefore also not eof}
```

```
          then {strip leading blanks}
            repeat read(input,ch)
            until (ch < > space) or eoln(input) {and also maybe eof}
          else ch := space;
          if ch = space {and therefore a double eoln exists}
          then ch := endofentry
          {else ch has the value of the next character}
        end
        else read(input,ch)
    END; {nextch}
```

Nextch carefully goes through each possible combination of the two signals and ensures that the end-of-entry marker gets sent across when they occur. It takes on the additional task of stripping off any leading blanks on a line. Where data consists of normal text, blanks may appear to make the data easier to read, and it is assumed that they do not form part of the strings to be stored.

One complication here is that getoneof assumes that ch has a value when it skips spaces. In order to ensure that this is so, ch must be primed by a call to nextch from the outside program.

Interlude—Looking ahead with input↑

Although common practice, priming a routine always seems messy. One way to avoid reading ch in advance is to use the buffer variable which is associated with every file, including input. The buffer variable is given the name of the file followed by the pointer symbol and contains the item about to be read. Thus input↑ is defined right at the start of the program, and we could rewrite nextch and all the routines that use it to refer to input↑ rather than ch. The only problem is that, quite understandably, input↑ cannot be altered, so that the trick used to replace ch by an end-of-entry marker could not be duplicated.

Both ch and input↑ therefore have their advantages and the only guideline is that you should stick to one or the other in any one program, or confusion will doubtless result.

The Data Structure

Before we consider the reading routines any further, we must carry on to step 4 in the design rules—set up the data structure to hold an entry. This is a clear case for a record, because there are several fields, all of different types. The definition follows the clues given already in the input scheme and the command module.

```
TYPE   yearrange = 1800. .2000;
       pagerange = 1. .pagemax;
```

```
books = record
  title,
  publisher,
  author     : string;
  date       : yearrange;
  pages      : pagerange;
  price      : real;
  illustrated : boolean;
  ISBN       : string
end;

VAR   book : books;
```

It makes no difference what order fields are listed in, so we choose a logical one, even though it means mentioning string twice. Illustrated is boolean, since a book is either illustrated or isn't, and as a result, there is no read routine for it: if an exclamation mark appears, illustrated is set to 'true'. The three numeric fields, date, pages, and price, all have different types, a fact which is reflected by the command module calling three separate routines for them.

Initializing

We are now in a position to work out the initializing of these fields. Initializing is another of those very valuable exercises that is usually neglected in haste. To be fair, there is another reason for shying clear of it, and that is that it is usually very difficult to decide what to initialize a field to! The problem is twofold: we have to find a value which could not otherwise occur and we have to be able to test for it. For example, we could set the price of each entry to zero, then when printing out the entry, if the price is still zero we know that it is unknown as yet and leave it blank. Price is an easy one; what about strings? A suitable value would be all spaces, but this is clumsy to test for, since it would have to be set up as a variable and assigned spaces to start with. The date presents a similar difficulty in that we have carefully set the limits which our catalogue will cover, but initializing will require us to include 1799 or 2001, without it being clear in the definition why this was so.

The answer to the problem is an old one: factorize. We shall factorize the information concerning presence or absence out of the fields themselves and set up a separate field to record this. This will be a set of names corresponding to the field names. If a name is in the set, then there exists a proper value for the field. If the name is not in the set, then no value is known for the field. Thus initializing for the whole entry is accomplished by setting the set to empty. This gives:

```
TYPE
fieldnames = (thetitle, thepublisher, theauthor,
              thedate, thepages, theprice,
              theillustrations, theISBN);
```

```
books = record
                thedata : set of fieldnames;
                title    : ...
                  .
                  .
                  .
        -     end;
```

and

```
        book.thedata := [ ];
```

A check for existence of a field will read quite nicely, for example:

```
        if theprice in thedata then . . .
```

The Reading Routines

This more or less completes the top level of the input design, and we can now proceed down to the actual reading routines. These fall into two categories—the string ones and the numeric ones. A string is exactly like a line and the reading and writing of one has already been covered. The adaptations to readline would include initializing and a slightly different end condition for the poetry-line. The end condition will in fact be based on the imminent appearance of a marker. The development of this routine is left as an exercise for the reader.

One extension to readline is worth considering. In its present form, it will store an end marker in every string. In order to find out how long the string is, a quick count will have to be done. If the length is going to be used often, for centring or adjusting, say, then it may be worth storing the length with the string. Since this information is known as each string is read, it can be stored immediately. The definition of a string then becomes:

```
TYPE string = record
                length : lineindex; {to allow for empty lines}
                data : packed array [linerange] of char;
            end;
```

Numeric Conversions

Let us begin by looking at numeric items in general. There is already a built-in Pascal routine to read a number. However, it does not guard against typing errors—one of the largest sources of invalid data. On an ordinary typing device, the numbers are in lower case, but * is in the upper case. It is quite possible for someone to miss lifting the shift key by a fraction of a second and type *!980 instead of *1980. This would be disastrous on three counts: it would probably get past a visual check, it would cause the read to crash, and it would create havoc in the command module since ! is a marker. We therefore have to forego the read routine as supplied and write our own.

```
PROCEDURE readinteger(var n : integer);
BEGIN
    n := 0
    Skip till the first digit
    repeat
        n := n*10 + the new digit
        Read on
    until no longer a digit
END; {readinteger}
```

The basis of the routine is the reading of characters, which are then converted into their numeric equivalent and accumulated to form the actual number. The conversion involves a type conversion from char to the ordinal value of that character. In most character sets, however, the ordinal value of the digits is not what one expects, i.e. ord('8') is seldom 8. It is more likely to be 248. The ordinal value must therefore be offset by the ordinal of zero. The routine becomes:

```
PROCEDURE readinteger (VAR n: integer);
BEGIN
    n := 0;
    getoneof (['0'. .'9'], 'digit');
    repeat
        n:=n*10 + ord(ch) − ord('0')
        nextch;
    until not (ch in ['0'. .'9']);
END; {readinteger}
```

(Note that strictly this is readnatural rather than readinteger.)

The next step is to incorporate this procedure in the other three. The blueprint for all of them is:

```
PROCEDURE readyear (var date : yearrange);
    var n : integer;
    BEGIN
        Read a number into n
        If it is in the required range,
            copy it into date and mark it as in the set
        Otherwise put out an error message and do not
            mark it as in the set
    END; {readyear}
```

This is a typical routine for checking that a number is in a given range. Reading a page follows the same pattern, except that we wish to be nice to the users and permit them to (perhaps absentmindedly) add a 'p' after the number of pages. Expanding out the comments of readyear in this context we get:

```
PROCEDURE readpages;
    VAR p : integer;
    BEGIN
        readinteger(p);
        if (p<1) or (p>pagemax) then
            error('length?');
        book.pages :=p;
        if ch='p' then nextch;
    END; {readpages}
```

Here we have introduced the error routine, which plays a large part in verification programs. Notice that we have to signal what kind of error has occurred, and a short alfa string serves very well.

The third numeric routine involves real numbers—with a difference. In fact, numbers may come in as any of

6.99   6.00   0.6   6   6.5   6.50   65p

All but the last conform to the general form of a real number, but the 'p' at the end stands for pence and cannot simply be ignored as was the 'p' for pages. Moreover, internationally speaking, the 'p' could be a 'c' (for cents) and the full stop in 6.99 could even be a comma! This increases the need for a tailor-made read routine. The companion to readinteger is therefore:

```
PROCEDURE readreal (var r : real);
    VAR integerpart : integer;
        significance : real;
    BEGIN
        readinteger (integerpart);
        r := integerpart;
        if (ch='.') or (ch=',') then begin
            nextch;
            significance := 0.1;
            while ch in ['0'. .'9'] do begin
                price := price + (ord(ch)–ord('0'))*significance;
                significance := significance * 0.1;
                nextch;
            end;
        end;
    END; {readreal}
```

and readprice uses this as follows:

```
PROCEDURE readprice (var price : real);
  CONST decimalsign = 'c'; {or 'p'}
  BEGIN
    readreal(price);
    if ch = decimalsign then begin
      nextch;
      price := price/100;
    end;
    price := price + 0.005;
  END; {readprice}
```

There is still one flaw in all these routines, but it is one which we can make a case for ignoring. This is the question of significance of numbers. An integer can only hold a number of a certain size, depending on the number of bits assigned to it. Thus a 32-bit integer can only support numbers of up to 9 digits safely. Our readinteger routine has no check on whether the machine's limit is exceeded. Such a check could be included, but it is highly unlikely that years or page lengths will exceed this, even with typing errors. Even though we started this chapter with a resolution to consider all possibilities, we realize that there are limits, and therefore, for the purposes of this explanation, significance checks will be ignored.

We might now wish to test these routines: in order to do so, we shall need corresponding output routines. This is the subject of the next section.

4.3   Printing a Catalogue—Output Formatting

In the last section, we came to the conclusion that for secure programs, the reading routines provided with the system were inadequate. Is this true for the writing routines? At first glance, the answer is no: writing does not have the uncertainty about the data that reading has. But as soon as we start trying to do anything that relies on knowing where we are in the line, we find that we have to build in more controls. For example, writing the price on the right-hand side of the page requires that we know how far along the line we are already, so that we can write out the intervening spaces. Inputting actually has more aids in this connection, particularly the buffer variable feature (input↑) and the end-of-line check (eoln). For controlled outputting, the best method is to submerge any writes under a layer of our own procedures, which will keep track of where we are on the page and on the line.

For reading, we used the following hierarchy:

```
readbook
  ↓
readstring
readpages
```

readprice
readyear
↓
readreal
readinteger

For writebook we shall employ something similar, plus an additional layer to control:

- automatic overflowing to a new line when the current one is full
- division into pages
- moving on so many spaces
- leaving only so many spaces on the right.

Low-level Printing Control

To maintain control over the printed page, both horizontally and vertically, we need three counters: the current page number, the current line number and the current position in the line.

```
CONST   space        = ' ';
        charmax      = 100;
        linenomax    = 75;

TYPE    charindex    = 1..charmax;
        linenoindex  = 1..linenomax;
        pagenorange  = 1..maxint;

VAR     position : charindex;
        lineno   : linenoindex;
        pageno   : pagenorange;
```

Print is the routine which will control the horizontal position. Each time a character is to be written, print goes through this sequence:

- check if the line is complete, and if so, call newline
- increment the position
- write the character.

The order of these three actions is important. In particular, newline is only called when an attempt is made to add the (charmax+1)'th character. The reason for the delay is that an item that coincides with the end of a line could well be followed by an explicit call to newline from the program using these routines. If newline was activated as soon as a line was full, the explicit call would cause an extra blank line.

Newline stands in a similar relation to newpage, with the additional responsibility of resetting the position. Its sequence is:

- check if the page is complete, and if so, call newpage
- increment the line number
- writeln
- reset the position.

Newpage has no higher-level routine to pass control to, so it starts at the second step by incrementing the page number, writing it out and resetting the line number. The five printing routines are therefore:

```
PROCEDURE newpage;
    VAR i : pagenorange;
    BEGIN
        pageno := pageno + 1;
        for i := lineno to linelength + 1 do writeln;
        writeln(space : charmax div 2 - 2, '-', pageno 1, '-');
        page(output);
        lineno := 0;
    END; {newpage}

PROCEDURE newline;
    BEGIN
        IF lineno = charmax then newpage;
        lineno :=lineno + 1;
        writeln;
        position := 0;
    END; {newline}

PROCEDURE print (ch : char);
    BEGIN
        IF position = charmax then newline;
        position := position + 1;
        write(ch);
    END; {print}

PROCEDURE move (n : charindex);
    BEGIN
        for n := n down to 1 do print(space);
    END; {move}

PROCEDURE leave (n : charrange);
    BEGIN
        IF n > (charmax - position) then newline;
        move (charmax - position - n);
    END; {leave}
```

Writebook

We can now set up a skeleton writebook procedure which will present the entries in the general form of:

title
  author   *date*
  publisher pages ill   *price*
  ISBN

Vacant fields should be replaced by others where feasible (e.g. publisher and price should be on line 2 if there is no author or date) and overrunning will happen automatically (e.g. with very long titles). Filling vacant fields relies on knowing which are vacant, which is where the set of field names comes in. To check for both the author and date missing we use set intersection as

if [theauthor, thedate]∗ thedata < > [ ] then newline;

Also, we wish to indent three spaces except on the first line. To do this, newline is altered to move in indent spaces and the value of indent (either 0 or 3) is controlled from writebook. Assuming the existence of suitable procedures for writing the fields, writebook becomes:

```
        PROCEDURE writebook (book : books);
             BEGIN with book do begin
                  indent := 3;
{line 1}  writestring(title);
             newline;
{line 2}  if theauthor in thedata then writestring(author);
             if thedate in thedata then begin
                  digits := 4;
                  leave(digits+2); move(2);
                  writeinteger(date,digits); END;
             if [theauthor, thedate]∗thedata < > [ ] then newline;
{line 3}  if thepublisher in thedata then writestring(publisher);
             if thepages in thedata then begin
                  Calculate the digits needed
                  move(2);
                  writeinteger(pages,digits); print('p'); END;
             if theillustrations in thedata then begin
                  move(2);
                  print('i');print('l');print('l'); END;
             if theprice in thedata then begin
                  Calculate the digits needed, and add 3
```

```
            leave(digits+2); move(2);
            writeprice(price); END;
         if [thepublisher, thepages, theprice, theillustrations]*thedata
            < > [ ] then newline;
{line 4}  if theisbn in thedata then begin
            print('I'); print('S'); print ('B'); print('N');
            print(' '); print('O'); print(' ');
            writestring(ISBN);
            newline; END;
         END;
         indent := 0;
         newline;
       END; {writebook}
```

For the date, we know that we need to leave four places at the end of the line, but for the price and pages we have to calculate the number of digits that will be printed. Fortunately, we remember that logs to the base 10 provide this information in the characteristic, so we have

```
digits := trunc (ln(n)/ln(10.0)) + 1;
```

For the price, we add three onto this figure—either for the decimal point and two decimal places, or for the two places and the 'c' (or 'p').

Writeprice and the other writing procedures are very similar to their reading counterparts and are not discussed in detail here. They appear in the full program listing in the Comprehension at the end of the chapter.

The Advantage of Write Routines

At this point the reader may be losing faith in the necessity for all these routines. Why not simply

```
write (pages : digits, 'p')
```

instead of

```
writeinteger (pages, digits); print ('p');
```

The trouble with the former is that it does not record the new position on the line of output. So how can we tab correctly when we print the price? A fix would be

```
write(pages : digits, 'p'); position := position+digits+1;
```

This is dangerous. It could so easily be forgotten, or maybe there are not (digits+1) spaces left on a particular line, in which case adding them to position will cause a 'value out of range' execution error. It is much better to leave the incrementing of the counters to the printing routines, which always check for potential overflows.

Printing in columns

The above justification for the print routines is a matter of style and good programming. There is also a practical reason why we route everything through these routines. As an extension of the problem it is required that the pages of book entries be printed in columns—a very common requirement in real-life printing, and especially in catalogues where the entries are relatively short. However, printing in columns is regarded as a tricky problem by programmers because the common solution does not always work. Intuitively, we would consider reading in enough information for all the columns on the page, then dividing it up and printing it in parallel. In pictures, we have

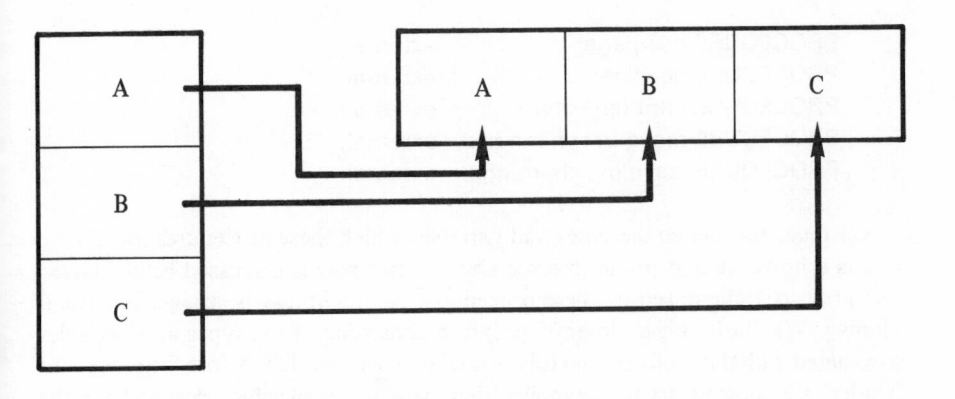

The disadvantage of this method is that it assumes that an array of the correct size can be set up and the information stored there. Relying on an array is unattractive if, for example, the information is already in a linked list. (Printing in columns is often used for Shakespeare's plays, which we saw were better off in this structure.) Although we did not discuss it in Chapter 3, we can see intuitively that dividing a linked list up into equal portions will require a couple of scans. A better solution is to delegate the entire printing process to the routines we have already. They will have an array big enough for a page of several columns. Each call to print will result, not in a write, but in the storing of the character in the array, which we shall call the *tray*. Newline does not write either: it simply lets lineno be incremented as before, thus opening up a new row of the tray. Finally, newpage increments the column number and if the maximum has been reached, it can now activate the printing of the tray. Printthetray employs a triple loop to unravel the columns side by side. The beauty of this method is that no program using the print routines need change or be at all concerned with the details of printing in columns, apart from specifying initially how many are required.

128

4.4 Packaging and Using Libraries

In the last section we saw that it was possible to build up a set of routines with a common purpose. In order for these to be available for other programs and other users, we have to put them in a library. In computer terms, a *library* is a file on some magnetic medium (disc or tape) which contains routines of general interest. To use these, we merely mention their names. When the compiler is finished with our program, it calls in the *linker* (or consolidator or collector), which works out which procedures are missing, fetches them out of a library, and joins them on to the program. We have to investigate exactly how to use a library, and then how to set one up with our own favourite routines.

Using is easy. The procedure heading of each library procedure that is to be used is written at the start of the program (after the declarations) and followed by the word 'external'. The parameters for the procedure (if any) are listed exactly as if we were defining them. The compiler uses these definitions to check that any calls to the procedures are correct. For our printing routines, we might define:

```
PROCEDURE newpage;              external;
PROCEDURE newline;              external;
PROCEDURE print (ch : char);    external;
PROCEDURE move (n : charindex); external;
PROCEDURE leave (n : charrange); external;
```

We must also define the types and variables which these procedures use. Doing this is a nuisance and prone to error and a better way is discussed below. Given this proviso, though, setting these procedures up in a library is straightforward, if clumsy. We start with a 'dummy' program consisting of the types and variables associated with the routines, and follow it with newpage. Just before the procedure header, we indicate to the compiler that here is a procedure destined for the library. This indicator is usually a special comment, e.g. (*$E+*), where E stands for external. The exact form may differ from computer to computer, but the idea will be the same. The routine and dummy program are compiled, and the process repeated for each of the other routines.

> Nothing is ever as simple as it looks.

The catch is that we have to inform the computer which library to store the routine in. This information is given outside the program in the job control statements (JCL or SCL). Murphy's law will ensure that this aspect of the task will take longer to get right than the rest put together!

Global, Local, and Shared variables

Now let us look at those types and variables that have to be defined every time we use the routines. In Pascal, declarations of variables (and by implication types and constants, too) are of two kinds: *global* and *local*. Global variables belong to the program and can be used by every procedure. Local variables are defined by a procedure for use by it and any procedures which it itself defines. The difference is illustrated in the diagram.

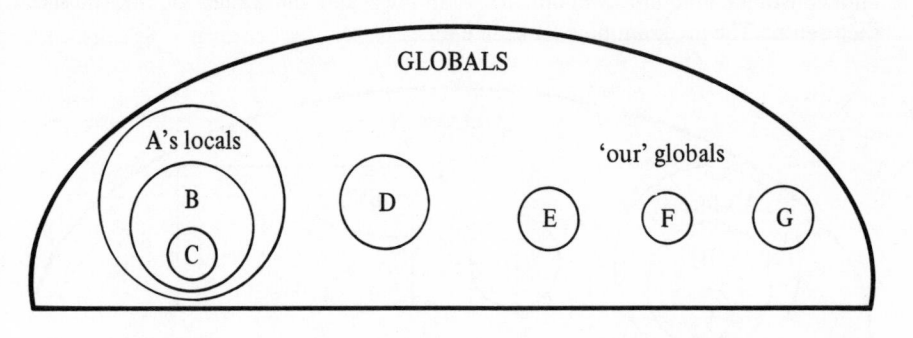

The locals defined by A can be used by it and by B and C. Together these three nested procedures form a self-contained entity. The problem arises when a collection of routines logically form an entity, but are physically separate because they can all be called individually. They might have variables which only they should have access to, but because declarations can only be global or local, these have to defined with all the other globals. Without any formal grouping, the shared variables are left open for (accidental) use by the other procedures.

Packages

Standard Pascal unfortunately does not provide a means for grouping shared variables. Languages which have been derived from Pascal (e.g. CLU, Euclid, Ada) recognize the need for this facility and allow one to define a *package*. Because some Pascal systems have been extended to include something like packages, it is worth discussing how they work. A package looks like this:

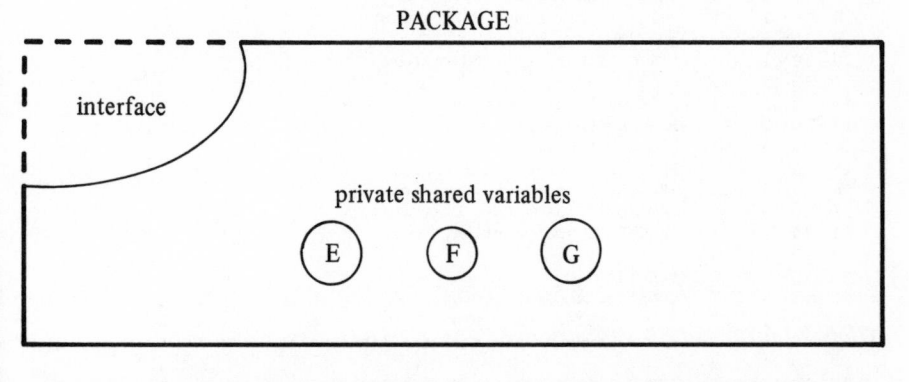

The private shared variables are globals which only the packaged routines can see and use. Those variables which are used by both the package and the program

130

are listed in the interface. An example of such a variable would be indent, which is set to 0 or 3 by writebook and used by newline to position correctly the start of the next line. It is not possible to declare indent as a parameter, because newline is also called from within the package itself. Also in the interface are listed the types and constants that are common to both sides and the names of the routines themselves. The program now looks like this:

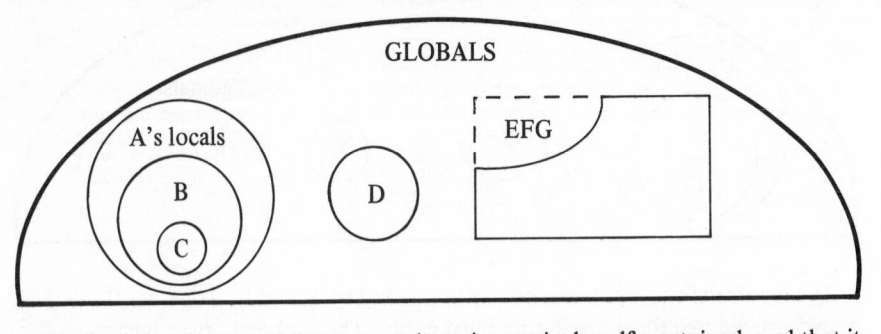

We now have to ensure that our package is genuinely self-contained, and that it can initialize itself. For the printing routines, we would have to include a procedure to initialize the counters—position, lineno, and pageno. By the same token, a finalizing routine should be called to empty any buffers that still have information in them. For the sake of completeness, Figure 4.2 gives the whole printing package here in one of the common packaging formats. (The format chosen is that of a widely used system for small computers called UCSD Pascal.)

```
UCSD Pascal Compiler at Wits University

  1  10  1    1 UNIT printunit;
  2  10  1    1
  3  10  1    1 INTERFACE
  4  10  1    1   CONST  space     = ' ';
  5  10  1    1          charmax   = 100;
  6  10  1    1
  7  10  1    1   TYPE   charrange = 1..charmax;
  8  10  1    1          charindex = 0..charmax;
  9  10  1    1
 10  10  1    1   VAR    indent    : charindex;
 11  10  1    2
 12  10  1    1   PROCEDURE startprinting;
 13  10  2    1   PROCEDURE newpage;
 14  10  3    1   PROCEDURE newline;
 15  10  4    1   PROCEDURE print (ch : char);
 16  10  5    1   PROCEDURE move  (n : charindex);
 17  10  6    1   PROCEDURE leave (n : charrange);
 18  10  7    1   PROCEDURE stopprinting;
 19  10  7    1
 20  10  1    1 IMPLEMENTATION
 21  10  1    2   CONST  linenomax  = 64;
 22  10  1    2          columnmax  = 4;
 23  10  1    2          traymax    = 256;   {linenomax*columnmax}
 24  10  1    2
 25  10  1    2   TYPE   linenorange = 1..linenomax;
 26  10  1    2          linenoindex = 0..linenomax;
```

```
27  10  1       2          columnrange = 1..columnmax;
28  10  1       2          columnindex = 0..columnmax;
29  10  1       2          pagenoindex = 0..maxint;
30  10  1       2          trayrange   = 1..traymax;
31  10  1       2          trayindex   = 0..traymax;
32  10  1       2          rows        = packed array [charrange] of char;
33  10  1       2
34  10  1       2   VAR
35  10  1       2   { limits } linelength : charrange;
36  10  1       3              pagelength : linenorange;
37  10  1       4              noofcolumns: columnrange;
38  10  1       5              gap        : charrange;
39  10  1       6   {counters} position   : charindex;
40  10  1       7              lineno     : linenoindex;
41  10  1       8              pageno     : pagenoindex;
42  10  1       9              traylevel  : trayindex;
43  10  1      10              column     : columnindex;
44  10  1      11   { buffers} row        : rows;
45  10  1      61              tray       : packed array [trayrange] of rows;
46  10  112861
47  10  1       1   PROCEDURE startprinting;
48  10  1       0     BEGIN
49  10  1       0       writeln('Linelength, pagelength, noofcolumns, gap');
50  10  1      60       readln(linelength, pagelength, noofcolumns, gap);
51  10  1     112       position := 0;
52  10  1     119       indent := 0;
53  10  1     126       lineno := 0;
54  10  1     133       column := 0;
55  10  1     140       pageno := 0;
56  10  1     149       traylevel := 0;
57  10  1     158     END; {startprinting}
58  10  1     170
59  10  8       1   PROCEDURE printthetray;
60  10  8       1     VAR columnsize,
61  10  8       1         L                : linenorange;
62  10  8       3         c                : charrange;
63  10  8       4         s                : columnindex;
64  10  8       0     BEGIN
65  10  8       0       columnsize := (traylevel + lineno) div noofcolumns;
66  10  8      16       for L := 1 to columnsize do begin
67  10  8      33         for s := 0 to noofcolumns-1 do begin
68  10  8      54           traylevel := s*columnsize;
69  10  8      65           for c:= 1 to linelength do write(tray[traylevel+L,c]);
70  10  8     124           write(space:gap);
71  10  8     136         end;
72  10  8     143         writeln;
73  10  8     151       end;
74  10  8     158       for L := columnsize to pagelength + 1 do writeln;
75  10  8     194       pageno := pageno + 1;
76  10  8     207       writeln (space : ((linelength + gap)*noofcolumns-gap)
77  10  8     226                         div 2 - 2, '-', pageno:1, '-');
78  10  8     275       {page (output);}
79  10  8     275       column  := 0;
80  10  8     282       traylevel:=0;
81  10  8     291     END; {printthetray}
82  10  8     312
83  10  2       1   PROCEDURE newpage;
84  10  2       0     BEGIN
85  10  2       0       column := column+1;
86  10  2      11       IF column = noofcolumns then printthetray;
87  10  2      22       traylevel := column * pagelength;
88  10  2      37       lineno := 0;
89  10  2      44     END; {newpage}
90  10  2      56
91  10  3       1   PROCEDURE newline;
92  10  3       0     BEGIN
```

```
 93  10  3    0     IF lineno = pagelength then newpage;
 94  10  3   11     lineno := lineno + 1;
 95  10  3   22     IF position < linelength then
 96  10  3   31        for position:=position+1 to linelength do
 97  10  3   57           row[position]:=space;
 98  10  3   80     tray[traylevel+lineno] := row;
 99  10  3  104     position := 0;
100  10  3  111     move(indent);
101  10  3  119   END; {newline}
102  10  3  134
103  10  4    1 PROCEDURE print {ch : char};
104  10  4    0   BEGIN
105  10  4    0     IF position = linelength then newline;
106  10  4   11     position := position + 1;
107  10  4   22     row[position]:=ch;
108  10  4   35   END; {print}
109  10  4   48
110  10  5    1 PROCEDURE move {n : charindex};
111  10  5    0   BEGIN
112  10  5    0     for n:=n downto 1 do print(space);
113  10  5   27   END; {move}
114  10  5   42
115  10  6    1 PROCEDURE leave {n : charrange};
116  10  6    0   BEGIN
117  10  6    0     IF n > (linelength-position) then newline;
118  10  6   13     move (linelength-position-n);
119  10  6   27   END; {leave}
120  10  6   40
121  10  7    1 PROCEDURE stopprinting;
122  10  7    0   BEGIN
123  10  7    0     if (column > 0) or (lineno > 0) then printthetray;
124  10  7   15   END; {stopprinting}
```

Figure 4.2   The print unit

We hasten to emphasize that:

THIS IS NOT STANDARD PASCAL

However, in advanced programming, we are forced out of the cocoon which is formed by a standard and are able to taste the forbidden fruits put before us by compiler implementors. In real life, we will constantly be placed in the position where, for the sake of efficiency, simplicity, or sheer desperation, we have to look beyond the confines of our language to what the whole computer system has to offer. The hallmark of a good programmer is that he knows his language inside out and can tune it to 90 per cent of his needs—far more than an amateur would think possible. But when the need arises, he is not afraid of using additional facilities, always bearing in mind the words of the Marriage Service:

'not by any to be enterprized, not taken in hand, unadvisedly, lightly or wantonly . . . but reverently, discreetly, advisedly and soberly . . .'

4.5   Comprehension—Books-in-Print

The program in Figure 4.4 together with its sample input (Figure 4.3) and output solves the basic problem of reading in coded bibliographic entries and printing them out in columns. The program uses two non-standard Pascal features which are easily explained:

1. 'USES printunit' calls in the printunit routines, as discussed in the previous section.
2. The data is stored in a file known as infile, and this file is reset using an extended form. Such extensions are discussed in Section 7.4. For our purposes, there is no difference between infile and input.

Read the program through once, marking (in coloured pens) the important procedures and actions, then answer the questions.

Improvements

The output does not look quite right. Words are split over two lines, as are the numbers of pages in some cases.

1. Do you think that avoiding these splits should be the task of:
    the writebook routines
or
    the printing routines?
Why?
Devise a solution to the problem and implement it. Run the program on the computer if possible.
2. In a similar way, entries are split over columns and pages. Do you think that it would be reasonable to try to avoid these splits? If not, why not? If so, do you think that the solution would be along the same lines as the previous one?
3. The data given is all correct. Alter it by introducing errors, and run the program to see how it reacts. It should detect several errors. Notice that the *error-reporting* routine gives the title of the book in error. This is because the columns facility means that entries are not printed as they are read in and the error message does not appear with the printed entry. However, the program has no *error-recovery* routines. Is it likely that one error in the input will cause others? If so, how, and where should recovery take place?

Extensions

Once the basic readbook and writebook routines are established, it is amazing how quickly one can extend or alter the formats from the user's point of view. Try the following three. (They were actual requests made by the publisher who used this program.)

4. The international standard book number (ISBN) has a particular format. It consists of ten digits with the last one possibly being an X meaning 10. This

last digit is a check digit: by adding up the other nine in a particular way and taking a modulus, we should arrive at this figure. If not, then there has been an error in entering the ISBN. The formula for the check is

$$\sum_{i=1}^{10} D_i *(11 - i)\ MOD\ 11 = 0$$

Write a procedure called readisbr which calls readstring and then performs this check.

5. The output format for the book entries is pleasing to the eye, but is very wasteful of space. In order to save on printing costs, one could sacrifice the nice format and simply print an entry as a continuous stream of items, separated by full stops or two blanks as appropriate. For example,

> *Cape Charade. Butler G.*
> *Balkema 3,50*

> *Capture and care of wild*
> *animals (The). Young E. ed.*
> *Human and Rousseau. ill.*
> *10,50 ISBN 0 949968 12 9*

would save one and two lines respectively. Altering writebook only, implement this change. Run the program with varying line lengths to see which seems to give the best saving (i.e. the lines do not have to be 30 wide).

6. It turns out that many books, particularly textbooks, belong to a series of which there is a title and then several subtitles, each with its own date, price, ISBN, etc. For example, two such composite entries are

> *A Re Bale %van Straik @Hoffman P. A. et al*
> *+Sub Std A / 56 ! *79 $55c #627 00941 7*
> *+Sub Std B /54 ! *76 $55c #627 00920 4*
> *+Std 1   /48 ! *78 $60c #627 00920 4*
> *+Std 3   /124 ! *77 $70c #627 00924 7*
> *+Std 4   /126 ! *77 $70c #627 00925 5*
> *+Std 5 (Mpato Wa Thlano) /129 ! $80c *77 #627 00926 3*

> *Civil practice and procedure in all Bantu courts in Southern Africa*
> *@Khumalo J. A. M. %Juta*
> *+Main volume *75 $25 #7021 0657 7*
> *+Supplement no 1 *76 #7021 0724 7 $2.5*
> *+Supplement no 2 *77 #7021 0825 1 $5*

Since reading the subtitle is exactly the same operation as reading a title, we can use last-line recursion to handle this extension. Pointers will also be needed to create a list of subtitles, as there could be any number of them. Devise the necessary changes to the book record and the readbook procedure and implement this new facility.

Candid Cape Town: a discreet guide to the Cape Peninsula @Michaelides
C.G. *1977 %Struik /161 ! $4.95 #86977 090 X

Cape charade @Butler G. %Balkema $3.5

Cape childhood (A) @Henshilwood N.G. *72 %David Philip /112 ! $7.95
#949968 02 1

*Cape Peninsula ferns: a guide to the fern species of the Cape Peninsula, with
black and white drawings and identification keys of all recognised species*
@Roux J.P. %National Botanic Gardens *79 /66 ! #620 03775 X $2.5

Capture and care of wild animals (The) @Young E. ed %Human and
Rousseau ! $10.50 #7981 0331 0

Caravan caravel @Philip M. *73 %David Philip /144 $2.85 #949968 12 9

Casey and Co.: selected writings of Casey 'Kid' Motsisi @Motsisi K. &
Mutloatse M. ed *78 ®Ravan /133 ! $3.85 #86975 088 7

Children's wildlife gallery *77 %Albany Museum /20 ! $40c #620 02964 1

Clive's lost treasure @Allen G. & D. *79 %Macmillan $12.5

Close to the sun: stories from Southern Africa @de Villiers G.E.
%Macmillan *79 /215 #86954 077 7 $2.95

Coat (The) @ Fugard A. %Balkema $3.5

Cold stone jug @Bosman H.C. %Human and Rousseau $4.25

Collector of treasures and other Botswana village tales (The) @Head B.A.
*77 %David Philip /109 $4.95 #949968 92 7

Figure 4.3   Data for books-in-print

```
UCSD Pascal Compiler at Wits University

 1   1  1    1 PROGRAM printbook (input,output);
 2   1  1    3
 3  10  1    3
 4  10  1    3 CONST  space    = ' ';
 5  10  1    3        charmax  = 100;
 6  10  1    3
 7  10  1    3 TYPE   charrange = 1..charmax;
 8  10  1    3        charindex = 0..charmax;
 9  10  1    3
10  10  1    3 VAR    indent   : charindex;
11  10  1    4
12  10  1    1 PROCEDURE startprinting;
13  10  2    1 PROCEDURE newpage;
14  10  3    1 PROCEDURE newline;
15  10  4    1 PROCEDURE print (ch : char);
16  10  5    1 PROCEDURE move  (n : charindex);
```

```
17  10  6    1    PROCEDURE leave (n : charrange);
18  10  7    1    PROCEDURE stopprinting;
19  10  7    1
20   1  1    1    USES printunit;
21   1  1    4
22   1  1    4    CONST  stringmax   = 180;
23   1  1    4           yearmin     = 1900;
24   1  1    4           yearmax     = 1981;
25   1  1    4           pagemax     = 1000;
26   1  1    4           endofentry = ']';
27   1  1    4
28   1  1    4    TYPE   stringrange= 1..stringmax;
29   1  1    4           stringindex= 0..stringmax;
30   1  1    4           strings    = packed array [stringrange] of char;
31   1  1    4           alfa       = packed array [1..8] of char;
32   1  1    4           pagerange  = 1..pagemax;
33   1  1    4           yearrange  = yearmin..yearmax;
34   1  1    4           charset    = set of char;
35   1  1    4           fields     = (thetitle, theauthor, thepublisher,
36   1  1    4                          thepages, theprice, thedate,
37   1  1    4                          theillustrations, theISBN);
38   1  1    4           books      = RECORD
39   1  1    4             title,
40   1  1    4             author,
41   1  1    4             publisher  : strings;
42   1  1    4             pages      : pagerange;
43   1  1    4             date       : yearrange;
44   1  1    4             price      : real;
45   1  1    4             illustrated : boolean;
46   1  1    4             ISBN       : strings;
47   1  1    4             thedata    : SET OF fields
48   1  1    4           END;
49   1  1    4
50   1  1    4    VAR
51   1  1    4           infile      : text;
52   1  1  305           book        : books;
53   1  1  671           markerset   : charset;
54   1  1  687           ch          : char;
55   1  1  688
56   1  2    1    PROCEDURE error (message : alfa);
57   1  2    6    var i : stringrange;
58   1  2    0    BEGIN
59   1  2    0      write(' **** Error in the ',message,' in ');
60   1  2   64      i:=1;
61   1  2   72      while book.title[i] <> '/' do begin
62   1  2   88        write(book.title[i]);
63   1  2  109        i:=i+1;
64   1  2  119      end;
65   1  2  121      writeln;
66   1  2  129    END;
67   1  2  144
68   1  3    1    PROCEDURE nextch;
69   1  3    0    BEGIN
70   1  3    0      if eof(infile)
71   1  3    7      then begin
72   1  3    9        error ('data eof');
73   1  3   22        ch := endofentry;
74   1  3   26      end
75   1  3   26      else
76   1  3   28      if eoln(infile)
77   1  3   35      then begin
78   1  3   37        readln(infile);
79   1  3   44        if not eoln(infile) {and therefore also not eof}
80   1  3   51        then {strip leading blanks}
81   1  3   54          repeat read(infile,ch)
82   1  3   64          until (ch <> space) or eoln(infile)
```

```
83   1  3   76                      {and also maybe eof}
84   1  3   76                 else ch := space;
85   1  3   85                 if ch = space {and therefore a double eoln exists}
86   1  3   88                 then ch := endofentry
87   1  3   92                 {else ch has the value of the next character}
88   1  3   92             end
89   1  3   96             else read(infile,ch)
90   1  3  108         END;
91   1  3  122
92   1  4    1  PROCEDURE readbook(VAR book : books);
93   1  4    2
94   1  4    2  VAR marker : char;
95   1  4    3
96   1  5    1     PROCEDURE getoneof (these : charset; description : alfa);
97   1  5    0        BEGIN
98   1  5    0           while ch = space do nextch;
99   1  5   16           if not (ch in these) then begin
100  1  5   28             write(´ **** Invalid ´,description,´. Skipping : ´);
101  1  5   91             while not eof(infile) and not (ch in these) do begin
102  1  5  112                write(ch);   nextch;
103  1  5  126             end;
104  1  5  128             writeln;
105  1  5  136           END;
106  1  5  136        END;
107  1  5  152
108  1  6    1     PROCEDURE readstring(VAR s : strings);
109  1  6    2     {Does not check for stored-string overflow}
110  1  6    2     VAR i : stringindex;
111  1  6    0     BEGIN
112  1  6    0        getoneof([´A´..´Z´,´a´..´z´,´0´..´9´],´alphabet´);
113  1  6   34        i := 0;
114  1  6   42        repeat
115  1  6   42           i := i+1;
116  1  6   52           s[i] := ch;
117  1  6   65           if eoln(infile)
118  1  6   72           then begin
119  1  6   74              while (i>1) and (s[i] = space) do i := i-1;
120  1  6  104              nextch;
121  1  6  106              if not (ch in markerset) then begin
122  1  6  119                 i := i+1; s[i] := space;
123  1  6  140              end;
124  1  6  140           end
125  1  6  140           else nextch;
126  1  6  144        until ch in markerset;
127  1  6  156        if s[i]<>space then i:=i+1; {else overwrite the space}
128  1  6  180        s[i] := ´/´;
129  1  6  191     END;
130  1  6  208
131  1  7    1     PROCEDURE readinteger (VAR n:integer);
132  1  7    0        BEGIN
133  1  7    0           n:=0;
134  1  7    3           getoneof ([´0´..´9´],´ digit ´);
135  1  7   30           REPEAT
136  1  7   30              n:=n*10 +ord(ch) - ord(´0´);
137  1  7   42              nextch;
138  1  7   44           UNTIL not (ch in [´0´..´9´]);
139  1  7   63        END;
140  1  7   78
141  1  8    1     PROCEDURE readyear;
142  1  8    1     VAR n : integer;
143  1  8    0        BEGIN
144  1  8    0           readinteger(n);
145  1  8    4           IF n<100 THEN n:=n+1900;
146  1  8   16           IF (n<yearmin) or (n>yearmax) then
147  1  8   29              error(´ date ´);
148  1  8   42           book.date := n;
```

138

```
149   1  8   57    END;
150   1  8   70
151   1  9    1    PROCEDURE readpages;
152   1  9    1      VAR p : integer;
153   1  9    0      BEGIN
154   1  9    0        readinteger(p);
155   1  9    4        IF (p<1) or (p>pagemax) then
156   1  9   15          error(´ length?´);
157   1  9   28        book.pages := p;
158   1  9   41        IF ch=´p´ THEN nextch;
159   1  9   50      END;
160   1  9   62
161   1 10    1    PROCEDURE readprice;
162   1 10    1      CONST decimalsign = ´c´;   { or ´p´}
163   1 10    1      VAR integerpart : integer;
164   1 10    2        significance : real;
165   1 10    0      BEGIN WITH book do begin
166   1 10    5        if (ch=´.´) or (ch=´,´) THEN
167   1 10   18          price:=0.0
168   1 10   22        ELSE BEGIN
169   1 10   32          readinteger (integerpart);
170   1 10   36          price:=integerpart;
171   1 10   44        END;
172   1 10   44        IF (ch=´.´) or (ch=´,´) THEN BEGIN
173   1 10   57          nextch;
174   1 10   59          significance := 0.1;
175   1 10   70          WHILE ch in [´0´..´9´] DO BEGIN
176   1 10   88            price := price +(ord(ch)-ord(´0´))*significance;
177   1 10  112            significance := significance*0.1;
178   1 10  127            nextch;
179   1 10  129          END;
180   1 10  131        END;
181   1 10  131        IF ch = decimalsign THEN BEGIN
182   1 10  138          nextch;
183   1 10  140          price := price/100.0;
184   1 10  159        END;
185   1 10  159        price:=price+0.005;
186   1 10  179      END;
187   1 10  179    END;
188   1 10  194
189   1 11    1    PROCEDURE addtodata;
190   1 11    0      BEGIN with book do
191   1 11    5        case marker of
192   1 11   10          ´@´ : thedata := thedata+[theauthor] ;
193   1 11   27          ´%´ : thedata := thedata+[thepublisher] ;
194   1 11   44          ´*´ : thedata := thedata+[thedate] ;
195   1 11   61          ´$´ : thedata := thedata+[theprice] ;
196   1 11   78          ´/´ : thedata := thedata+[thepages] ;
197   1 11   95          ´!´ : thedata := thedata+[theillustrations] ;
198   1 11  112          ´#´ : thedata := thedata+[theISBN] ;
199   1 11  131          endofentry : ;
200   1 11  133        end;
201   1 11  262      END;
202   1 11  276
203   1  4    0    BEGIN
204   1  4    0      WITH book DO BEGIN
205   1  4    3        thedata := [thetitle];
206   1  4   12        readstring (title);
207   1  4   18        REPEAT
208   1  4   18          getoneof(markerset,´ marker ´);
209   1  4   39          marker := ch; nextch;
210   1  4   46          CASE marker OF
211   1  4   49            ´@´ : readstring(author);
212   1  4   56            ´%´ : readstring(publisher);
213   1  4   61            ´/´ : readpages;
214   1  4   65            ´*´ : readyear;
```

```
215   1  4   69              ´$´ : readprice;
216   1  4   73              ´!´ : illustrated := true;
217   1  4   81              ´#´ : readstring(ISBN);
218   1  4   89            endofentry : ;
219   1  4   91          END;
220   1  4  220          addtodata;
221   1  4  222        UNTIL marker = endofentry
222   1  4  223      END;
223   1  4  227    END;
224   1  4  244
225   1 12    1    PROCEDURE writebook (book : books);
226   1 12  368      TYPE numberrange = 0..9;
227   1 12  368      VAR  digits : numberrange;
228   1 12  369
229   1 13    3      FUNCTION whole (n : real) : numberrange;
230   1 13    0        BEGIN
231   1 13    0          whole:= trunc(ln(n)/ln(10.0))+1;
232   1 13   24        END;
233   1 13   36
234   1 14    1      PROCEDURE writestring(VAR s : strings);
235   1 14    2        VAR i : stringrange;
236   1 14    0        BEGIN
237   1 14    0          i := 1;
238   1 14    8          while s[i] <> ´/´ do begin
239   1 14   22            print(s[i]);
240   1 14   35            i := i+1;
241   1 14   45          end;
242   1 14   47        END;
243   1 14   62
244   1 15    1      PROCEDURE writeinteger (n,d : integer);
245   1 15    3        VAR g, x : integer;
246   1 15    0        BEGIN
247   1 15    0          x:=1;
248   1 15    3          FOR g:=2 to d do x:=x*10;
249   1 15   26          FOR d := d downto 1 DO BEGIN
250   1 15   37            print (chr (n div x + ord(´0´)));
251   1 15   45            n:=n mod x;
252   1 15   50            x:=x div 10;
253   1 15   55          END;
254   1 15   62        END;
255   1 15   78
256   1 16    1      PROCEDURE writeprice (p : real);
257   1 16    3        VAR n : integer;
258   1 16    0        BEGIN
259   1 16    0          n:=trunc((p-trunc(p))*100);
260   1 16   19          IF p>0.999 THEN BEGIN
261   1 16   34            writeinteger(trunc(p),digits-3);
262   1 16   48            print(´,´);
263   1 16   52          END;
264   1 16   52          writeinteger(n,2);
265   1 16   56          IF p<1 THEN print(´c´);
266   1 16   70        END;
267   1 16   82
268   1 12    0      BEGIN WITH book DO BEGIN
269   1 12    6        indent := 3;
270   1 12   12        writestring(title);
271   1 12   17        newline;
272   1 12   20        IF theauthor in thedata THEN writestring(author);
273   1 12   32        IF thedate in thedata THEN BEGIN
274   1 12   40          digits := 4; leave(digits+2); move(2);
275   1 12   65          writeinteger(date,digits); END;
276   1 12   73        if [theauthor, thedate]*thedata <> [ ] then newline;
277   1 12   88        IF thepublisher in thedata THEN writestring(publisher);
278   1 12  100        IF thepages in thedata THEN BEGIN
279   1 12  108          digits:=whole(pages); move(2);
280   1 12  129          writeinteger(pages,digits); print(´p´); END;
```

```
281  1 12  141      IF theillustrations in thedata THEN BEGIN
282  1 12  149         move(2);
283  1 12  156         print('i'); print('l'); print('l'); END;
284  1 12  168      IF theprice in thedata THEN BEGIN
285  1 12  176         IF price<1 THEN digits := 3
286  1 12  187                   ELSE digits:=whole(price)+3;
287  1 12  213         leave(digits+2); move(2);
288  1 12  231         writeprice(price); END;
289  1 12  238      if [thepublisher, thepages, theprice, theillustrations]
290  1 12  238         *thedata <> [ ] then newline;
291  1 12  253      IF theisbn in thedata THEN BEGIN
292  1 12  261         print('I'); print('S'); print('B'); print('N');
293  1 12  277         print(' '); print('0'); print(' ');
294  1 12  289         writestring(ISBN);
295  1 12  294         newline; END;
296  1 12  297      END;
297  1 12  297      indent := 0;
298  1 12  303      newline;
299  1 12  306   END; {writebook}
300  1 12  318
301  1  1    0   BEGIN
302  1  1    0      reset(infile,'BOOKDATA.TEXT');
303  1  1   43      markerset:=['@','%','/','*','$','!','#',']'];
304  1  1   65      nextch;
305  1  1   67      startprinting;
306  1  1   70
307  1  1   70      WHILE not eof(infile) DO BEGIN
308  1  1   80         readbook(book);
309  1  1   85         writebook(book);
310  1  1   90      END;
311  1  1   92
312  1  1   92      stopprinting;
313  1  1   95   END.
```

Candid Cape Town: a discreet g
uide to the Cape Peninsula
Michaelides C.G.   1977
Struik   161p ill   4,95
ISBN 0 86977 090 X

Cape charade
Butler G.
Balkema   3,50

Cape childhood (A)
Henshilwood N.G.   1972
David Philip 112p ill
                          7,95
ISBN 0 949968 02 1

Cape Peninsula ferns: a guide
to the fern species of the
Cape Peninsula, with black
and white drawings and iden
tification keys of all reco
gnised species
Roux J.P.   1979
National Botanic Gardens 6
6p ill   2,50
ISBN 0 620 03775 X

Capture and care or wild anima
ls (The)
Young E. ed

Human and Rousseau ill
                         10,50
ISBN 0 7981 0331 0

Caravan caravel
Philip M.   1973
David Philip 144p   2,85
ISBN 0 949968 12 9

Casey and Co.: selected writin
gs of Casey 'Kid' Motsisi
Motsisi K. & Mutloatse M. e
d   1978
Ravan 133p ill   3,85
ISBN 0 86975 088 7

Children's wildlife gallery
                          1977
Albany Museum 20p ill
                          40c
ISBN 0 620 02964 1

Clive's lost treasure
Allen G. & D.   1979
Macmillan   12,50

Close to the sun: stories from
Southern Africa
de Villiers G.E.   1979
Macmillan 215p   2,95

Coat (The)
    Fugard A.
    Balkema   3,50

Cold stone jug
    Bosman H.C.

Collector of treasures and oth
   er Botswana village tales (
   The)
   Head B.A.   1977
   David Philip 109p   4,95
   ISBN 0 949968 92 7

Figure 4.4   The Books-in-Print program

Chapter 5

Algorithms (Part 2)—Sorting and Searching

The need to sort things into order is very common in computing (and in real life). We need to sort things into numerical order, into alphabetical order, by categories, or by dates. It is very important to realize that whatever the criterion for sorting, the sorting operation itself remains fundamentally the same. Coupled with sorting is the idea of searching: if things are in some known order, then finding a particular item can be done more efficiently than the simple linear search employed in Chapter 2. In this chapter we consider some of the classic sorting and searching methods and compare their relative efficiency. Because the array is the data structure on which these methods are based (Chapter 6 examines others), this chapter ends with a treatise on the storing and accessing of arrays and tables.

5.1 The Sorting Process

The very first algorithm considered in this book was called 'Picking and Choosing', and we saw how it could be used to shuffle a pack of cards. We pointed out that shuffling could be viewed as the transformation of a sequence of cards from one order into another. Sorting is exactly the same kind of transformation, viewed as going from disorder to order. In the shuffling algorithm, a card was repeatedly selected from an ever-decreasing list, with the basis for the selection being a random function. Sorting can be done similarly by repeatedly selecting an item from those remaining, with the basis for the selection being 'the next in order'. No matter what the items are that are being sorted, or whether the order is ascending, descending or whatever, the sorting operation remains the same.

Since the items to be sorted must all be of the same type, we shall declare

```
TYPE   range = 1 . .n;
       index = 0. .n;
       table = array [range] of items;
```

A suitable multi-purpose sorting procedure can then be defined, working straight from the picking and choosing algorithm, as

```
PROCEDURE sort (var a : table;
                n : range;
                function ordered (x, y : items) : boolean);
```

```
VAR i, j : range;
BEGIN
    for i := 1 to n do begin
        j := nextinorder(a, i, n);
        exchange (a[j], a[i]);
    end;
END;
```

Nextinorder is a simple looping function of the 'find the largest' kind:

```
FUNCTION nextinorder (a        : table;
                      from,n : range;
                      function ordered (x,y : items) : boolean);
    VAR j,k : range;
    BEGIN
        j := from;
        for k := j + 1 to n do
            if not ordered (a[j], a[k]) then j := k;
        nextinorder := j;
    END; {nextinorder}
```

We have increased the generality by parametrizing nextorder, making the ordering function to be used a formal function. Unfortunately, this now invalidates the higher-level procedure sort: this is an example of the backtracking and iteration that characterizes top-down design in real life. The necessary changes are made in the final version of the program, shown in Figure 5.1.

A Question of Efficiency

Now we should look critically at this program. The sort procedure itself is 25 lines long and includes two internal routines, exchange and nextinorder. In the development of the sort, this division of labour helped us to formulate the solution. Doing things properly, we set up the routines with parameters that seemed relevant and that enhanced readability. With hindsight we can set to reducing the sort procedure to a more streamlined form. The basis for doing this is:

1. The use of procedures is only essential if they are called from more than one place.
2. Parameters are only necessary if different calls are provided with different variables.

Taking nextinorder, we see that both the table and its size are part of its environment and always correspond to the table and value of n defined, by the sort procedure header. Similarly, the ordering function can be accessed by nextinorder directly. Although the from parameter is always equivalent to i, the change of name in the interests of readability is a possible reason for retaining it as a parameter. By point 1, though, both routines are redundant anyway.

144

```
 1    PROGRAM Sorting (input, output);
 2
 3    CONST max = 100;
 4          maxhead = 22;
 5
 6    TYPE  range = 1..max;
 7          index = 0..max;
 8          items = char;
 9          table = array [range] of items;
10          heads = packed array [1..maxhead] of char;
11
12    VAR   scores : table;
13          maxscores : range;
14
15    {The ordering functions for characters ignore the case
16     of the letter.  Reducing the ord of each by mod 32 copes
17     with most collating sequences.}
18
19    FUNCTION ascending (a, b : items) : boolean;
20      BEGIN
21        ascending := ord(a) mod 32 < ord(b) mod 32;
22      END; {ascending}
23
24    FUNCTION descending (a,b : items) : boolean;
25      BEGIN
26        descending := ord(a) mod 32 < ord(b) mod 32;
27      END; {descending}
28
29    PROCEDURE sort (VAR a : table; n : range;
30                       FUNCTION ordered (x,y : items) : boolean);
31      VAR i,j : range;
32
33      FUNCTION nextinorder (a : table; from, n : range) : range;
34        VAR j,k : range;
35        BEGIN
36          j := from;
37          for k := j+1 to n do
38            if not ordered(a[j],a[k]) then j:=k;
39          nextinorder := j;
40        END; {nextinorder}
41
42      PROCEDURE exchange (var x,y : items);
43        VAR temp : items;
44        BEGIN
45          temp := x;  x := y;  y := temp;
46        END; {exchange}
47
48      BEGIN {sort}
49        for i := 1 to n-1 do begin
50          j := nextinorder (a,i,n);
51          exchange (a[i],a[j]);
52        end;
53      END; {sort}
54
55    PROCEDURE print(heading:heads; t : table; n : range);
56      VAR i : 1..maxint;
57      BEGIN
58        for i := 1 to maxhead do write(heading[i]); writeln:
59        for i := 1 to n do write(t[i]:2);
60        writeln; writeln;
61      END; {print}
62
63    PROCEDURE obtain(var t:table; var n : range);
64      VAR i : range;
```

```
65      BEGIN
66          readln(n);
67          for i := 1 to n do read(t[i]); readln;
68      END; {obtain}
69
70      BEGIN {Main program Sorting}
71          obtain(scores, maxscores);
72          print('UNSORTED                   ',scores,maxscores);
73          sort (scores, maxscores, ascending);
74          print('SORTED ASCENDING    ',scores,maxscores);
75          sort (scores, maxscores div 2, descending);
76          print('HALF SORTED DESCENDING', scores, maxscores div 2);
77      END.
```

Figure 5.1   The sorting program

We notice also that on the last scan through the list, *i* is *n* and *j* is *n* and nextinorder simply returns *n*, which then causes $a[n]$ to be exchanged with itself. Reducing the number of times the whole list is scanned gives the full *selection sort* procedure:

```
PROCEDURE selectionsort (var a : table;
                         n : range;
                         function ordered (x,y : items) : boolean);
    VAR i, j, k : range;
        temp    : items;

    BEGIN
        for i := 1 to n − 1 do begin
            j := i;
            for k := 1 + 1 to no do
                if not ordered (a[j], a[k]) then j := k;
            temp := a[i];
            a[i] := a[j];
            a[j] := temp;
        end;
    END; {selectionsort}
```

The 25 lines have shrunk to 15. This exercise illustrates the dual role of a programming language. On one hand it is there to assist in finding a solution, by providing a convenient yet precise way of expressing our thoughts. On the other hand, it is the means of communicating with the computer and often we like to do this in as efficient a way as possible. In general, a compact algorithm such as the one above will be more efficient than a modular, top-down one. What we lose is the additional information about the solution which was contained in the procedure and parameter names.

Ordering Functions

As we have seen, the sorting process is quite independent of the nature of the items being sorted: all reference to the details of the things is confined inside the comparison function. To the sort, this is a formal parameter and the definition of the actual parameter is within the scope of the procedure that calls the sort. In practice, we often have to sort a table of composite items, using one field (or part of a field) as the *key*.

Suppose we have student records containing names and marks for various courses. A typical definition might be:

```
TYPE    studentrange  = 1 . .n;
        courserange    1 . .coursemax;
        markrange     = 0 . .100;
        coursenumbers = 200. .299;
        marks = record
                    course : coursenumbers;
                    score  : markrange;
                end;
        Students = record
                    name : string;
                    results : array [courserange] of marks;
                    total   : markrange;
                end;
        classlist = array [studentrange] of students;
```

We may wish to sort the class list into alphabetical order, or numerical order on a total mark, or possibly on the mark for a particular course. We would then set up three ordering functions. The two for the numeric comparisons are:

```
FUNCTION totalorder(a,b : students) : boolean;
BEGIN
    totalorder := a.total > b.total;
END; {totalorder}
FUNCTION courseorder(a,b : students) : boolean;
BEGIN
    courseorder := a.results[i].score > b.results[i].score;
END; {courseorder}
```

Note that for sorting on a particular course, the index to the results array is assumed to be non-local to the function. It cannot be a parameter because all the ordering functions must have the same two (and only two) parameters.

Alphabetic ordering is more complicated because names can contain upper and lower case letters, spaces, and punctuation. So as not to lose sight of the sorting problem itself, the question of how to handle alphabetic data properly is left to Chapter 7. However, we observe that comparisons are done many times during a sort and if they are going to involve a lot of work, it may be better to include in the item a compressed version of the name which can be used as the key. This compressed version could be all in one case, with punctuation removed so that the ordinary < or > operations will produce a suitable result. Because of the difficulty of ordering alphabetic data correctly, records often contain a numeric field which is used as the key instead. Examples of such keys are student numbers, bank account numbers, and even the course numbers in the above example.

Exchange Procedures

After comparison, the second essential part of a sort is the exchange procedure. If the things that have to be exchanged are at all large, exchanging them will be time-consuming, but it can be avoided by the following elegant device.

Sorting defines a permutation, which if applied to the items would render them into sorted order. The trick is to generate the permutation, while leaving the objects themselves in their original positions. We define

    VAR perm : array [range] of range;

and initialize it so that $perm[i] = i$ for $i = 1..n$. Then instead of comparing $a[i]$ with $a[j]$ we compare $a[perm[i]]$ with $a[perm[j]]$. Then when the exchange has to be done, we simply exchange $perm[i]$ and $perm[j]$, instead of the whole large items. At the end of the sorting, perm will hold the desired permutation, and the items in the table can be retrieved by accessing the ith thing as $a[perm[i]]$.

Analysis of Performance

Now let us look at the performance of the selection sort, in particular how it behaves for large values of n. There are three factors which contribute to the performance:

● the number of passes through the list
● the number of comparisons
● the number of exchanges.

The list is considered $n - 1$ times and for each pass, one exchange is made. This gives

No. of passes $= n - 1$
No. of exchanges $= n - 1$

On each pass, the list is reduced by one, making the number of comparisons

$$(n - 1) + (n - 2) + (n - 3) + \ldots + 1$$

$$= \frac{n(n - 1)}{2}$$

148

which is of the order ($\frac{1}{2}n^2$), usually written O($1/2n^2$). This is disquieting. We should always be wary of processes whose time varies with size in a worse-than-linear way. While $\frac{1}{2}n^2$ is acceptable (as opposed to $n!$), there are good theoretical arguments to suggest that we should be able to do the job in a time of O($n\ log_2n$).

What is perhaps worse is that even if the table is actually in the correct order, the procedure takes the same time as for a randomly or inversely ordered sequence. On the other hand, this algorithm is easy to produce, simple to understand, and you are unlikely to make any mistakes in actually programming it. What is more, the effort of producing a better algorithm is non-trivial, to say the least. So you have to exercise judgement in choosing whether or not to use this simple sort.

To illustrate exactly how selection sort achieves this performance, Figure 5.2 shows the steps through the sorting of 10 numbers.

SORTING TEST ON : 7 2 6 9 5 4 1 0 3 8
$n = 10$, $n(n - 1)/2 = 45$

SELECTION SORT

```
7 2 6 9 5 4 1 0 3 8
. ^ . . . . . . . . . . . . . . . ^ . . . . . . . . . .
0 2 6 9 5 4 1 7 3 8
    . ^ . . . . . . . . . . . . . ^ . . . . . . . . .
0 1 6 9 5 4 2 7 3 8
        . ^ . . . . . . . . . . . ^ . . . . . . . . .
0 1 2 9 5 4 6 7 3 8
            . ^ . . . . . . . . . ^ . . . .
0 1 2 3 5 4 6 7 9 8
                . ^ . . ^ . . . . . . . . . .
0 1 2 3 4 5 6 7 9 8
                        . . . . . . . . . . . . . .
0 1 2 3 4 5 6 7 9 8
                            . . . . . . . . . . . .
0 1 2 3 4 5 6 7 9 8
                                . . . . . . . . .
0 1 2 3 4 5 6 7 9 8
                                    . ^ . . . ^ .
0 1 2 3 4 5 6 7 8 9
```

45 comparisons and 6 exchanges.

...   indicates a comparison
.^.   indicates an exchange

Figure 5.2 Illustration of selection sort

5.2 Alternative Sorting Methods

As we have seen, the sorting process can be described simply as

- deducing the correct place in the sequence for each item
- moving it there.

There are many different ways of performing this process and each has its own strengths and weaknesses. There are excellent books on sorting available, notably *Sorting and Searching* by Knuth, which is still the most complete treatise on the subject, and Wirth's *Algorithms + Data Structures = Programs*, which describes all the methods in Pascal. Figure 5.3 categorizes the most well-known sorts. The one which we have discussed is on the far left, being a straight internal sort. External sorts are those that are done not in memory, but using discs or tapes; the usual reason for selecting such methods is that there are too many items to fit in memory. These sorts are discussed in Chapter 7. In this section we will describe the other internal sorts mentioned, except for *treesort*, which is found in Chapter 6. The emphasis is on capturing the sense of the different algorithms in a few lines, and then exploring their performance and advantages.

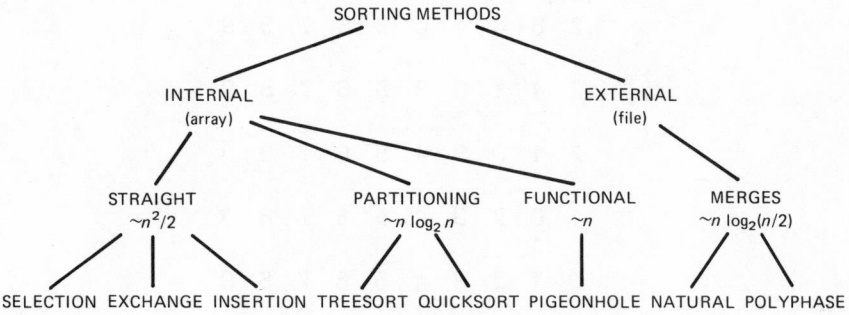

Figure 5.3   Various sorting methods

Exchange Sort

The *exchange sort* (often called the *bubble sort*) attempts to take advantage of any pre-existing ordering of the items. Suppose we go through an unsorted table comparing pairs of adjacent items and exchanging them if they are not in order. Let the highest key be $a[k]$. When it is compared with $a[k + 1]$ it will be exchanged, and will be found to be out of order on every subsequent comparison. It will thus finish in its correct position at the end of the list, and the amount of work (exchanges) required to get it there will be proportional to its initial distance from its correct position. With the highest key in position we now have to sort a table of $n - 1$ items, and the same algorithm can be applied. It thus seems that the more nearly sorted the table is, the less work the exchange sort will do. The method is as follows:

1. Consider each list $a[1]. .a[j]$, where j starts at n and works back to 2.
2. For each pair $a[i]$ and $a[i + 1]$ in the list, exchange them if they are out of order.
3. When no exchanges take place, stop—the table is sorted.

The method is illustrated in Figure 5.4.

SORTING TEST ON : 7 2 6 9 5 4 1 0 3 8
$n = 10, n(n - 1)/2 = 45$

EXCHANGE SORT

```
7  2  6  9  5  4  1  0  3  8
.^. .^. .^. .^. .^. .^. .^. .^. .^. .^.
2  6  7  5  4  1  0  3  8  9
 . . . .^. .^. .^. .^. .^. .^. . . . .
2  6  5  4  1  0  3  7  8  9
 . . . .^. .^. .^. .^. .^. . . . . . .
2  5  4  1  0  3  6  7  8  9
 . . . .^. .^. .^. .^. . . . . . . . .
2  4  1  0  3  5  6  7  8  9
 . . . .^. .^. .^. . . . . . . . . . .
2  1  0  3  4  5  6  7  8  9
 . .^. .^. .^. . . . . . . . . . . . .
1  0  2  3  4  5  6  7  8  9
 .^. .^. . . . . . . . . . . . . . . .
0  1  2  3  4  5  6  7  8  9
 . . . . . . . . . . . . . . . . . . .
0  1  2  3  4  5  6  7  8  9
```

44 comparisons and 28 exchanges.
...   indicates a comparison
.ˆ.   indicates an exchange

Figure 5.4   Example of exchange sort

The procedure for the sort is:

```
PROCEDURE exchangesort (var a : table;
                                    n : range;
                        function ordered (x,y : item) : boolean);
        VAR last, i : range;
            inorder : boolean;
```

```
BEGIN
    last := n;
    repeat
        inorder := true;
        for i := 1 to last − 1 do begin
            if not ordered (a[i], a[i + 1]) then begin
                exchange (a[i], a[i + 1]);
                inorder := false;
            end;
        end;
        last := last − 1;
        if last < 2 then inorder := true;
    until inorder;
END;
```

Notice that termination is forced as soon as only one item is left. Without this condition, last would have gone out of range.

With the conditional termination, the best and worst cases for the exchange sort are easily obtained:

	Best case	Worst case
Passes	1	n
No. of comparisons	$n - 1$	$\dfrac{n(n-1)}{2}$
No. of exchanges	0	$\dfrac{n(n-1)}{2}$

Thus with the list in order (the best case), the exchange sort performs much better than the selection sort. Intuitively, it seems that the performance should also be better for a partially sorted list, but the average performance is in fact disappointing. It can be shown by detailed analysis that on average,

$$\text{No. of passes} = n - Cn/2$$

$$\text{No. of comparisons} = \frac{n(n - K - \ln n)}{2}$$

$$\text{No. of exchanges} = \frac{n(n - 1)}{4}$$

where C and K are constants. Therefore, the sort is still performing at order n^2. Moreover, the number of exchanges is very large and since an exchange is likely to be a more costly operation than a comparison, this is a severe drawback. In fact, this sort has very little to recommend it except its catchy nick-name—the bubble sort. (The name comes from the way in which successive exchanges cause the last item to 'bubble' up to the end of the list.)

Before leaving the exchange sort, we note that there is one improvement that can be made. When a pass through the list results in more than one item landing in its correct place, then the next pass can ignore all of these items, not just the rightmost one. In the example in Figure 5.4, the second pass results in 7 and 8 being in their correct positions. Therefore the third pass need only consider the list from the first to the sixth item. The redundant comparisons can actually be seen in the diagram. The algorithm can be revised by recording the position of the last exchange made in each pass and using it to set the length for the next pass. By experiment, one can see that this will give about 10 per cent improvement in comparisons, and less than this on exchanges.

Insertion Sort

The next sort is one that is used by many card players. It turns out to have better performance than either of the methods so far discussed. Suppose that the first j items have been sorted into correct order. We take the next item $a[k]$, $k = j + 1$, and compare it in turn with the preceding items until its correct position is reached or until we reach the start of the table. In either case we can now insert $a[k]$ in its correct place. Of course, arrays are not elastic, so we cannot actually insert $a[k]$ in this way. In fact we achieve the same effect by comparing $a[k]$ with $a[k-1]$ and exchanging them if they are not in order, then repeating the process comparing $a[k]$ with $a[k-2]$ and so on, stopping when the correct place for $a[k]$ is found. The complete algorithm is:

```
PROCEDURE insertionsort (var a : table;
                         n : range;
                         function ordered (x,y : item) : boolean);
        VAR i,j : index;
            state : (scanning, ended, positioned);
            x : item;

        BEGIN
            for i := 2 to n do begin
                x := a[i];
                j := i - 1;
                state := scanning;
                repeat
                    if j = 0            then state := ended else
                    if ordered (a[j], x) then state := positioned
```

```
        else begin
          a[j + 1] := a[j];
          j := j − 1;
        end
      until state < > scanning;
      if i < > (j + 1) then a[j + 1] := x;
    end;
END; {insertionsort}
```

Figure 5.5 gives an example of the sort in action.

SORTING TEST ON : 7 2 6 9 5 4 1 0 3 8
$n = 10, n(n − 1)/2 = 45$

INSERTION SORT

```
7   2   6   9   5   4   1   0   3   8
.−. .−.
2   7   6   9   5   4   1   0   3   8
... .−. .−.
2   6   7   9   5   4   1   0   3   8
......
2   6   7   9   5   4   1   0   3   8
... .−. .−. .−. .−.
2   5   6   7   9   4   1   0   3   8
... .−. .−. .−. .−. .−.
2   4   5   6   7   9   1   0   3   8
.−. .−. .−. .−. .−. .−. .−.
1   2   4   5   6   7   9   0   3   8
.−. .−. .−. .−. .−. .−. .−. .−.
0   1   2   4   5   6   7   9   3   8
... .−. .−. .−. .−. .−. .−.
0   1   2   3   4   5   6   7   9   8
... .−. .−.
0   1   2   3   4   5   6   7   8   9
```

34 comparisons and 14 exchanges.
... indicates a comparison
.−. indicates a move (3 moves make a exchange)

Figure 5.5   Example of insertion sort

Unlike the other two sorts, the insertion sort does not use an exchange procedure as such. Instead of counting exchanges, we count the number of moves made during the shifting process, and then divide by 3. This gives a figure for the work required in terms of exchanges. The performance of the sort can be established as

	Best case	Average	Worst case
No. of passes	$n - 1$	$n - 1$	$n - 1$
No. of comparisons	$n - 1$	$\dfrac{n(n - 1)}{4}$	$\dfrac{n(n - 1)}{2}$
No. of exchanges	0	$\dfrac{n(n + 5)}{12}$	$\dfrac{n(n + 3)}{6}$

This sort has a definite edge on the others on comparisons, though the number of exchanges is more than for the selection sort. We see, however, that the crux of the insertion sort is finding the correct place for the new item. This is a searching problem, and in the next section we shall investigate more efficient ways of 'finding and keeping'.

Quicksort

We now turn our attention to the partitioning sorts, the most famous of these being quicksort, which was proposed by Hoare in 1967. Quicksort works on the principle that if exchanges are to be made then they should be made over long distances. We have already seen that the selection sort achieves $O(n)$ exchanges in this way. To do the same, but with far fewer comparisons, quicksort divides the list into two parts and gets all the lower items in the left part and all the higher items in the right part. At each division, the possible number of items that can be compared is significantly reduced (although it is not always halved). Spelt out, the method is:

1. Choose an item in the list as the pivot.
2. Move all items less than it on to its left.
3. Move all items more than it on to its right.
4. Repeat for the left part if it has more than one item.
5. Repeat for the right part if it has more than one item.

The long exchange in steps 2 and 3 is accomplished as follows:

Move:

1. Scan with i from the left until $a[i] > pivot$.
2. Scan with j from the right until $a[j] < pivot$.
3. Exchange $a[i]$ and $a[j]$.
4. Repeat until $a[i]$ and $a[j]$ overlap.

The process is illustrated in Figure 5.6. Quicksort is neatly expressed as a

SORTING TEST ON : 7 2 6 9 5 4 1 0 3 8
$n = 10, n = (n - 1)/2 = 45, n \log_2 n = 33$
QUICKSORT

```
   [              *                    ]
   7   2   6   9   5   4   1   0   3   8
   .^.             ...           .^.....
   3   2   6   9   5   4   1   0   7   8
   ....^          ...           .^.
   3   2   0   9   5   4   1   6   7   8
                 .^.....        .^.
   3   2   0   1   5   4   9   6   7   8
                 .^...^.
   [       *       ]
   3   2   0   1   4   5   9   6   7   8
   .^.         .^........
   0   2   3   1   4   5   9   6   7   8
   .........
      [   *       ]
   0   2   3   1   4   5   9   6   7   8
             .^...^......
      [   ]
   0   2   1   3   4   5   9   6   7   8
      .^...^.
             [   ]
   0   1   2   3   4   5   9   6   7   8
                 ......
                     [       *       ]
   0   1   2   3   4   5   9   6   7   8
                     ....^...^........
                     [   ]
   0   1   2   3   4   5   6   9   7   8
                     ......
                             [   *   ]
   0   1   2   3   4   5   6   9   7   8
                             .^...^....
                             [   ]
   0   1   2   3   4   5   6   7   9   8
                             .^...^
   0   1   2   3   4   5   6   7   8   9
```

39 comparisons and 10 exchanges.

...   indicates a comparison
.^.   indicates an exchange
[ ]   indicates the partition under consideration
*   indicates the pivot

Figure 5.6   Example of quicksort

recursive algorithm:

```
PROCEDURE quicksort (var a : table;
                     n : range;
                     function ordered (x,y : item) : boolean);
    PROCEDURE sort (L,R : index);
    VAR i,j,k : index;
        x    : item;
    BEGIN
        i := L; j := R;
        k := (L + R) div 2;
        x := a[k];
        repeat
            while ordered (a[i],x) do i := i + 1;
            while ordered (x,a[j]) do j := j - 1;
            if i < j then exchange (a[i],a[j]);
            if i ≤ j then begin
                i := i + 1;
                j := j - 1;
            end;
        until i > j;
        if L < j then sort(L,j);
        if i < R then sort(i,R);
    END;

BEGIN
    sort(l,n);
END;
```

If we work through the example, we see that it is possible for the pivot itself to be involved in the exchange. The pivot for the next division is taken as the point at which the two scans overlap. So in the example, the second pivot, 0, was the lowest value in its partition: it was exchanged with 3 and at the next level the partitions were {0} all by itself and {2 3 1 4}.

The performance of quicksort depends on the choice of pivot. If the pivot turns out to be the median value in the list, then the partitions will be equal. If this happens repeatedly, then

$$\text{No. of passes} = log_2 n$$

Within each partition, each item is compared with the pivot, giving

$$\text{No. of comparisons} = n\ log_2 n$$

Following Wirth, we determine the number of exchanges in a partition as the number of elements to the left of the median-pivot, $(i - 1)$, times the probability of it having to be exchanged, $(n - i + 1)/n$. This gives the approximate relation

No. of exchanges $= n/6 \; log_2 n$

This analysis relies on the assumption that the pivot is the median, and the probability of this happening is only $1/n$. The average performance for quicksort is less than these figures, but Wirth puts the degradation at a factor of only $2 \; log_e 2$ for random pivots. In the worst case, the pivot will be the largest value in each partition, causing the subsequent partitions to be of length 1 and $n - 1$. If this happens, quicksort degenerates to an $O(n^2)$ process. To avoid this happening, it might be worth while selecting three possible pivots and choosing the middle value of these.

Finally, we note one aspect of performance which has not been mentioned so far, which is the additional requirements made by the sort on memory. The straight sorts have the characteristic that they sort *in situ* and do not use any extra storage. On the face of it, neither does quicksort, but this is a false impression. The recursion associated with the quicksort procedure requires the parameters and local variables to be stacked at each level, and this is a significant for large n.

Comparison

For competeness sake, Figure 5.7 gives comparative figures for the four sorts mentioned so far for a list of 100 items. The test was run with both exchanges and comparisons calling procedures to increment the counts. The items were scalar values. While the superiority of quicksort was not evident for 10 items, it is quite clear that as n^2 becomes a much bigger number than $n log_2 n$, it quickly outstrips the others. Selection sort is particularly good on exchanges, but it does not beat insertion sort on overall speed. Exchanges are less of a factor than comparisons, anyway, as a permutation can usually be used to avoid costly moving of large items.

The lesson of this section is that one should memorize the quicksort process and use it. Failing that, insertion is the one to go for.

	Time ratio	Comparisons	Exchanges
Quicksort	1.0	845	159
Insertion	3.6	2768	953
Selection	4.4	4950	96
Exchange	6.0	4845	2675

Figure 5.7   A sorting test

5.3 Searching and Table Look-up

Closely related to sorting is searching. Given a table of pairs {key, item}, the problem of searching (or table look-up) is to locate the item with a given key, or to ascertain that no such entry exists. In this latter case, we may record failure, or we may add the entry to the table for future reference. The techniques used during searching will, as always, depend on the nature of the data and on the operations required. Thus, relevant factors include:

- the size of the table
- whether the size is constant
- if not, the frequency with which items are added to the table and the frequency with which items are removed from the table.

In what follows, we shall assume that our table is an array of records, each record containing a key and other fields which we shall collectively refer to as 'item', i.e.

```
TYPE things = record
                key  : keytype;
                item : anytype;
              end;
    table = array [range] of things;
```

As we saw with sorting, the key can be one of the regular fields, or it can be a specially constructed field which incorporates information from one or more other fields. If the key is numeric or of any other scalar type, then the comparisons can be expressed simply with the $<$, $>$, or $=$ operations, rather than with an ordering function. Naturally, for more complex keys, an ordering function can be substituted.

Although we have made the things in the table into records, we have already seen in Section 3.6 that an array of records can be replaced by parallel arrays, one for each field. The searching techniques discussed here are therefore quite general and could be used with any programming language, not just Pascal.

Linear Search

The linear search has been discussed in detail in Section 2.2. Here we examine its performance. The performance of a searching method is measured by the average number of comparisons required to locate a random key. A linear search for a random key in the table is often stated as requiring $n/2$ tests. In fact the correct figure is $(n + 1)/2$ since for a single random access the probability of k tests is

$$p_k = 1/n,$$

giving

$$\bar{k} = \sum_{K=1}^{N} kp_k$$

$$= (n + 1)/2$$

Another index of performance in a search method is the number of comparisons required to determine that a key is not in the table. For the linear search this takes n comparisons, which is acceptable if adding new items to the table is an infrequent requirement.

The performance of a linear search can be improved by ensuring that the most commonly accessed items come early in the table. If the frequency of access cannot be predicted, each entry can include an extra field in which the number of times that entry has been accessed is recorded. The table can then be reordered at intervals to place the items in order of frequency of use. It is necessary to balance the gain in performance against the overheads of keeping and updating the counts, and reordering the table.

Binary Search

In real life, data is more often than not arranged in some natural order. Within the computer, we can exploit this order to speed up our search. The method used is one we use unconsciously when consulting a telephone directory. To look up an entry, we compare its key with the key of the entry at a random point, and by using the ordered property of the keys we can confine the search to one or other part of the table. Repeated application of the technique rapidly locates the desired entry, or confirms its absence. Since the method depends on the ordering of the items, it is only appropriate when the table is already ordered, or when updating is a very rare occurrence.

The performance of the binary search can be visualized by first considering a table containing p entries, where p is a power of 2. If $p = 2^m$, then it is easy to see that m partitions will be sufficient to locate any item. In general, if the table contains n entries, the number of partitions required is $[log_2 n] + 1$, where $[x]$ is the smallest integer that is not less than x.

There are many possible variations in programming the binary search: one possibility is given here:

```
CONST nplus1 = ...;
TYPE orders = (before, after, same);
PROCEDURE binarysearch (a      : table;
                        n      : range;
                        x      : keytype;
                        var ans : index;   {returns 0 if not found}
                        function ordering (x,y : keytype) : orders);
```

```
TYPE cover = 0. .nplus1;
VAR mid,
   left, right : cover;
   state      : (searching, found, notthere);
BEGIN
   left := 1; right := n;
   state := searching;
   repeat
      mid := (left + right) div 2;
      case ordering(a[mid].key, x) of
         before : left := mid + 1;
         after  : right := mid - 1;
         same   : state := found;
      end;
      if left > right then state := notthere;
   until state < > searching;
   case state of
      found    : ans := mid;
      notthere : ans := 0;
   end;
END; {binary search}
```

There are a few points to note about this procedure:

1. The left and right indices must eventually overshoot the range of the table on both sides. Hence we define a new type called cover which extends one index on either side of the range.
2. The type of the ordering function has been changed from boolean to the three-valued orders because the three cases are treated differently. In sorting, the distinction was simply between being in order or not in order, with equal items being taken as being in order.
3. The state variable searching technique has been used. The loop could indeed have been phrased otherwise, but the alternatives have their drawbacks. Either the indices go out of range at the same time as a check on an element of the array is done, or the ordering function has to be called twice, once to alter the indices and once to check if the loop can terminate.

Indexed Search

Sometimes the form of the key allows us to partition the table into regions such that one part of the key identifies a region, and the other part acts as a key for a search within a particular region. Although the keys in any one region are not in order, we arrange that all the keys in region i are less than any of the keys in region j for $i < j$. The table is then prefixed by an array called the index in which entry k is the index in the table of the first item in region k. Table look-up now

INDEX	1	0
	2	6
	3	14
	4	21
	5	27
	6	31
	7	32
	8	33
	9	34

1	IF	22	BEGIN
2	DO	23	UNTIL
3	OF	24	WHILE
4	TO	25	ARRAY
5	IN	26	CONST
6	OR	27	LABEL
7	END	28	REPEAT
8	FOR	29	RECORD
9	VAR	30	DOWNTO
10	DIV	31	PACKED
11	MOD	32	PROGRAM
12	SET	33	FUNCTION
13	AND	34	PROCEDURE
14	NOT		
15	THEN		
16	ELSE		
17	WITH		
18	TYPE		
19	CASE		
20	FILE		
21	GOTO		

Figure 5.8   An indexed table of reserved words

involves locating the appropriate region in the index and then searching the table entries in that region.

Any method can be used for the two searches, and indeed they might well be handled differently. The choice of method will depend on whether the index and the table are ordered, whether there is an even spread of entries in each region, and how big the regions are. As an example of this method, consider the problem of eliminating reserved words from the frequency list which was set up in the program of Figure 2.2. In order to ascertain whether a word is reserved or not, a list of such words must be consulted. In Pascal, there are some 35 such words ranging in length from 2 letters (e.g. if, do, to) to 9 letters (procedure). The table could be set up with an index based on the length of the word, giving the picture in Figure 5.8. The region can be found from the index simply by indexing it with the length, i.e. no searching is necessary in the first part. Then the table itself is searched from $Index[k-1] + 1$ to $Index[k]$. Since the most words in any region is eight, a linear search will be quite efficient enough. Another reason for using a linear search is that the entries can then be arranged in frequency order, as is the case in Figure 5.8.

Computed Entry Tables

An effective method of combining rapid look-up with easy updating is afforded by the computed entry table, also known as a key-transformation table or hash table. Consider a table of m entries with keys k_i, $i = 1..m$. Suppose there exists a function $H(k)$ with the property that H maps the keys k_i onto the integers $1..m$ in a one-to-one fashion. (highly improbable, but just suppose.) If we store the entry with key k_i at position $h = H(k_i)$ in the table, we can subsequently access the item in one probe by accessing the table at $H(k_i)$.

In general, it is not possible to find such a function, but it is often possible to devise a function with less restrictive properties as follows:

- $H(k)$ maps the keys k_i onto the range
  $1..m'$ $(m' > m)$.
- The mapping is fairly uniform over the range
  $1..m'$, but it is not necessarily unique.

Suppose we take our table of m entries and store them in a table large enough for m' entries in the following way:

```
for i := 1 to m do begin
    compute h := H(k_i)
    if table slot h is empty
    then store k and the item in table entry h
    else examine successive slots and store the entry in the first empty slot.
end;
```

In examining successive slots in the else clause, the table is treated as circular, i.e. succ (table[m']) is table[1]. Assume for the moment that there will always be an empty slot. If the table has been built up in this way it can be accessed by a similar procedure. To locate the entry with key k we have:

```
Compute h := H(k)
while (slot h not empty) and (table[h].key < > k)
    do h := (h + 1) mod m';
if table[h].key = k
then the entry has been found
else the entry is not there,
    but we have found where to put it.
```

1	AND	21	–	41	TYPE	
2	ARRAY	22	–	42	UNTIL	
3	BEGIN	23	LABEL	43	VAR	
4	–	24	–	44		–
5	CASE	25	MOD	45	WITH	
6	CONST	26	–	46	WHILE	
7	DO	27	NOT	47		–
8	DIV	28	–	48		–
9	END	29	OF	49		–
10	ELSE	30	OR	50		–
11	FOR	31	PACKED	51		–
12	FILE	32	PROGRAM	52		–
13	GOTO	33	PROCEDURE			
14	DOWNTO	34	–			
15	FUNCTION	35	REPEAT			
16	–	36	RECORD			
17	IF	37	SET			
18	IN	38	–			
19	–	39	TO			
20	–	40	THEN			

Figure 5.9   A hash table of reserved words

As an example, Figure 5.9 shows how the reserved words of Figure 5.8 might be stored in such a hash table. The key for each word is taken as the initial letter, and the hash function is

$$H\,(initial) := (initial - ord(`A')) * 2 + 1$$

so that $H(`A') = 1$, $H(`B') = 3$ and $H(`Z') = 51$. The size of the table, m', is 52.

The entries have been added in the order given in Figure 5.8. Three of the entries did not get into the two slots set aside for those initials: UNTIL should have been on 41, but the three T's (TO, THEN, and TYPE) came in first and overflowed. More serious is the case of DOWNTO which should have been at 7 but got pushed all the way down to 14. This in itself caused FUNCTION to be in 15, rather than in 11 or 12.

Handling clashes

We see that if the key k maps uniquely onto a value h we shall retrieve our item in one shot: if more than one key maps onto the same h we shall need more shots, but on average the number of shots rarely exceeds 2. When two or more keys map onto the same h we say that a *clash* occurs. When this happens, we make a linear search of part of the table, enabling this method to be viewed as a variant of the indexed table search: here we compute a starting point for the search instead of getting it from a table.

The performance of this method of table look-up clearly depends on the probability of a clash being reasonably low. This is in part a function of the hashing algorithm (the function H) but it will also be influenced by the proportion of the table slots that are unoccupied, which in turn will depend on the size of the table. As a rule of thumb, we usually make $m' = 3m/2$, so that when all entries are in the table only 60 per cent of the slots are used. Some justification for this figure will appear shortly.

The method as described suffers from the disadvantage that once a clash has occurred the probability of another clash increases. Thus suppose slot $h1$ is occupied, if another key maps onto $h1$ a clash occurs: suppose we store this item at $h1 + 1$. Clashes will now occur for keys that map into $h1$ or $h1 + 1$. As soon as one such occurs, $h1 + 2$ becomes occupied also and there are now three slots for which clashes can occur. This phenomenon is known as *primary clustering* and is avoided by a technique known as *quadratic hash*.

If slot h_0 is found to be occupied, then successive shots are made in slots $h_i = (h_0 + i^2) \bmod m'$, $i = 1, 2 \ldots (m' - 1)$. This requires very little extra work since we don't actually have to multiply to generate i^2: remembering that the second differences of a second-degree polynomial are constant, we can use the recurrence relation

$$h_{i+1} = h_i + d_i$$
$$d_{i+1} = d_i + 2$$

with $h_0 = 0$, $d_0 = 1$.

It is not obvious that this sequence will cause all the slots in the table to be examined. In fact it won't, but it turns out that we can guarantee to examine at least half the slots by the simple device of making m' a prime number. To see why this should be so, first observe that if the ith and jth shots coincide on the same table slot, then

$$(i^2 - j^2) = 0 \bmod m'$$

Since $i \neq j$, it follows that

$$(i + j) = 0 \bmod m',$$

i.e. $(i + j)$ is a multiple of m'. If m' is prime, then either i or j must be at least $m'/2$. It is still the case that the table may appear to be full when there are in fact some empty slots, but this is rarely of any significance. It can be shown that every slot will be visited by examining slots $(h + i^2) \bmod m'$ and $(h - i^2) \bmod m'$ for $i = 1, 2, \ldots, (m' - 1)/2$, and making m' a prime of the form $4k + 3$.

Choosing a hash function

The hash function H needs to be chosen with care. An effective way of ensuring that its value lies in the range 0 to $m' - 1$ is to make it the remainder after division by m'. If $ord(k)$ is the ordinal number of k in the set of all possible keys, then a good function is

$$H(k) = ord(k) \bmod m' + 1$$

It is necessary for quadratic hashing, and generally desirable, for m' to be a prime. Useful primes of the form $4n + 3$ are 11, 19, 23, 31, 59, 127, 251, 503, 1019.

When using alphabetic keys for ordering, one can form an ordinal value from the first or first two letters. For small values of m, the initial works well when multiplied by 2, as was seen in Figure 5.9. For larger data, one could take

$$H(k) = ord(k[1])*26 + ord(k[2])$$

which gives 676 possibilities, but of course not all of them are equally probable or even possible. In this case, one would resort to a more robust mathematical analysis, as can be found in Knuth.

Deleting in a hash table

Although we are here strictly only concerned with searching, data stored in tables can be updated in between searches, and this includes deletions. Deleting an item from a hash table is not very easy. Suppose the item maps onto slot $h1$. If we wipe it out, then a search for any other items which also mapped onto $h1$ but were stored elsewhere will be abandoned. If we regard the item that occupied its genuine slot as the head of a chain of late-comers, then it is clear that we cannot simply remove the head without losing access to all the rest. The answer is to maintain an indicator in each slot, which can be set to 'deleted'. The searching process will detect this and continue until a genuine empty slot is found. The adding process on the other hand, can actually reuse the slot with a deleted indicator set.

Analysis of key transformation

A measure of the performance of a key-transformation algorithm is the average number of probes required to insert an item (since the same number of probes will be required for subsequent retrieval of the item). We are particularly interested in how the performance varies as the table fills up. Let A denote the proportion of slots occupied, thus $A = 0$ indicates an empty table, while $A = 1$ indicates a completely full table. If we assume that all keys are equally likely, and that the hashing function distributes them uniformly over the table, we can show that in the absence of clashes the average number of probes to insert or find an item is $(-1/A)\ln(1 - A)$. If we assume clashes and a linear scan to find a free slot, the average becomes $(1 - A/2)/(1 - A)$.

The following table gives some representative values of these averages:

A	$(-1/A)\ln(1 - A)$	$(1 - A/2)/(1 - A)$
0.1	1.05	1.06
0.5	1.39	1.50
0.75	1.85	2.50
0.9	2.56	5.50
0.95	3.15	10.50

As was expected, performance deteriorates as the table fills up, but it is still surprisingly good when the table is 75 per cent full. The figures in the table also justify the rule-of-thumb that a table of n entries should have $3n/2$ slots.

Pigeonhole Sort

There is clearly a close correlation between searching and sorting techniques. Most searching techniques rely on the data being in order to gain speed. A hash table, on the other hand, is actually a means for creating an ordered version of the data. If there is a one-to-one correspondence between the keys of the items being sorted and the indices of the table, then items can arrive in random order and be slotted directly into their correct positions. This is known as a *pigeonhole sort*, since it is reminiscent of the pigeonholes typically used to sort letters in post offices.

However, if clashes occur, then the table will not be in order (as can be seen in Figure 5.9) and in fact it will live up to the epithet 'hash'. There are various ways of dealing with clashes while maintaining order. For example, the items causing the clash can be shifted forwards or backwards to allow the new item to slot in. This increases the average number of shots to insert an item, but if the keys are sufficiently evenly distributed, the increase will not be significant and the performance of the sort will still be better than $n\log n$ and will be more of the order of n.

Once all the items have been inserted, the final stage of the sort is to compress the table so that all the empty slots are removed. The pigeonhole sort therefore requires additional storage, which the straight sorts did not.

5.4 Array Storage Techniques

The array is a naturally occurring structure in scientific programming. It is used widely for linear algebra calculations and for the solution of partial differential equations. Large arrays can occupy significant amounts of storage, for example a 100×100 matrix of real values, each value needing four bytes, would require 40 000 bytes or 40K. These days, many microcomputers have a limit of 64K bytes of storage, a portion of which is reserved for system routines and, of course, the program. Fitting a 40K array into the remainder might be quite a squeeze. On large computers, such constraints do not apply, but there is still an attitude in dealing with such arrays that seeks for more efficient storage use.

Fortunately, in many cases, it turns out that a large number of the elements of an array are zero, or that there is some natural symmetry whereby half of the elements are duplicates. The way is therefore open to eliminate some of the elements and to store only the unique or non-zero ones. In this section we investigate ways of storing and accessing such arrays efficiently.

Classification of Arrays

The first classification criterion is the rank of an array. Arrays of rank 1 are known as *vectors*, and those of rank 2 as *matrices*. Further classifications are given in Figure 5.10.

The diagrams indicate the form of the array. As can be seen, the important distinction is whether elements are repeated (as in a symmetric array) or whether large numbers of them are zero. The banded arrays are those which have values along one or more diagonal bands. The best-known example is the unit matrix, which has values along the main diagonal. A jagged array has rows which are of varying size and the variation is not systematic. An array is regarded as 'sparse' when upwards of 80 per cent of the elements are zero and the non-zero elements occur in an unsystematic manner.

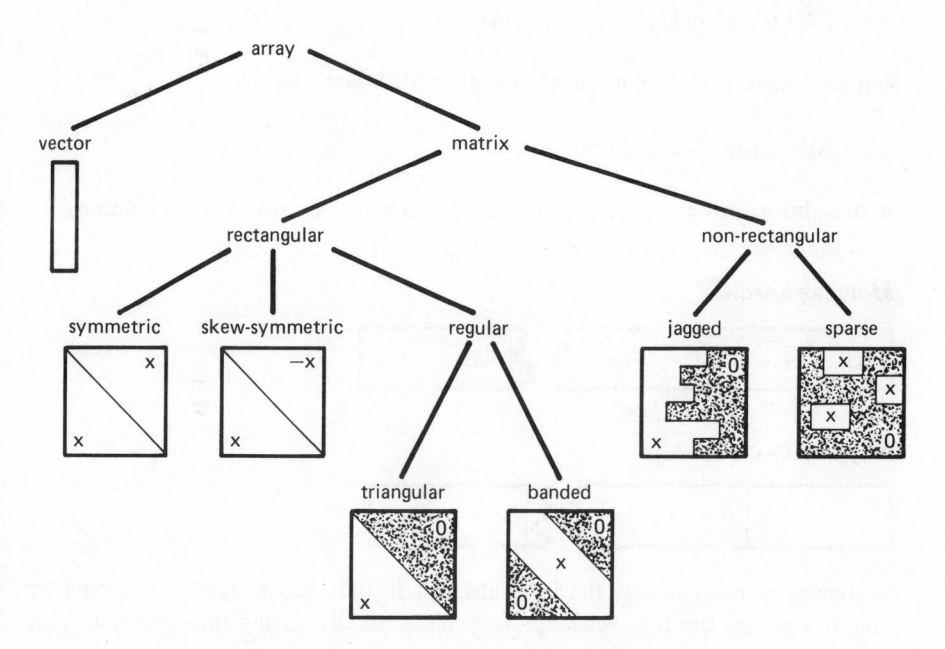

Figure 5.10   A classification of special arrays

Mapping Functions

We recall that an array consists of an aggregate of values identified by a single name, with individual components specified by indexing. The rank of an array can be thought of as the number of subscripts required to locate an element. A particularly illuminating concept is to view the array as a mapping: in the case of an array of rank 2 it is a mapping from the set of all possible pairs of subscripts onto a set of values. Thus an array is a function defined by a table of values rather than by an algorithm. If the mapping is a systematic one, then it is possible to replace an array by a function. The prime example of this technique is the unit matrix defined by

$$u[i,j] \Rightarrow 1 \text{ if } i = j$$
$$0 \text{ if } i \neq j$$

The matrix can be represented instead by a function:

```
function u (i, j : range) : real;
    begin
        if i ≠ j then u := 0 else u := 1;
    end;
```

In general, suppose we have the rectangular array

```
VAR A : array [1. .n, 1. .m] of real;
```

and we wish to map it on to the vector of length $N = n \times m$, i.e.

```
AV : array [1. .N] of real;
```

A straightforward mapping can be done in two ways: 'by rows' or 'by columns'.

Mapping by rows

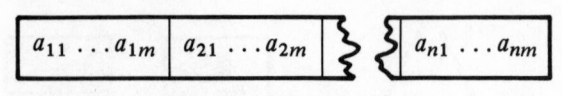

Mapping by columns

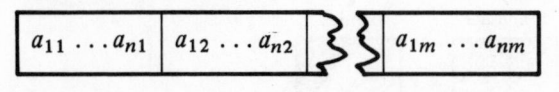

Mapping by rows causes the last subscript to vary most rapidly; mapping by columns makes the first subscript vary most rapidly. Using this principle, 'row order' and 'column order' mappings for arrays of rank 3 and above can be obtained. Note that mapping by rows is the more natural way, since it reflects the order in which the values for a matrix are usually written down.

We can now define a function for each mapping. If we map by rows, the element in row i, column j will appear at position

$$M_{\text{row}}(i,j) = (i-1)*m + (j-1) + 1$$
$$= (i-1)*m + j$$

in the linear array. Thus we have

$$A[i,j] \Rightarrow AV[M(i,j)]$$

For column order, the mapping is

$$M_{\text{col}}(i,j) = (j-1)*n + i$$

This technique of mapping can be used to take advantage of arrays with special structure. For example, a *triangular* array as defined by

$$A[i,j] \Rightarrow 0 \text{ if } i < j$$

can be placed into AV as follows:

a_{11}	$a_{21}a_{22}$	$a_{31}a_{32}a_{33}$	$a_{41} \ldots a_{44}$	$a_{1m} \ldots a_{nm}$

Then since the ith row contains i elements, rows 1 to $i-1$ occupy

$$1 + 2 + 3 + \ldots + (i-1)$$
$$= i*(i-1)/2 \quad \text{spaces}$$

The mapping function is

$$M_{\text{tri}}(i,j) = i(i-1)/2 + j$$

As another example, consider one of the banded matrices known as *tridiagonal* which is defined as

$$A[i,j] \Rightarrow 0 \text{ if } |j-1| > 1$$

(such matrices occur in the calculation of eigenvalues and eigenvectors, and in the solution of partial differential equations). The elements will be positioned in a vector in groups of three except for the first and last rows which have only two elements. The diagram is as follows:

$a_{11}\,a_{12}$	$a_{21}\,a_{22}\,a_{23}$	$a_{32}\,a_{33}\,a_{34}$	$a_{43}\,a_{44}\,a_{45}$

Then a_1 is at position 1 in the linear array, a_{22} at position 4, a_{33} at position 7, and in general a_{ii} is at position $1 + 3(i - 1)$. For a stored element $|i - j| = 0$ or 1, hence the mapping function is

$$M_{3di}(i,j) = 1 + 3(i - 1) + (j - 1)$$

which simplifies to

$$M_{3di}(i,j) = 2(i - 1) + j$$

General Methodology for Storing Arrays

We can now place the mapping function idea in context by developing a method for storing and accessing matrices as vectors in as efficient a way as possible, If we are sure that in the algorithm that deals with the array only values of i,j corresponding to the stored part of the array arise, then occurrences of $A[i,j]$ can simply be replaced by $AV[M(i,j)]$. For example, for a tridiagonal matrix, $A[i,j]$ becomes $AV[2*(i - 1) + j]$. However, it is more likely that we have an algorithm to operate on a rectangular array, but wish to conserve storage space by only storing part of the array. For example, if A is a skew-symmetric matrix, we might wish to store only the lower triangle. We could replace all references to $A[i,j]$ by references to $AV[M(i,j)]$, taking care to interchange i,j and the sign of the value for any elements in the upper triangle. However, changes such as these are highly error-prone and hide the real intent of the algorithm.

A better method is to keep the details of the checking of i,j in a function. This leads us to four steps in the general method for storing arrays as linear vectors:

1. Decide on a *storage strategy*. Elements can be omitted because they are zero (as in triangular and tridiagonal arrays) or because they are duplicates (as in symmetric and skew-symmetric). Set up the vector AV of the appropriate size to hold all the unique non-zero elements.
2. Define the *mapping function* $M(i,j)$ such that the stored elements of A are mapped onto AV as

$$A[i,j] \Rightarrow AV[M(i,j)] \text{ for certain } i,j$$

3. Design an *access function* AF that will check the values of i and j and return either the appropriate value from the linear array or one of {zero, $-$value,

error} depending on the properties of the array being mapped. An outline for the function is:

```
FUNCTION AF (i,j : range) : item;
BEGIN
    if i,j correspond to an element actually stored
    then AF := AV[M(i,j)]
    else deliver zero or deduce the value as appropriate
END; {AF}
```

4. Design an *update procedure AP* that will alter the value for given subscripts, when this is permissible. (A procedure is needed since a function cannot return the destination of an assignment.) The outline is:

```
PROCEDURE AP (i,j : range; x : item);
BEGIN
    if i,j correspond to an element actually stored
    then AV[M(i,j)] := x
        else error if value should be zero
        or deduce value to update
END; {AP}
```

The distinction between the access function and update procedure introduces us to the general notion that in dealing with a structure there are two different operations involved—selecting a value and updating a value. With this methodology we can systematically deal with the various kinds of arrays, as in Figure 5.11.

Non-rectangular Arrays

The significant properties of the non-rectangular arrays, which distinguish them from the rectangular ones discussed so far, are that:

● there is no systematic pattern to the stored elements
● the number of stored elements may vary.

The first property means that our mapping functions will have to be more complex and will probably result in a drop in efficiency of access. The second property has a fundamental effect on the whole array storage methodology: if the number of elements is going to vary, then an array is not an appropriate structure at all. As was discussed in Chapter 3, variable structures require the techniques of dynamic storage, i.e. pointers and linked lists. Our approach here will be to consider the case of the fixed number of elements, and then by building on the work of Chapter 3, to show how the ideas which have been developed can be adapted to the more general case.

Symmetric

Store lower triangle
$M(i, j) = i*(i–1)/2 + j$

AF: **if** $i \geqslant j$
  then $AF := AV[M(i,j)]$
  else $AF := AV[M(j,i)]$

AP: **if** $i \geqslant j$
  then $AV[M(i,j)] := x$
  else $AV[M(j,i)] := x$

Skew-symmetric

Store lower triangle
$M(i,j) = i*(i–1)/2 + j$

AF: **if** $i \geqslant j$
  then $AF := AV[M(i,j)]$
  else $AF := -AV[M(i,j)]$

AP: **if** $i \geqslant j$
  then $AV[M(i,j)] := x$
  else $AV[M(j,i)] := -x$

Lower triangular

Store lower triangle
$M(i,j) = i*(i–1)/2 + j$

AF: **if** $i \geqslant j$
  then $AF := AV[M(i,j)]$
  else $AF := 0$

AP: **if** $i \geqslant j$
  then $AV[M(i,j)] := x$
  else *error*

Tridiagonal

Store three diagonals
$M(i,j) = 2*(i–1) + j$

AF: **if** $|i–j| \leqslant 1$
  then $AF := AV[M(i,j)]$
  else $AF := 0$

AF: **if** $|i–j| \leqslant 1$
  then $AV[M(i,j)] := x$
  else *error*;

Figure 5.11   Array storage schemes

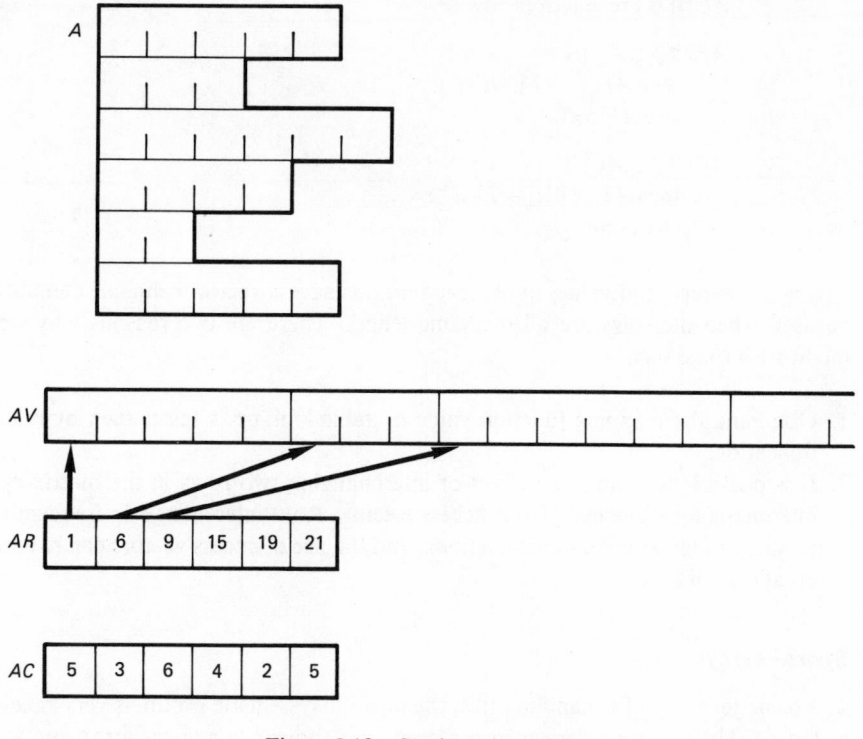

Figure 5.12   Storing a jagged array

Jagged Arrays

Consider first the jagged arrays, that is, arrays in which the rows are of irregular length. We can place the rows in a linear array but there is no longer a simple mapping function from A to AV. However, just as an array is a function defined by a table of values, so we can define the mapping function by a table of values. We do this by setting up a *row access vector*, called AR, which records the starting position in AV for each row. Thus if a_{i1} is found at position m_i in the linear array AV, then $AR[i] = m_i$. To access $A[i,j]$ we need only write $AV[AR[i] + j - 1]$. This is satisfactory, provided that we can ensure that j has a legal value. If we add an extra element on to AR, then j can be checked against $AR[i + 1] - AR[i]$. Alternatively, we can continue with the array-as-a-function idea and keep another vector of row lengths in a check vector, AC. Figure 5.12 shows this arrangement.

Following the program schemas given in Figure 5.11 for the access function and updating procedures, we have:

Jagged

> Store non-zero elements
> $AR[i]$ is the start of row i in AV

$AC[i]$ is the length of row i

AF: **if** $j \leqslant AC[i]$
    then $AF := AV[AR[i] + j - 1]$
    else $AF := 0$

AP: **if** $j \leqslant AC[i]$
    then $AV[AR[i] + j - 1] := x$
    else *error*

It is of interest (and value) to observe that this access vector technique can also be used when the rows are all the same length. There are two reasons why we might wish to do this:

1. Obtaining the mapping function value by table look-up is faster then by multiplication.
2. It is possible to obtain the effect of interchanging two rows in the matrix by interchanging elements of the access vector. Row interchange is frequently required in linear algebra calculations, and the use of access vectors can save a great deal of time.

Sparse Arrays

The basic technique for handling this, the most unsystematic group, is very much as before. The non-zero elements are stored contiguously in a linear array and we have a row access vector to indicate the start of each row. Because the elements in each row are interspersed with zero elements, access to the jth element cannot be done by the formula $AV[AR[i] + j - 1]$, as was the case for the more uniform jagged arrays. Instead, each element must carry with it its column subscript. AV therefore becomes an *array table*, AT, with two fields—the column subscript, j, and its corresponding value, v. In order to find an element, we find the start of row i, as given by $AR[i]$, and then search linearly for the required j. So what kind of structure is this? An index sequential table, of course! Following on from the earlier discussion of this kind of structure, we set up AR with the value of the index before each row, with $AR[1]$ being 0. The example in Figure 5.13 shows the representation of a sample sparse matrix.

For the sake of completeness, we give the corresponding schema:

Sparse

Store non-zero elements with column subscripts in AT
$AR[i]$ is the start of each row minus 1.

AF: Search AT from $AR[i - 1] + 1$ to $AR[i]$
    for the given j, returning k.
    If found **then** $AF := AT[k].v$
        else $AF := 0$

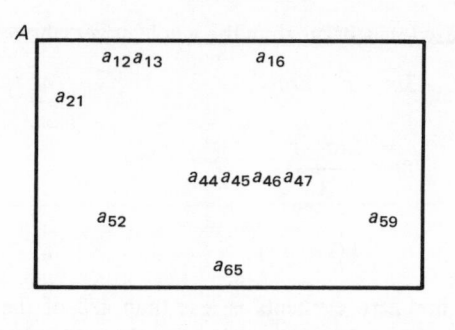

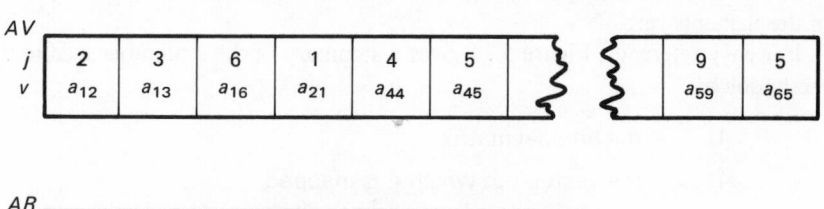

Figure 5.13   Storing a sparse array

AP: Search AT from $AR[i-1] + 1$ to $AR[i]$
for the given j, returning k.
If found **then** $AT[k].v := x$
else error

How efficient is this method? The overall efficiency of access is going to depend on the expected access patterns, i.e.

- systematic access to elements in a row
- random access to elements anywhere.

If access is systematic, then this method is no less efficient than if the whole array had been stored. However, for random access to elements, there is a linear search through the elements of each row. It is indeed an important lesson that

Every facility has its price

How much space do we save? Let us assume that A has r rows and c columns, and that the items require 2 units of storage each, while an integer requires 1. Then to store the full array would require $2rc$ units. Let m be the number of non-zero elements. Then this method uses $3m$ units for the elements in AT and r units for AR. The method will be use less storage than the whole array when

$$3m + r < 2rc$$

$$m < \frac{2rc - r}{3}$$

$$= \tfrac{1}{3}(2rc - r)$$

Thus when the number of non-zero elements is less than 1/3 of the total, this method will give a saving in storage. In other words, 'break-even' is at 66 per cent of the elements zero.

For easy reference, Figure 5.14 gives a summary of the structures used in this methodology.

A –   the original matrix

AV –   the vector into which A is mapped

AT –   the table in which A is stored with column subscripts

AF –   the access function which returns a value from AV or AT given subscripts of A

AP –   the update procedure which changes a value in AV or AT given subscripts of A

AR –   the row access vector which indicates the start of each row of A as it is stored in AV

AC –   the row check vector which gives the length of each row of A

Figure 5.14   Summary of the array methods terminology

Variable Sized Arrays

We now consider how these methods can be adapted to handle arrays where the number of elements in each row varies with time. Instead of the vector AV or AT, we set up a series of linked lists, one for each row. Access to the lists is through the row access vector, which consists of actual Pascal pointers, rather than numerical indices. The only change to the array-oriented schemas is for jagged arrays: because we cannot do arithmetic on these pointers, we cannot use the formula $AV[AR[i] + j - 1]$ to go immediately to the jth element of the row. The jth element must be found by linking through $j - 1$ nodes, giving the same algorithms as for sparse arrays. For illustration, Figure 5.15 shows the matrix of Figure 5.13 using linked lists.

Clearly, updating is very simple using the standard linked-list techniques of Chapter 3. The efficiency of access depends on the same criteria as does the array method. The amount of storage, however, is larger (for the links) and gives a break-even of 75 per cent zero elements—slightly higher than the array method.

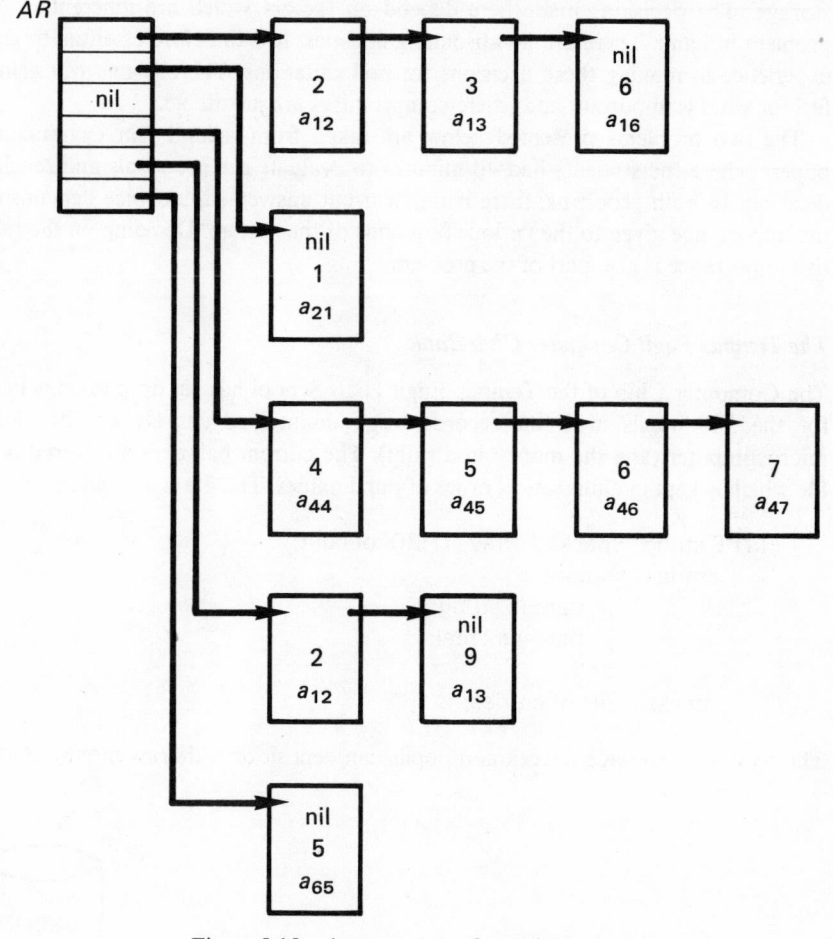

Figure 5.15   A sparse array for variable elements

This leads us to the final moral of this chapter:

> There is a trade-off between
> ease of updating and
> speed of access.

In other words, you can't have it all ways!

5.5   Analysis—Which Method to Use?

The overriding message of this chapter is that one is always faced with a choice: which sorting method to use, whether to search with hash tables or index sequential, and whether or not it is worth while to use linked rather than sequential storage. The decisions made here depend on factors which are inherent in the problem in hand. There are no absolute guidelines. It is therefore essential to gain experience in making these decisions for real situations. Thereby one will gain a feel for what is important and where compromises are justifiable.

The two problems presented below are taken from second-year examination papers where the students had 40 minutes to evaluate the proposals and reach a decision. In both problems, there is no clear-cut answer—the choice depends on the importance given to the various functions of the system. Deciding on the relative importance is also part of the problem.

The Tempus Fugit Computer Club Bank

The Computer Club of the Tempus Fugit High School has set up a savings bank for the 500 pupils, with the records being maintained entirely on the club's microcomputer (and the money in a safe!). The current balances are stored on a file which is kept in alphabetical order of pupil names. The file is defined as

```
TYPE string = packed array [1..20] of char;
     entries = record
                 name : string;
                 balance : real;
               end;
     banks = file of entries;
```

The bank is open once a week and pupils can deposit or withdraw money. At the

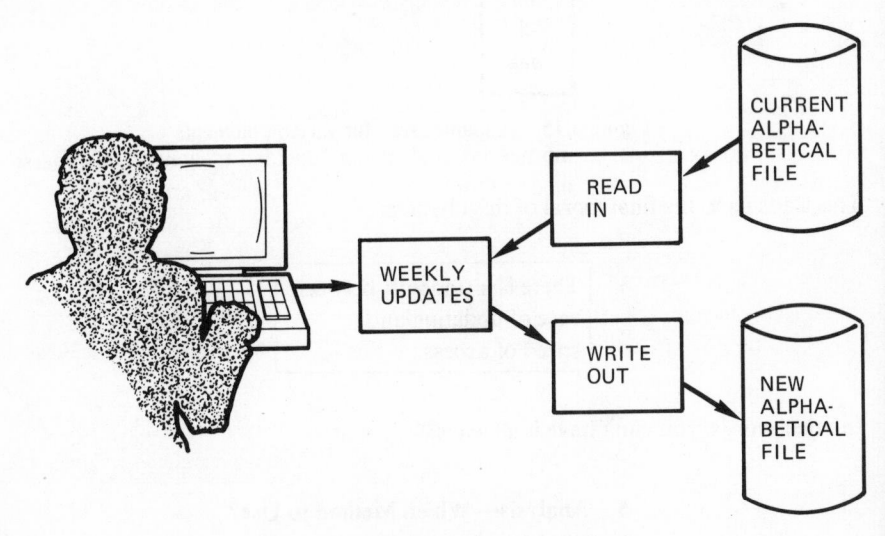

Figure 5.16   System chart for the bank

end of each banking session, a new alphabetical file is created with the new balances. Any new clients are slotted in correctly and anyone with a zero balance is left out. The system chart for the bank's operation is shown in Figure 5.16.

During the development of the system, there were two suggestions as to how the file should be represented in memory while the update session lasted.

KATHRYN: Set up a hash function based on the first two letters of the surname and store the entries in a hash table.

THOMAS: Store the entries in a linked list in alphabetical order and maintain an index to the first and last entry for each letter of the alphabet.

Answer the following questions:

(a) Describe and evaluate each of these proposals with regard to:

    Method of creation
    Overhead of additional storage
    Ease of insertion and deletion
    Speed of searching
    Ease of producing a new alphabetical file.

(b) On the basis of your evaluation, choose either Kathryn's or Thomas's suggestion, giving reasons for your answer. Write the Pascal declarations for all the necessary data structures for the method of your choice and give the Pascal hash (Kathryn) or indexing (Thomas) expression.

(c) For your chosen method, write a procedure to add a new name with a given balance to the structure.

Gnillajt Ampy's Sparse Arrays

Gnillajt Ampy, the famous numerical analyst, has decided to convert his sparse matrix manipulation programs to work on a medium-sized microcomputer. He has established that reasonably sized matrices will fit in the micro's memory, provided only the non-zero elements are stored. He now has to decide on the most efficient method of arranging the matrices. There are two suggestions:

LUCY: Store the non-zero elements in any order in a vector and maintain an access table of {row, column, vector-index}.

ALLAN: Store the non-zero elements in linked lists, one for reach row, with the elements kept in order, and maintain a row access vector of pointers to the start of each list.

Answer the following questions:

(a) Draw diagrams to show how each method would store the matrix

$$\begin{bmatrix} 0 & 4 & 0 & 0 & 9 & 0 \\ 0 & 0 & 0 & 0 & 0 & 0 \\ 0 & 0 & 5 & 7 & 0 & 1 \\ 3 & 0 & 0 & 0 & 0 & 0 \end{bmatrix}$$

(b) Define the Pascal data types and variables necessary to implement each proposal.

(c) Describe and compare the methods with regard to
Overhead of space as a function of the non-zero elements
Ease of adding and removing elements
Speed of finding the value of an element given the subscripts
Ease of interchanging two rows.

(d) On the basis of your evaluation, choose either method and write a Pascal procedure to print out the contents of the matrix, including all the zeros. (You may ignore the problem of a row not fitting on one printer line.)

Chapter 6

Data Structures (Part 2)—Trees

In the first part of this course we looked at what are strictly linear structures—arrays and linked lists. There is an equal wealth of techniques and applications areas for the non-linear structures, the archetype of which is the tree.

6.1 Introducing Trees

In the last chapter we saw several algorithms for sorting. Except for quicksort, they all had the common property that they rearranged the items in a linear array *in situ*. Although the items start in a linear array and must finish in a linear array, this does not mean that the data must stay in an array while it is being sorted. Instead of trying to devise algorithms that are more clever, let us see whether we can get better results by changing the data structure.

Sorting is a matter of ordering, and we make our breakthrough by thinking of two-dimensional ordering, where the position of an item *vis-à-vis* its left and right neighbours carries some of the information. Left and right are viewed as being 'derived' from the item, so that we have

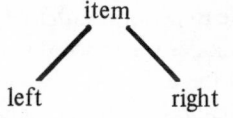

which is a structure known as a tree. Because of this term, there are a host of other botanical terms associated with trees, the main ones that interest us being

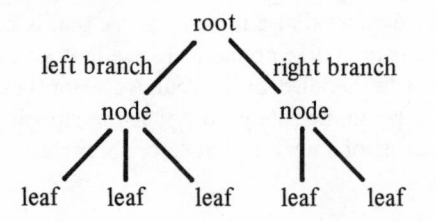

(The exact definition of trees and all these terms is delayed till the next section. We note, however, that drawing trees upside-down is a mere convenience—as they get larger they can grow with the direction of writing.)

181

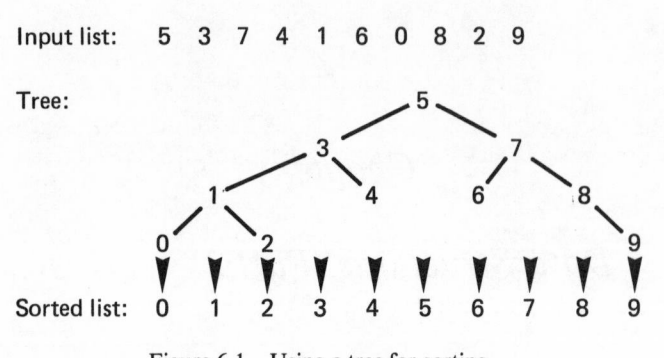

Figure 6.1 Using a tree for sorting

Now, we can assign items to the tree such that by following the left branch from a particular node we only encounter items that come before the starting node. Then by a deft operation, we flatten the tree by removing all the lines and squashing the tree between its root and its leaves. This process is illustrated in Figure 6.1. While such an arrangement constitutes a sorting, it will only be of practical use if we can easily construct the tree, and equally easily recover a linear sorted list. We shall first look at these problems informally.

Constructing a Tree

We can see more easily how to construct such a tree by considering how we would add an item to an existing tree. We know that if the item to be added is less than the root item then it will be added to the left of the root, while if it is greater than the root item then it will be added on the right of the root. We can thus select the left or right branch from the root. If we note that the node so reached is itself the root of a tree, then we have to perform *exactly the same operation* to select the left or right branch from this node. We proceed in this way until we reach a node that has no more branches in the direction in which we wish to go, and then we add *x* to the left or right as appropriate. (To check that you understand this process, see if you agree that 5.5 would go on the left branch of 6.)

To construct the whole tree, we start off by making the first item the root and successively adding items as just described. Here we have an example of a recursive process, based on the fact that a node of a tree that is not a leaf is itself the root of another tree. It is of course no mere chance that a structure with a recursive description should be handled by a recursive algorithm. Remembering the lessons of Section 2.3, we immediately note that the stopping condition for this process is the encountering of a node with no more branches.

Flattening the Tree

We now turn to the problem of recovering the sorted list from the tree. From the way in which the tree was constructed, we can initially break the process down as follows:

1. List in correct order all the items on the left branch of the root.
2. List the item at the root.
3. List in correct order all the items on the right branch of the root.

If the left branch is a leaf, then step 1 is trivial. If not, we can regard the first descendent node as the root of a subtree and apply the whole process over again to this subtree. Similar considerations apply to the right branch. Here we have another example of a recursive process.

We can thus see that trees can provide quite an exciting new way of looking at data. The essential ingredient for a tree is the lateral relationship, which in this case was sorting order, but may be many things. To emphasize the utility of trees, we list some of their uses in computing.

Uses of Trees

1. *Expression trees.* An ordinary mathematical formula (or expression) can be put onto a tree such that brackets are unnecessary and yet the order of evaluation is still maintained (Figure 6.2a). Sub-expressions which were in brackets are represented as subtrees, and the lower down a subtree is, the earlier it must be evaluated.
2. *Game trees.* Many two-person games can be illustrated by a tree which shows the various possible moves that can follow a given move (Figure 6.2b). Here we see that a branch indicates a choice and that certain choices may have different advantages.
3. *Recognition trees.* Often commands to a computer system do not have to be typed in full and any portion will be accepted provided the abbreviation is not ambiguous. A recognizer for such words can be built around a tree that indicates the possible letters that can follow each other, and includes a space (b) at the appropriate points to permit abbreviations (Figure 6.3c).

What we notice about these trees is that the number of branches from any one node is unlimited. Also, there are many different ways of laying out the trees: some are nicely symmetric like the expression tree, some are bushy like the game tree, and some are sort-of lopsided like the recognition tree. The trick is to draw the tree in a way which communicates its meaning.

6.2 Tree Transformations and Traversals

The non-linear nature of trees makes them quite complex structures and as a result they have been studied in great detail by computer scientists. The results of these studies are definitions and algorithms relating to important tree variations and the useful manipulations of them. These will now be described in a semi-formal way, covering all the common terms and techniques used in tree applications.

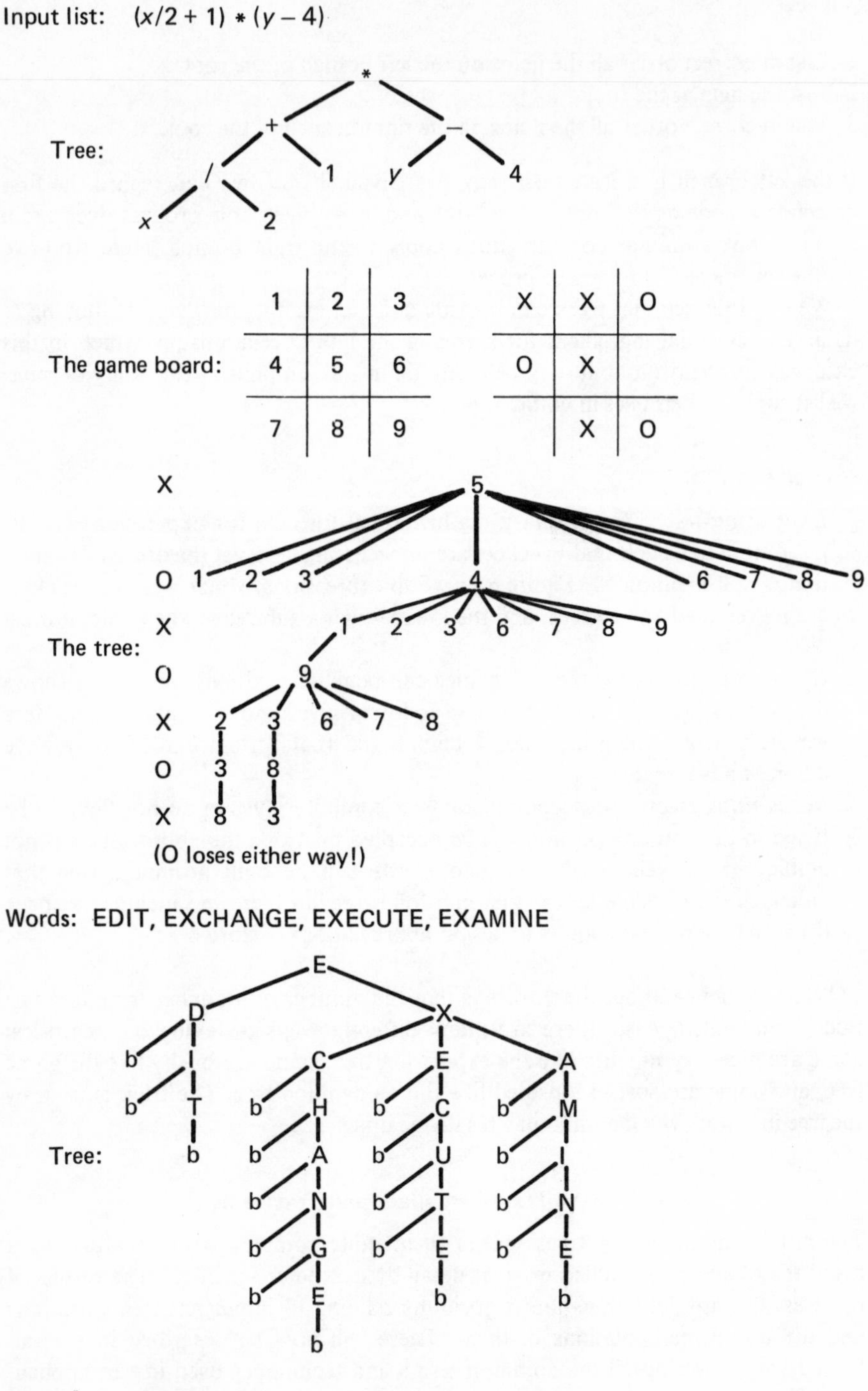

Input list: $(x/2 + 1) * (y - 4)$

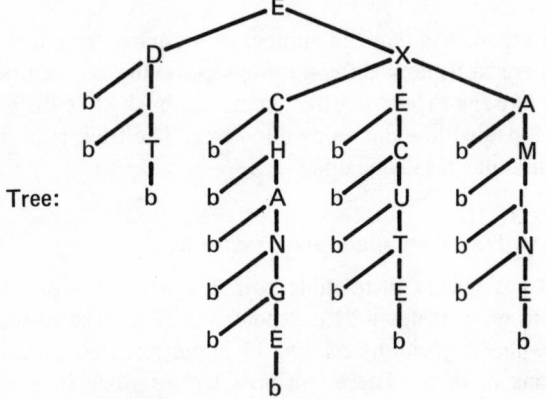

Tree:

The game board:

	1	2	3
	4	5	6
	7	8	9

	X	X	O
	O	X	
		X	O

The tree:

(O loses either way!)

Words: EDIT, EXCHANGE, EXECUTE, EXAMINE

Tree:

Figure 6.2   Uses of trees
  (a) An expression tree   (b) A game tree   (c) A word tree

Definition. A *tree* is a set of *nodes* such that:

(a) there is a specially designated node called the *root*;
(b) any other nodes are partitioned into disjoint trees which are called *subtrees* of the root.

Recursive definitions like this can be mind-boggling so let us go through it step by step.

A tree is a set of nodes

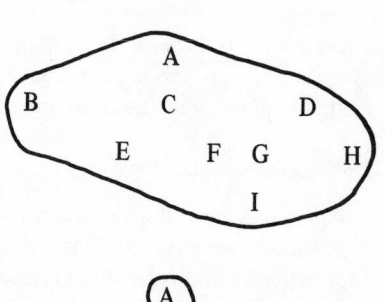

One of the nodes is the root and the others are partitioned into sub-trees

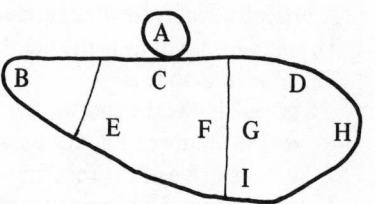

Now each subtree is also a tree, so taking each in turn we divide its set of nodes into a tree and subtrees.

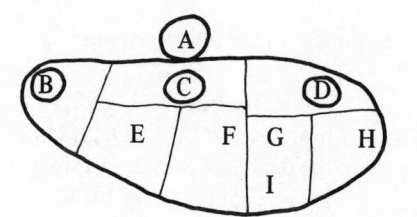

B's subtree is completed because there are no subtrees, but the others are refined further.

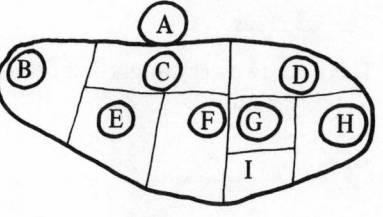

Finally, at the fourth 'level', we establish I as a tree all by itself.

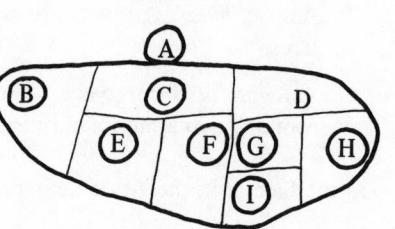

The above diagrams are illustrative, but as we have already seen, there is a neater way of drawing trees as directed graphs of connected nodes i.e.

Notice that there is a stopping condition for this recursive definition: when there is only one node in a tree or subtree, it becomes the root and there is no further expansion of the definition.

Definitions

A *forest* is a set of disjoint trees.
A *leaf* (or *terminal* node) is a node which has no subtrees.
A *branch* (or *non-terminal* node) is any node which is not a leaf.
The *degree* of a node is the number of subtrees it has.
The *level* of a node is:
- one if it is the root
- the number of nodes passed through on a path from the root to the node (inclusive of the root and the node) otherwise.

A tree is *empty* if it has neither root nor branches.

Example. In the tree given above,

leaves are B, E, F, I, and H
branches are A, C, D, and G
the degree of A is 3, of F is 0
the level of C is 2, of I is 4.

Special Trees

There are two very important definitions concerning the refinement of the original tree definition.

Definitions

A *strict binary tree* is a tree in which each node has exactly zero or two sub-trees.

A *Knuth binary tree* is a set of nodes which is either empty or consists of a root and two Knuth binary trees.

On the face of it, these two definitions are remarkably similar, since both restrict the subtrees of a node to at most two. The difference is that a strict binary tree insists on two or none, whereas a Knuth binary tree allows two, one or none. Thus we have

Strict binary tree   Knuth binary tree

(Notice that the Knuth binary tree definition is recursive. Can you spot its stopping condition?)

These special trees are going to be useful (as we shall see) and it is therefore essential to be able to transform the more general trees into these forms. There are two such algorithms, which strangely enough benefit from terminology related to family trees rather than trees in nature. The terms are:

Each root is the *father* of the roots of its subtrees, which in turn are *sons* of the father. The leftmost subtree is the *eldest son* of the root. The roots of the subtrees of the same father are said to be *brothers*.

For those with feminist tendencies, this rubric can also be phased in a non-sexist way, i.e.:

Each root is the *parent* of the roots of its subtrees, which in turn are *children* of the parent. The leftmost subtree is the *firstborn* of the root. The roots of the subtrees of the same parent are said to be *siblings*.

Transforming a forest to a Knuth binary tree

Algorithm

1. Link together all the roots of the trees in the forest.
2. Link together all the brothers.
3. Remove all links from a father to his sons except that to the eldest son.
4. Make the root of the first tree in the forest the root of the Knuth binary tree and tilt the tree by 45°.

Example

The trees:

1. and 2.

3.

4.

The application of this transformation is followed up in the Family Tree Project at the end of this chapter.

Transforming a tree to a strict binary tree

Algorithm

1. If the tree has a single node, the strict binary tree is just that node.
2. Otherwise, cut the branch between the root and the firstborn. Form a new node which is a root with the firstborn as its left subtree and the old root as its right subtree.
3. Repeat these steps recursively for each subtree.

Example. For the first application of steps 1 and 2 we get

Repeating them, we find that B conforms to the conditions of step 1, so we cut between A and C, and so on.

We notice that the original root, A, has moved all the way down the tree as successive cuts were made. Now, for interest's sake (and because we have schooled ourselves to check boundary conditions) we'll apply the algorithm to a tree that is already a strict binary tree:

How unexpected! The algorithm has transformed the already strict binary tree into a different one. The difference is that the new tree has data only on the leaves. In earlier texts on data structures, this is often assumed to be a necessary constraint, but modern programming languages allow us to represent trees in such a way that this restriction becomes unnecessary. A small change to step 2 of the algorithm, viz.:

2. Otherwise, if there are not exactly two subtrees, cut . . .

solves the problem. Using the revised algorithm on the first tree, we get:

which also conforms to the definition of a strict binary tree, but has 7 nodes, rather than 9 as in the first version.

Traversing a Tree

After considering tree-to-tree transformations, we go on to tree-to-list transformations. The essence of the problem is to reduce a tree to a linear list in such a way that we can then rebuild the tree exactly as it was. These algorithms go under the general heading of traversals, which term is defined as follows.

Definitions. A *traverse* is an ordered walk around a tree such that each node is visited once and only once.

There are a variety of such orders, so we shall just list them alongside the resulting list for the tree

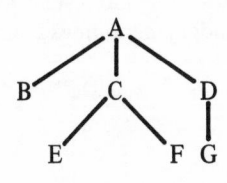

In each case, we assume that nodes or subtrees are considered from left to right.

Definitions

> *Topdown*   A B C D E F G
> Start at the root and
> visit nodes on each level.

> *Bottom-up*   E F G B C D A
> Start furthest from the
> root and visit nodes on
> each level.

The next two definitions are recursive and have the stopping condition that a traverse of an empty tree is a null operation.

Definitions

> *Preorder* (prefix)   A B C E F D G
> Visit the root
> Traverse each subtree

> *Postorder* (postfix)   B E F C G D A
> Traverse each subtree
> Visit the root

Now we consider the question as to whether we can reconstruct our tree from any of these lists. In the first two, we picked up nodes without any direct connections between them, such as G following F. It will be very difficult to build a tree from data which has been obtained by visual inspection. The situation with preorder and postorder is more hopeful since our path always followed the existing links. But there is still no inherent information in BEFCGDA that tells us which the subtrees are.

In order to rebuild a tree from a list, the list needs to retain the basis on which it was originally built. Our example was chosen at random, not according to any definite rules. Instead, let us consider an example of an expression tree, e.g.

List: $d := b*b - 4*a*c$

Tree:

The tree is set up such that operators of higher precedence are further down the tree. That is a fair enough basis to work on. A postorder traverse of the tree gives us

Postorder: $d\,b\,b * 4\,a * c * - :=$

which is a form well known to pocket calculator users. From this we can define the reconstruction algorithm as follows.

Algorithm—construct a tree

1. Scan the list from left to right
2. If an operator is found, construct a tree with the operator as root and the two previous items as left and right subtrees, and replace all three with this tree.

Example $d\,b\,b * 4\,a * c * - :=$ $\Rightarrow$

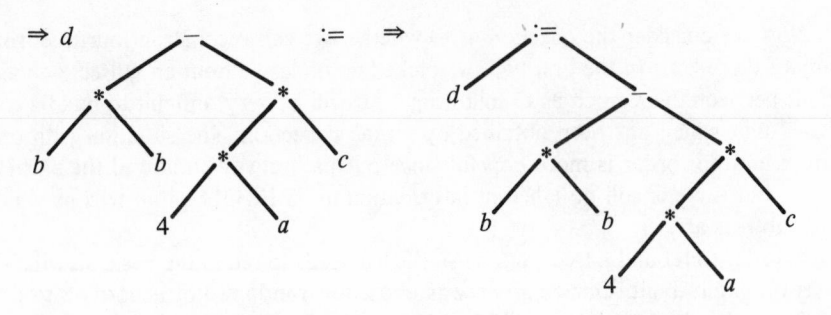

We leave it as an exercise for the reader to develop a similar reconstruction from preorder. It is more difficult, not because preorder is inherently unwieldy, but rather because it is not suited to the particular rules governing operator precedence. As will be seen in the Family Tree Project, preorder is the preferred method for constructing father–son–brother relationships.

To complete the picture, we define a third recursive traversal order which is a companion to preorder and postorder, but will only work on binary trees (strict or Knuth), because it relies on being able to identify subtrees as either left or right of the root. Such a distinction is meaningless with more than two subtrees.

Definition

   Inorder (infix)
      Traverse the left subtree
      Visit the root
      Traverse the right subtree

For the expression tree above, an inorder traverse yields

$$d := b * b - 4 * a * c$$

which should not be a surprise since the normal way of writing an expression is with the operator in between two operands and is known as infix form.

6.3 Sorting and Searching with Trees

Armed with these definitions, we can return to the sorting problem to see how a tree is actually represented in Pascal. As the diagrams suggest, the classic representation of a tree uses a record for each node and pointers for the links. With a sorting tree, there are only ever two links from each node, so that we can define:

```
TYPE tonodes = ↑nodes;
     nodes = record
               data : item;
```

```
                left,
                right : tonodes;
            end;
```

To declare the tree, we would use

```
    VAR tree : tonodes;
```

and immediately set

```
    tree := nil;
```

Treesort

We saw in Section 6.1 that tree sorting involved constructing a tree from the list of input items, and then flattening it back into the list. In outline the construction algorithm is as follows.

Algorithm—construct tree:

> If *the tree is empty*
> then *make this item the tree*
> else *compare the item to the root and*
> > if *it comes before then add to the left branch*
> > if *it comes after then add to the right branch.*

If the item is a duplicate, we could add it to either branch, or simply ignore it: this depends on the particular kind of tree being created. As each node is added to the tree, its fields will be undefined. It is good practice to initialize all the fields immediately, using a makenode procedure, as in:

```
PROCEDURE makenode (var node : tonodes; value : item);
    BEGIN
        new(node);
        node↑.data := value;
        node↑.left := nil;
        node↑.right := nil;
    END; {makenode}
```

The astute reader will already have realized that the flattening process is in fact equivalent to an inorder traverse of the tree. Putting together the two algorithms, we can define treesort, with an example as in Figure 6.3. As in the straight sorting program (Figure 5.1), the listing is not compiled. It uses two interesting ordering functions, and the same input and output routines as before.

We notice that the index used during flattening is declared and initialized to 1 outside the flatten procedure itself. This is because when we enter a recursive

194

```
 1   PROGRAM Treesorting (input, output);
 2
 3   CONST max = 100;
 4         maxhead=21;
 5
 6   TYPE   range  = 1..max;
 7          index  = 0..max;
 8          items  = char;
 9          table  = array [range] of items;
10          ordering = (before, same, after);
11          heads = packed array [1..maxhead] of char;
12
13   VAR    scores : table;
14          maxscores : range;
15
16   FUNCTION eithercase (a, b : items) : ordering;
17     VAR amod, bmod : integer;
18     BEGIN
19       amod:=ord(a) mod 32; bmod:=ord(b) mod 32;
20       if amod < bmod then eithercase := before else
21       if amod > bmod then eithercase := after  else
22                           eithercase := same;
23     END; {ascending}
24
25   FUNCTION caseconscious (a, b : items) : ordering;
26     BEGIN
27       if a < b then caseconscious := before else
28       if a > b then caseconscious := after  else
29                     caseconscious := same;
30     END; {ascending}
31
32   PROCEDURE treesort (VAR a : table;
33                           n : range;
34                       function comparison (a,b : items) : ordering);
35
36     TYPE tonodes  = ^nodes;
37          nodes    = record
38                       data  : items;
39                       left,
40                       right : tonodes
41                     end;
42
43     VAR  tree : tonodes;
44          i    : index;
45
46     PROCEDURE makenode (VAR node : tonodes;  value : items);
47       BEGIN
48         new(node);
49         node^.data := value;
50         node^.left := nil;
51         node^.right := nil;
52       END; {makenode}
53
54     PROCEDURE addtotree (VAR root : tonodes; value : items);
55       BEGIN
56         if root = nil
57         then makenode (root, value)
58         else
59           case comparison(value, root^.data) of}
60             before : addtotree (root^.left, value);
61             same,
62             after  : addtotree (root^.right, value);
63           end;
64       END; {addtotree}
```

```
65
66        PROCEDURE flatten (root : tonodes);
67          BEGIN
68            if root <> nil
69            then begin
70              flatten (root^.left);
71              i:=i+1;   a[i] := root^.data;
72              flatten (root^.right);
73            end;
74          END;  {flatten}
75
76        BEGIN {treesort}
77          tree := nil;
78          for i := 1 to n do addtotree (tree,a[i]);
79          i := 0;
80          flatten (tree);
81        END; {treesort}
82
83      BEGIN {Main program Sorting}
84        obtain(scores, maxscores);
85        print('UNSORTED              ',scores,maxscores);
86        treesort (scores, maxscores, eithercase);
87        print('SORTED CASE-FREE     ',scores,maxscores);
88        treesort (scores, maxscores, caseconscious);
89        print('SORTED CASE CONSCIOUS',scores,maxscores);
90      END.
```

Figure 6.3   The tree sorting program

invocation of a procedure, we get a new set of local variables and parameters. If i had been declared in flatten, we would keep on getting a new copy of i, initialized to 1 each time, and the resulting table would be a mess.

The Efficiency of Treesort

We should now see whether this process is going to give the expected gain in efficiency. It looks promising, because in a full binary tree (i.e. no empty branches) N terminal nodes can be accessed using only $\log_2 N$ comparisons. If we take the example of Figure 6.1, we note that there are 11 nodes, and that there are 12 places at which new nodes can be added, i.e. on both sides of each leaf. (There will always be one more new place than nodes, since when we add a new item we replace a space by a node and two more spaces.)

If the items in the input table are randomly ordered, all the spaces are equally likely candidates for the next item to be added, so for this configuration, the average number of comparisons to add a new item is obtained by simple arithmetic. It is

$$((4 \times 4) + (4 \times 3) + (4 \times 4))/12 = 44/12 = 3.67$$

which is not greatly different from $\log_2 12$. This logarithmic performance can be confirmed in the general case, though the derivation is too complicated to pursue here.

Tree Search

We saw in Section 5.3 that the key-transformation (hash table) search is very effective, the search time being independent of the size of the table, and depending only on the ratio of the number of occupied slots to the total number of slots. However, there are two situations where it has disadvantages: deleting items is difficult and producing a sorted list of the items requires a complete subsequent sort. A method of storing data that gives a reasonably fast look-up, ease of insertion and deletion, and retains the ordering, is a tree-structured table.

We begin by extending the definition of a node to include a key (in case this differs from the item itself) and we trivially modify the addtotree procedure to incorporate the key. Searching the tree for a given key follows the same pattern:

Algorithm—search a tree:

>If *the key sought is less than the root's key*
>   then *search down the left branch*
>   else *search down the right branch.*

As we saw before with searching, it is convenient to put the algorithm in a function which can return either the node containing the key, or nil if the key does not exist on the tree. This gives

```
FUNCTION treesearch (root : tonodes; key : keys) : tonodes;
  BEGIN
      if root = nil then treesearch := nil
      else
      if key = root↑.key then treesearch := root else
      if key < root↑.key then treesearch := treesearch (root↑.left,key)
                          else treesearch := treesearch (root↑.right,key)
  END; {treesearch}
```

(We have built the ordering into the function. For generality we ought to use an ordered (x,y) function, but we're only human.)

We know from our discussion of sorting, that as long as the tree is reasonably balanced, performance for the search will be logarithmic. Thus we get the same performance as a binary search, with the added bonus of being able to add items freely. (The binary search relied on an array with the items fixed in their original order.)

Deleting Items from a Tree

Although not as tedious as deleting in a linear list, deleting an item from a tree does have its problems. There are two approaches to deleting:

- deleting a complete subtree
- deleting a node, while maintaining its subtree

To delete a subtree, we find the node and then recursively delete all nodes to its left and right. The reader should be able to write this procedure with ease. In the second approach, if the node is a leaf, deleting it will be a simple matter, but removing a node in the thick of a tree is going to require a little more care. There are three cases to consider.

1. The node is a leaf. This is trivial, e.g.:

2. The node has only one branch. Here the branch takes the place of the node, as in:

3. The node has two branches. This is the tricky one. Consider the position of the node with the largest key that is less than the one to be deleted—this is the node that must take X's place. It must be in the left subtree of X (since its key is less), and it must be the rightmost node in that subtree (since it is the largest). It follows that to the rightmost, it must be a leaf, or have only a left subtree. If it is leaf, the substitution is straightforward:

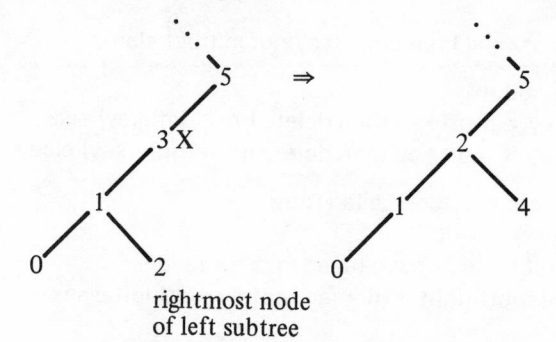

rightmost node
of left subtree

If the rightmost node has a left subtree, all the nodes on this subtree must be more than the left branch of X and therefore can happily remain there, even if their largest member moves. By redrawing the previous tree slightly, we illustrate this move:

5 X
1   7
4 rightmost node
  of left subtree
3
0   2

⇒

4
1   7
3
0   2

The actual deletion algorithm is therefore not as complicated as first appeared, and the special cases of moving the leftmost node can be well handled with a neat recursive design. The complete procedure to handle all cases is:

```
PROCEDURE delete (var root : tonodes; key :keys);
    VAR rootwas : tonodes;

    PROCEDURE rearrange (var leftsubtree : tonodes);
    BEGIN

        {Find rightmost node of left subtree}
        if leftsubtree↑.right < > nil
        then rearrange(leftsubtree↑.right)

        {Replace node to be deleted by this rightmost node}
        else begin
            rootwas↑.key := leftsubtree↑.key;
            rootwas := leftsubtree;
            leftsubtree := leftsubtree↑.left;
        end;
    END; {rearrange}

BEGIN
    if root = nil then error {key not in tree} else

{Find the node}
    if key < root↑.key then delete (root↑.left,key) else
    if key > root↑.key then delete (root↑.right,key) else

    {Delete the node called root}
    begin
        rootwas := root; {used in dispose later}
        if root↑.right = nil then root := root↑.left else
```

```
          if root↑.left = nil then root := root↑.right else
          rearrange(root↑.left);
          dispose(rootwas);
       end;
  END;
```

Balancing the Tree

Despite the logarithmic nature of its performance, tree sorting has one disadvantageous property. Whereas the linear sorting methods were designed to work better when there was a partial ordering initially, the tree sort is like quicksort in that the presence of ordering makes it worse. Consider the list of partially ordered numbers

    3 4 5 6 1 2 7 8 9 0

The tree for this list is

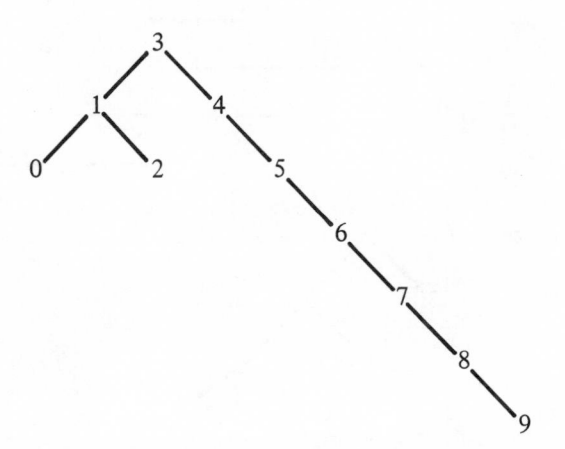

which is very unbalanced, since the partial ordering gives a very long tail of right branches. The logarithmic performance of partitioned sorts derives from the fact that at each node we discard approximately half of the possible successor nodes. If the tree develops a long tail, then this will not be the case. If the tree is to be used for searching, it may well be worth while to rearrange it so that it is balanced. This is quite a difficult process, although the underlying idea is quite simple.

Consider the nodes marked 4 and 5 in the tree above. Suppose 5 became the root with 4 as its left descendent. Then there will be one less node on the long tail and one more on the left side. Such manipulations can be done successively, and are adequately described in Wirth, 1976. Of more interest to us is the next subject, weighted trees.

200

Weighted Trees

While it is desirable to have a balanced tree if access to nodes follows a random pattern, trees of fixed data usually have the property that some nodes will be accessed with a higher frequency than others. For example, referring to the frequency count done in Figure 2.2, we see that the reserved words 'begin' and 'end' occur more often than 'type' and 'var', for instance. It would thus be advantageous to have an unbalanced tree with the popular items nearer the top.

We have defined the level, l, of a node as being the number of nodes from it to the root. The sum of all the levels for each nodes is the *path length*. We now assign to each node a weight, w_i, and we set about minimizing the weighted path length, $\Sigma w_i l_i$. One way of doing this is to apply Huffman's algorithm, which works by combining the lowest available weights to form a new weight, then repeating the process until all nodes have been considered. This process is illustrated in Figure 6.4.

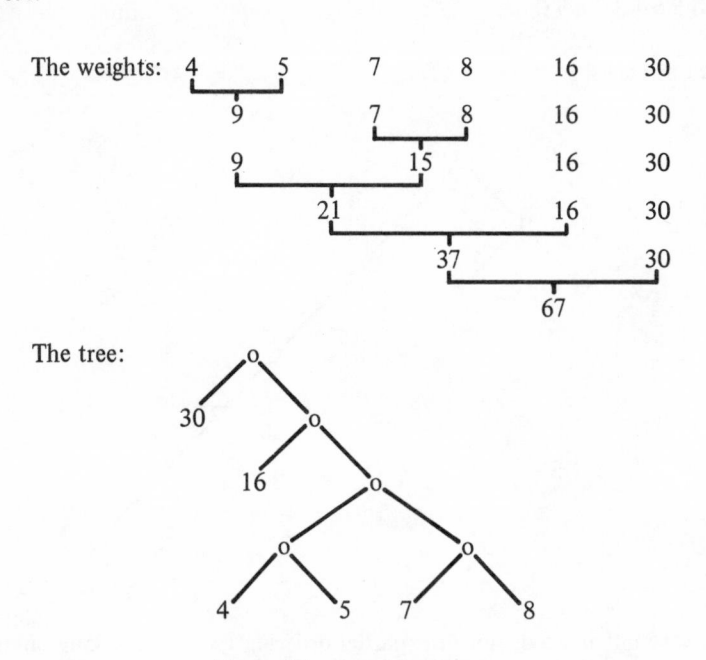

Figure 6.4   A weighted tree

6.4   Sequential Representation of Trees

Just as linked lists could be adequately represented in a linear structure, so too can trees. One might ask why one would want to do this. In the case of linked lists, there was very little justification other than that the techniques would be useful if one didn't have pointers in the language. With trees, there is a much greater variety of linear forms, as we have already seen, and most of these give benefits in one way or another. We shall look at four of these methods here.

Three-array Method

If the classic method for storing binary trees is called the two-pointer method, then its exact linear equivalent requires three arrays, one each for the data, the left link, and the right link. The algorithms to handle a tree in this way, and even its definition, are so similar to those developed in Section 3.6 that they are not expanded here.

Everything that can be done with the two-pointer method—sorting, searching, traversing—can also be done with three arrays. However, if the language being used does have dynamic storage, then there is clearly no advantage in using arrays, with their inherent finiteness.

Level–position Method

If the binary tree is static, with no additions or deletions envisaged, then traversing and searching can be speeded up by employing the array-as-a-function principle.

Each node can be labelled with a two-part label giving its level and position in that level, numbering from the left. Both parts start at 0 for the root. This gives

A requirement of this method is that the tree is full, i.e. that all leaves are at the same level. If there are missing nodes and leaves, these must be inserted with dummy values, making the tree complete. We now use the same general methodology developed in Section 5.4, by storing the tree in a linear array

VAR tree : array [treerange] of item;

and defining a mapping function to get to and from the original tree. At level i there are 2^i nodes, labelled $(i,0), (i,1) \ldots (i,2^i - 1)$. The item at level i, position j, is therefore given by

$$T(i,j) = 2^i + j$$

Because no nodes have been omitted in the copying of the tree into the array (the mapping function wouldn't work if they had), the access function (TF) and the update procedure (TP) are very simple:

$TF : TF := tree(T(i,j))$
$TP : tree(T(i,j)) := x$

In fact, there is no need to have special functions: we simply apply the mapping when necessary.

Looking at traversing, we see that we need to be able to follow the left and right branches, and to know when we have reached a node with no more subtrees. The position of the left subtree of a node at (i,j) is given by

$$L(i,j) = T(i + 1, 2^*j)$$
$$= 2^{i+1} + 2^*j$$
$$= 2(2^i + j)$$
$$= 2^* T(i,j)$$

By similar calculations, the right subtree is found at

$$R(i,j) = 2^*T(i,j) + 1$$

If $T(i,j) = k$, i.e. the node is at position k in the array, then its left and right subtrees are found at $tree[2^*k]$ and $tree[2^*k + 1]$ respectively. In order to know when we have reached the bottom of the tree, we have to know the maximum level, and compare i to it. Putting all this together, we can write an inorder tree traversal for this representation.

```
PROCEDURE inorder (i,j : treeindex);
BEGIN
    if i ≤ maxlevel
    then begin
        inorder (i + 1, 2*j);
        addtotable (tree[2**i + j]); {or expanded without **}
        inorder (i + 1, 2*j + 1);
    end;
END; {inorder}
```

Searching follows a similar pattern. The important advantage of this method is that it uses no extra storage for links. Provided there are not a significant number of dummy nodes needed to fill the tree, it can be extremely effective.

Parent-node Method

Apart from traversing and searching, a typical operation on trees is to find a path from one node to another. Pointers and recursion would enable this to be done quite elegantly, but neither of the other two methods so far make it easy to move back up the tree. In this method we do not store links at all, but instead record the parent of each node. Consequently, we are not bound to binary trees, and can handle multi-link trees without first transforming them.

We start by numbering every node in sequence. We then set up an array with two fields: the data at that node, and the number of its parent, i.e.

```
VAR tree : array [treerange] of record
            data    : item;
            parent : treeindex;
       end;
```

A parent of zero characterizes the root. Figure 6.5 shows this representation.

The idea of discovering whether a path exists from one node to another (other than via the root) stems from the notion of subtrees: if such a path exists, then the nodes are in the same subtree. One can imagine this question being relevant to a family tree, say. A simple algorithm for finding the path is as follows

Algorithm: Finding a path

1. Record the node numbers from the node $n1$ to the root.
2. Record the node numbers from the node $n2$ to the root.
3. If the common part of the two paths is more than just the root, then such a path exists.

Example. From I to H we have

> path I = {9, 7, 4, 1}
> path H = {8, 4, 1}
> Common part = {4, 1}

Therefore a path exists, and I and H are on the same subtree (of node 1).

Put into Pascal, the algorithm is

> TYPE paths = set of treeindex;

The tree:

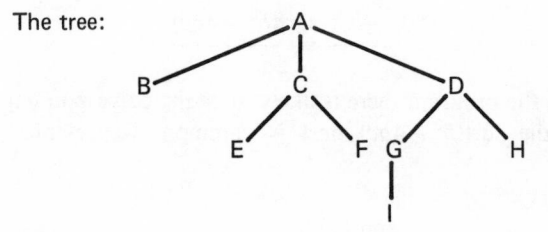

Its representation:

k	1	2	3	4	5	6	7	8	9
tree[k].parent	0	1	1	1	3	3	4	4	7
tree[k].data	A	B	C	D	E	F	G	H	I

Figure 6.5   A parent-node tree representation

```
PROCEDURE pathbetween (n1, n2 : treeindex) : boolean;
   VAR p1, p2 : paths;
   BEGIN
      findpath (n1, p1);
      findpath (n2, p2);
      pathbetween := (p1*p2) < > [ ];
   END; {pathbetween}
```

The set expression at the end is interpreted as 'If the intersection of the two paths (not counting the root) is not empty'. The findpath procedure is actually independent of the representation, but with parent nodes it is particularly easy, i.e.

```
PROCEDURE findpath (n : treerange; var p : paths);
   VAR current : treeindex;
   BEGIN
      current := n; {start at the last node}
      p := [ ];        {empty path}
      while current < > 0 do
      with tree[current] do begin
         p := p + [parent];
         current := parent;
      end;
   END; {findpath}
```

Terminating Binary Sequence

Another operation which would be useful would be the ability to determine whether two binary trees are the same, or whether parts of them are similar. This question is relevant in compiler writing where the compiler may be requested to optimize the space used. If it can detect that parts of a program are repeated, it can make one copy for general use. Take for example the expression

$$\frac{-b + \mathrm{sqrt}(b^2 - 4ac)}{2a}$$

Somewhere in the program there is likely to be the corresponding expression with $-$sqrt. Thus the sqrt($b^2 - 4ac$) part is common. Represented as a tree, this becomes

None of the methods so far is amenable to a straightforward tree comparison because they either maintain links or have none. What is needed is a blueprint of the tree which gives a formula of the link structure. This can be provided by means of a terminating binary sequence. The algorithm to convert a tree to such a sequence is as follows.

Algorithm: Terminating Binary Sequence

1. Convert the tree to a strict binary tree
2. Traverse the tree in reverse preorder, i.e.
   Visit the root
   Traverse the right subtree
   Traverse the left subtree
   recording a 1 for every branch and a 0 for every leaf.
3. Simultaneously record the data items encountered in a separate list.

Figure 6.6 shows the strict binary tree and its corresponding terminating binary sequence (TBS).

The tree:

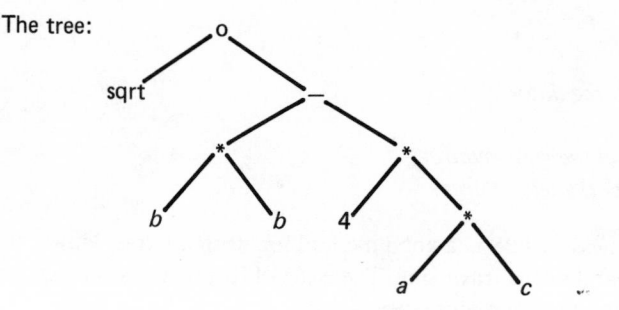

The TBS:

TBS	1	1	1	1	0	0	0	1	0	0	0
data		−	*	*	c	a	4	*	b	b	sqrt

Figure 6.6   A terminating binary sequence

To understand the meaning of the sequence, consider a small subtree, say

This is represented by 100 (a 1 for the branch node and two 0s for the leaves). Thus a simple subtree is identified by finding a 1 followed by two 0s. Once this has been done, the subtree is replaced by a 0, indicating a 'virtual' leaf, and is used in subsequent scans to find higher-level subtrees. This process is illustrated by:

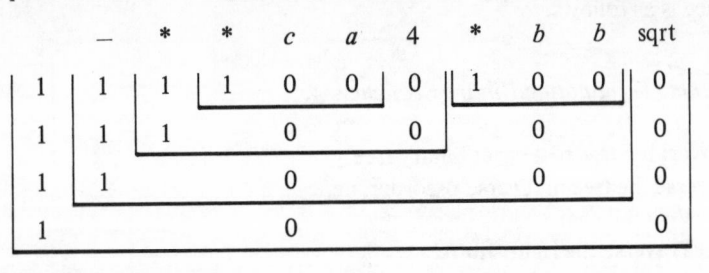

The binary patterns can be compared to those for other trees and a direct answer as to the structural equivalence can be obtained. Subsequently, the data can also be compared to establish complete equivalence of two subtrees. For example, the trees for $b*b-4*a*c$ and $x*x-2*y*z$ would have the same TBS and be structurally equivalent, but would have different data sequences. The amount of equivalence required will depend on the application.

A terminating binary sequence is a minimal representation for a tree with no information lost. To prove this, we give the algorithm to build it back into a linked tree.

Algorithm—reconstruct:

> *Make a node with the data*
> If *the next bit is 1*
> > then *reconstruct the right subtree*
> > else *reconstruct the left subtree.*

Because of its compactness, a TBS is a good method for storing a tree. However, it cannot be used for searching or traversing. The issue of storing trees is taken up again in the next chapter when we discuss files.

6.5 Family Tree Project

Introduction

Pascal belongs to the latest generation of high-level programming languages designed in the 1970s. One of the main advances over the languages of the 1960s (FORTRAN, ALGOL 60, BASIC) is the provision for data structures other than sequential arrays. Record definitions with named fields were used in COBOL for business data processing, but their true worth shows in the area of linked-list processing. Not only can a record consist of items of several different types, but it can also point to other records.

This project is concerned with the creation and manipulation of a data structure representing a family tree of the type shown in Figure 6.8. Family trees have been

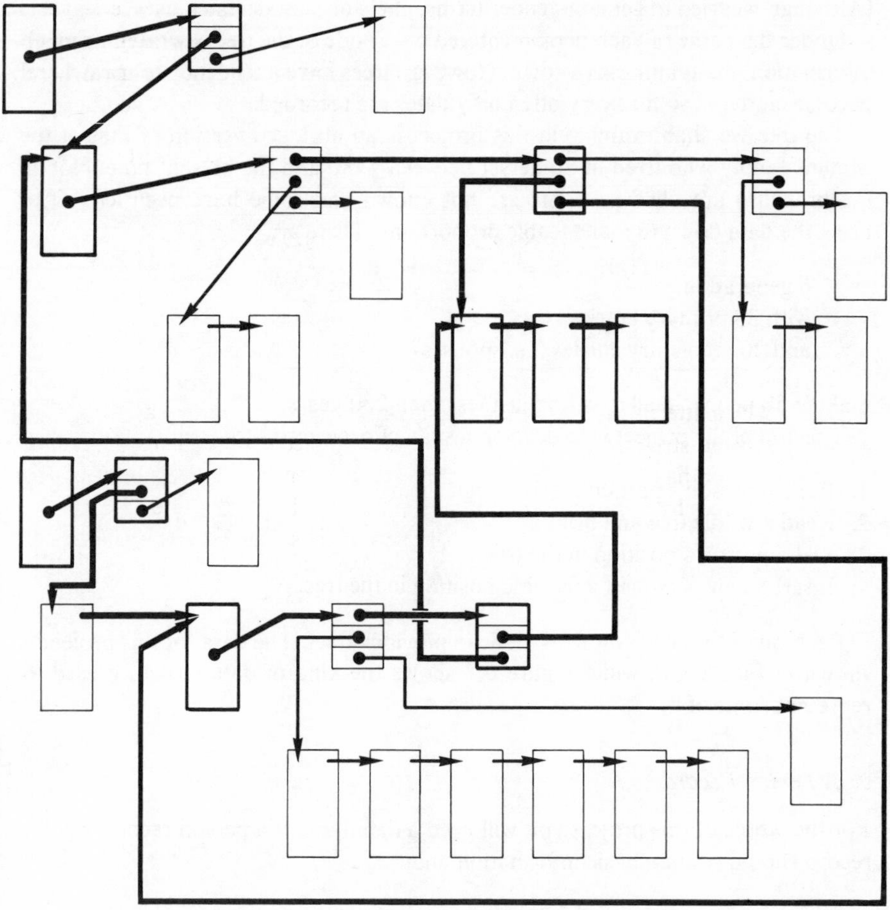

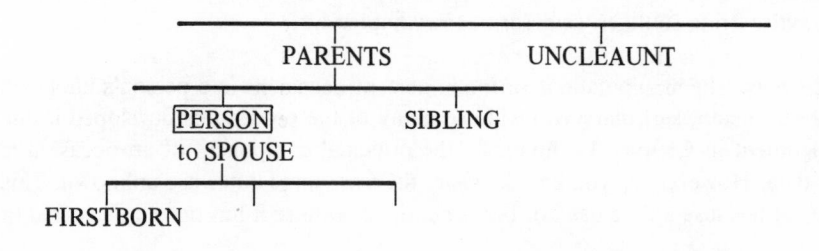

Figure 6.7   Example of a data structure for a family tree

kept and drawn as directed graphs since the early Middle Ages. A large amount of information is implied by the straight lines, which do not normally have arrows. Vertical lines indicate descendants, horizontal lines indicate siblings, which are always in chronological order. Certain terms correspond to relations as indicated in this diagram of PERSON's relations.

PARENTS   UNCLEAUNT

PERSON   SIBLING
to SPOUSE

FIRSTBORN

(Although we tried to get non-gender terms, uncle or aunt defeated us!)

Under the name of each person entered on a node of the tree is written as much information about him as is known. However, trees have a tendency to sprawl and become cluttered so that very often only dates are recorded.

The tree we shall examine in this project is an abridged version of that of the Mullins family who lived in Somerset between 1780 and the present time. Not all the branches are filled in: some are not known and some have been left off to bring the data down to manageable proportions. There are

> 6 generations
> with 38 primary entries
> and 20 secondary entries (i.e. spouses)

making 58 people in all covering just less than 200 years.

The aim of the project is to develop a suite of procedures to:

1. Read a person's particulars and print them.
2. Read a whole tree and print it.
3. List a person's position in the tree.
4. Insert a new person in a feasible position in the tree.

Each question builds on work done in previous ones. The data for this project is shown in Figure 6.8, while Figure 6.7 shows the kind of data structure used to represent some of it.

0. A Person Record

For the whole of this project you will need a definition of a person record. Such a record should contain basic information about

- the names of the person
- important occasions in his life
- his relationship to his family
- which generation he belongs to.

Names. Pascal provides a predefined type for holding eight or ten alphanumeric values, namely alfa. However, that is not enough, and we must set up our own string type to hold the names of the people. Such a type will be a packed array of characters. Fortunately, assignment, comparison and ordering are defined for packed arrays of characters, but you will have to include versions of readstring and writestring routines, as described in Chapter 4.

Occasions. The manipulations of the important occasions in a person's life (such as birth, death, and marriage) will use many of the procedures developed in the assignment in Chapter 1. Obviously the principal component of an occasion is the date. However, as you can see from the tree, some dates are unknown. This may be because a date has not been found, or because it has not yet occurred (a

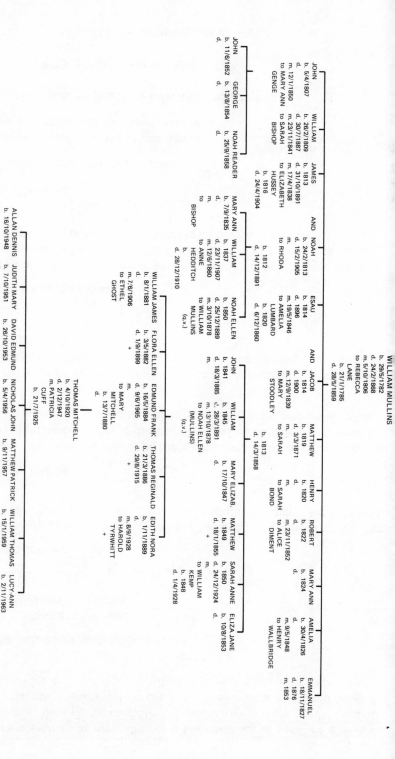

Figure 6.8 The Mullins family tree

current person's death) or never did occur (the marriage of someone who died young). All these facts can be established from the data and are worth including for future reference. Think about the concept of the status of a date and design a suitable record for an occasion. You will need procedures to readoccasion and writeoccasion.

Relationships. Given the declarations

```
TYPE   relative = ↑person;
VAR    thisperson : relative
```

a person can be created by

```
new (thisperson)
```

thisperson is now a pointer to a record with space for all the details of his life. The record can also have pointer fields which refer to other people. One such field might be

```
spouse : relative
```

Think about what other links might be needed but don't spend too much time on this as it will be covered further in Exercises 2, 3, and 4. It will be useful, however, to distinguish between primary entries in the tree and spouses, who are secondary entries.

Generations. A person can be partially identified by his generation or level on the tree. For example, William L01 refers to the first one; William L06 refers to William Thomas on the lowest level.

1. Readperson and Printperson

By now you should have defined a person record and written procedures to readoccasion and writeoccasion. The first exercise is to read in data about a person and print it out in a neat way, similar to an entry on the tree.

Exercise 1
(a) Write the body for

```
PROCEDURE readperson (p : relative);
```

The data is to be entered in the format described in the following Interlude. For this exercise use only the people shown in the sample.

Hints 1.   The procedure should have the following structure:

```
PROCEDURE readperson (p : relative);
var ...
PROCEDURE readstring (var s : string);
```

```
                    var . . .
                    begin
                       .
                       .
                       .
                    end;
          PROCEDURE readoccasion (var occ : occasion);
                    begin
                       .
                       .
                       .
                    end
          PROCEDURE readspouse (majorentry : relative);
                    begin
                       .
                       .
                       .
                    end;
                    begin
                       .
                       .
                       .
                    end; (*readperson*)
```

Interlude—Family data format

1. Each person is typed on a separate line in free format with items identified by markers.
2. Because some of the markers are letters and may appear in names, the name items end with a space, as a non-conflicting marker. Otherwise spaces are ignored.
3. Only items whose values are known are present.
4. The first item is the name.
5. Details of a spouse, if there is one, follow the primary entry.
6. The last marker is E.

Marker	Item	Type	Trailer
≠	first name	string	space
+	second name	string	space
B	birth date	⎫ K – date ⎫	
D	death date	⎬ H – year ⎬ next marker	
M	marriage date	⎭	
L	generation	integer ⎭	
&	spouse following	– ⎫ next marker,	
E	end of person	– ⎭ but must be #.	

Sample for Exercise 1												

```
#WILLIAM    BK     29   5   1782   DK   24     2   1868   MK   5  10  1806  L01  &
#REBECCA    BK     21   1   1785   DK   28     5   1859   E
#SARAH   +ANNE     BH       1850   DK   24    12   1924   L03  &
#WILLIAM +KEMP     BH       1848   DK    1     4   1928   E
#EMMANUEL   BK 18  11       1827   DH 1876    MH   1853   L02  E
#LUCY-ANN   BK  2  11       1963   L06   E
```

2. Because the spouse is a person, readspouse can call readperson recursively.
3. Use readdate inside readoccasion.

(b) Write the body for

PROCEDURE printperson (p:relative);

which has a similar structure to readperson. The block of data representing a person should be indented across the page depending on the level number. Also calculate and print out the age in years at death (if the date of death is known).

(c) Write a program to read in the four sample people, WILLIAM, EMMANUEL, SARAH ANNE, and LUCY-ANN together with their spouses where applicable, and print them out.

2. Readtree and Printtree

A family tree can be represented in a systematic way as in (a) below. Then if it is tilted 45°, it becomes a binary tree as in (b), and the traversing techniques can be applied.

(a)

(b)

So that

leftlink corresponds to firstborn

and

rightlink corresponds to sibling.

Listing this fragment of the tree is preorder gives

```
William 1
  John 2
    John 3
    George 3
    Noah Reader 3
  William 2
  James 2
```

Exercise 2
(a) Write the body for

PROCEDURE readtree (root : relative);

which is called after William and Rebecca have been read in, and reads in all their descendants, setting up appropriate links.
(b) Write the body for

PROCEDURE printtree (root : relative);

which is called after readtree, and prints out all the people in the tree in preorder, suitably indented.

Interlude—What is expected

The last exercise marked the end of carefully guided classwork. The statement of parts 3 and 4 will be more general and open-ended. It will be up to you to decide on how far to take the solution, what procedures you will need and what output to produce. It will therefore be necessary for you to explain to the examiner in a document accompanying your listings exactly *what* your programs do, as well as how they do it, although the latter may not amount to much if your Pascal is sufficiently readable.

Obviously higher marks will be given for a greater amount of work. However, it is more important to *understand* the whole problem and select a portion of it which can realistically be completed in the time available, than to hand in ambitious systems which only half work. As has been emphasized all along, marks will be given for initiative, clear style, layout, and readability.

3. Ancestry

Once the tree structure has been created, the next step is to be able to move about it freely and answer queries about existing people. The scope of queries is nearly infinite, but the following is a reasonably comprehensive one:

> Given a name and date of birth, print out all the particulars of the person (if he/she exists) plus the ancestry and a summary of descendants.

Example:

> EDMUND FRANKE
> b. 16/5/1884
> d. 9/6/1865 aged 81
> m. ?
> to MARY MITCHELL
> b. 13/7/1880
> d. ?

1 son
7 grandchildren (5 boys, 2 girls)

He is the 3rd child of WILLIAM (1845) and NOAH ELLEN
who was 2nd son of MATTHEW (1819) and SARAH
who was 7th son of WILLIAM (1782) and REBECCA.

4. Tree Integrity

The data in a family tree forms a data base which conforms to certain axioms. Some of these are

birth before death
birth before marriage
marriage before death

marriage before firstborn↑.birth[1]

death after or equal to child↑. birth

yearsbetween (birth, sibling↑. birth) > 1[2]

yearsbetween (birth, mothers↑. birth) < 50

yearsbetween (birth, death) < 100

yearsbetween (birth, marriage) ⩾ 18

You can probably think of more. The values given here are appropriate to the data and can be assumed to be correct.

The first task would be to build a program to verify each person in his position in the tree. Once you can do this, try and read in a new person and find him a place in the tree. Of course, there may be more than one feasible position! If you decide to do this, here is some test data consisting of real people who were deliberately left out of the tree.

THOMAS	CAROLINE MARY	JOHN WALTER
b.21/10/1810	b.30/10/1850	b.7/11/1846
d. 6/5/1830		d.
		m.14/8/1875
		to ANN PERHAM

WILLIAM ROBERT	NORMAN	KATHRYN AMY
b.28/5/1869	b.24/12/1908	b.14/2/1980
d. 9/12/1937	d.25/4/1925	
m.		
to SARAH-ANN SUMMERS		

LOUISA	WILLIAM
b.1849	b.21/3/1853
d.18/1/1855	

5. Statistics (if time allows)

(* DO NOT ATTEMPT 5 UNLESS 3 AND 4 ARE COMPLETE *)

It would be interesting to have some statistics about the people on the tree. For example:

What is the average age at death? at marriage?

What would the average age be, excluding those who died young (before 18)?

A sort program would also be useful so that the complete list of people could be printed out in chronological order.

---

1. Note that this axiom only requires that the marriage take place before the birth—not 9 months before. (See William and Rebecca's firstborn).

2. You may assume that where there are twins then both people are already known and adjacent in the sibling list. This axiom should read

$(\ldots > 1)$ **or** $(daysbetween(birth, sibling\uparrow. birth) = 0)$

Chapter 7

Input–Output (Part 2)—Files

The essentials of computation are the program and the memory. So far, we have assumed that the memory is infinite, and that it exists merely for the duration of the program. We must now consider the practicalities of a finite memory, and of data existing beyond the lifetime of a program so that it can be re-input, or sent to another program. These requirements are met by having memory—or storage—which is external to the computer's processor. Such memory is also 'external' to the Pascal language and it is necessary to consider how we interface with the operating system, and with users of our programs. This chapter covers such practicalities as well as the more traditional aspects of file organization and sorting.

7.1 Files in Pascal

In Pascal, *file* is the name given to the sequence abstraction. We have already met this data structure in Chapter 3, where we defined sequential lists and the operations on them (Figure 3.2). For files, the operations are:

↑	access the current item
reset	make the file available for reading from the beginning
rewrite	make the file available for writing from the beginning
get	move onto the next item while reading
put	write the current item
eof	test whether the end of file has been reached while reading.

Files are variables, and therefore have a name and a type. All the items stored on the file are of that type. Pascal files are therefore *homogenous.*

Classes of File

There are two classes of file in Pascal. The difference is based on whether the data is humanly readable or whether it is intended to be read only by another program (or the same program, later on). Humanly readable data is entered into a computer via, say, an editor, and consists fundamentally of lines of characters. In the same way, results are presented back to humans in lines of characters. This class of files are known as text files and are defined to be of

TYPE   text = file of char;

There are two predefined text files in Pascal—input and output. To Pascal, information held on these files is simply sequences of characters. To the human, however, there is a logical structure and meaning to the characters, in particular those that represent numbers. Pascal therefore provides *conversion routines* which will take numbers in character form and convert them to numbers—integer or real—in the machine's internal form.

These routines are built into the two standard procedures, read and write. Although we take the work that they do for granted, it is instructive to remember that the conversion takes time. For inputting data from the outside world and for producing results, this conversion is necessary. If, however, the file is to be used for storing data between runs of programs, then the second class of file is more

```
PROGRAM readin (input, store);

    VAR store : file of integer;
        n     : integer;

    BEGIN
        rewrite(store);
        while not eof(input) do begin
            read(n);  { converts characters to an integer}
            store↑ := n;
            put(store);
            while (input↑=space) and not eof(input) do get(input);
        end;
    END.

PROGRAM writeout(store, output);

    VAR store : file of integer;
        n     : integer;

    BEGIN
        reset(store);
        while not eof(store) do begin
            n := store↑;
            write(n);   {converts an integer to characters}
            get(store);
        end;
        writeln;
    END.
```

Figure 7.1   Using files

appropriate. These are files of items of any type except char, and they hold the data without conversion.

The use of machine-readable files such as a file of integer saves on time, but it may not always save space. Suppose an integer is stored in 16 bits. Characters are usually stored in 8 bits each, so that a file of integer will save space once the numbers exceed two digits.

To emphasize the difference, suppose we wish to read in and store a sequence of numbers and then later on print them out using another program. Figure 7.1 gives the two programs required.

There are several points of detail to note here:

1. Although the current item on the file, indicated by ↑, is technically a variable, many systems treat it specially and it is often not possible to use it as one would a variable. For example, in writeout, n is not strictly necessary because one could say

   ```
   write(store↑);
   get(store);
   ```

2. The second loop in readin emphasizes that input is composed of characters and that there may well be some after the last number (spaces, for instance). If this is the case, then the eof condition is not true once the last number has been read, but only after all the characters have been read. Therefore we must skip over the spaces between numbers each time, just in case.

3. Input and output also have to be reset and rewritten, respectively, but this is done by the system prior to the program starting. It is actually not possible to perform these operations during the program.

Files of Records

Files of single types are quite unusual: the most common use of machine-readable files is in storing records of data of different types. For example, we could declare

```
TYPE books = record
            title,
            publisher,
            author     : string;
            data        : yearrange;
            pages       : pagerange;
            price       : real;
            illustrated : boolean;
            ISBN        : string;
        end;
    VAR catalogue : file of books;
```

If the record has variants, then it is worth noting that most Pascal systems cannot take advantage of any variation in the size of the items sent to the file, and they will all be padded out to the size of the largest variant.

Why Files?

To summarize, there are three reasons for using files:

1. *Communicating* with the outside world. This is done through text files, of which the archetype (but not only) files are input and output.
2. *Storing* information for later use by the same or other programs. This is usually most efficiently done, in terms of speed and space, by means of machine-readable files defined to be of the exact type of items being stored.
3. *Accommodating* large amounts of data, larger than can fit in memory. This requires special techniques to complement those learnt in earlier chapters.

7.2   File Searching

There are two aspects to processing data on a file:

- the organization of the items, and hence the access method
- the formation of keys, and hence the ordering function.

In theory, any of the searching methods discussed in Chapters 5 and 6 could be used with files, but only those that follow a sequential access pattern are really feasible. Let us consider the five methods in turn, and thereby develop the additional techniques needed for file searching.

Linear Search

This is, of course, the natural way to scan a file and can be used effectively in many applications. Typically, we have a *master file* of items, several of which need to be interrogated. If we first sort the requests into the same order as the master file, then the entire operation can be performed in one scan. If the items accessed also need to be updated, then it is necessary to create a new master file as we go along. This process is known as *master file update*. Although simple in concept, a perfect algorithm for it is not easy, and has been the source of much correspondence in the literature.

Clearly, a linear search is not suitable if repeated access to random items on the file is to be made. In this circumstance, a more powerful organization of the file is required.

Binary Search

This method is not at all good for file processing because it relies on being able to jump back and forth in the data. On to better things . . .

Indexed Search

This is a favourite method for file searching and goes by the name 'indexed sequential'. The simplest way to implement it on files is to have separate files for the index and for each region. Access to a given item then involves a linear scan of the index file, resetting the appropriate region file, and a further linear scan. In addition to the time taken for the linear scans, there could be a considerable overhead in the resetting procedure which would make the method untenably slow.

If resetting is a drawback (as it would be if the files were on tape rather than disc), then an alternative is to have the index and regions in a single file. In order to access the regions via the index, we introduce the idea of an *item number*. Each item in the file has an implied serial number, starting from 1. The entries in the index then consist of the item numbers of the first item in each region. Having obtained the first entry's number by a linear search of the index, we then proceed to read the file in 'fast forward' mode, skipping the appropriate number of items. This is faster than a normal scan, where the keys are compared.

It may also be possible to introduce a still faster version, by making use of a *seek* procedure provided by the operating system. Such a procedure uses machine-code instructions to jump directly to a given item number on a file. It is not a bad thing to make use of such a procedure for efficiency's sake, because it is possible to implement its function in pure Pascal (the reader should try this as an exercise).

Hashed Search

The same considerations apply here as for the indexed search. If a seek procedure is available, then hash searching could be effective, provided the method of handling clashes results in items being stored further down the file.

Tree Search

One of the most efficient methods of searching is tree search, which also has the property that the search moves onwards in the structure, making it appropriate for adaptation to a file. Since the file is a sequential structure, we simply implement the sequential version of tree representation, using the item numbers as links. In addition, each item keeps its item number for identification. Thus we define

```
CONST null = 0;
TYPE itemnumbers = 0. .maxint;
     items          = record
        key             : . . .;
        data            : . . .;
        number,
        left,right : itemnumbers;
     end;
VAR treefile : file of items;
```

To access an item given its item number, we must read over the items between it and where we are at the time. So now we define

```
PROCEDURE fastforward (n : itemnumbers);
    VAR i : itemnumbers;
    BEGIN
        for i := 1 to n do get(treefile);
    END;
```

and the search procedure is

```
PROCEDURE treesearch (root : itemnumbers; key : keys);
    {Positions treefile at the required item}
    BEGIN
        if root < > null then begin

        {First move on to the root}
        fastforward (root-treefile↑.number);
        if key < > treefile↑.key then
        if key < treefile↑.key then treesearch (treefile↑.left,key)
                              else treesearch (treefile↑.right,key);
    END; {treesearch}
```

B-trees

When we are dealing with very large files (e.g. a million items), the look-up time will be entirely dominated by the physical access time. We therefore need to be sure that we can get a good chunk of the relevant part of the file at each file access. This suggests a short bushy tree as opposed to the long straggling tree characteristic of binary tree search. Moreover, it is necessary that the tree should show controlled growth; we must be able to guarantee that the tree remains squat and bushy.

All these requirements are satisfied by the B-tree, which has the following properties:

A B-tree is a multiway tree in which each node may contain several items and may have several successors. More precisely, for a B-tree of order d:

1. Every node contains not more than $2d$ items.
2. Every node except the root contains at least d items.
3. A node may have no successors, but if a node has immediate successors it must have one more than it has entries.
4. All terminal nodes appear at the same level.

Rules 1 and 2 ensure balanced growth. Rule 3 allows us to generalize the sorting order implied by a binary tree. Let the keys at a particular node be denoted by

$k_1, k_2, \ldots, k_m$ and let the successors be denoted by the pointers $p_0, p_1, \ldots, p_m$. Then p_0 points to keys less than k_1, p_j points to keys between k_j and k_{j+1} ($j = 1, \ldots, m$), and p_m points to keys greater than k_m. Pictorially we have:

Binary tree:

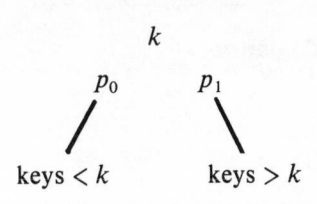

B-tree:

$$k_1 \quad k_2 \ldots k_m$$

$$p_0 \quad p_1 \quad p_2 \cdots p_{m-1} \quad p_m$$

keys $< k_1$ $k_1 <$ keys $< k_2$ $k_{m-1} <$ keys $< k_m$ keys $> k_m$

Searching for a node in a B-tree follows this algorithm:

> *Search (key, root) :*
> > *If key not contained in root's keys*
> > *then*
> > > *if key $< k_1$ then search (key, p_0) else*
> > > *if key $< k_2$ then search (key, p_1) else*
> > > *. . .*
> > > *search (key, p_m);*

Adding items to a B-tree is very elegant. By a search procedure similar to the one above, we find the appropriate node. If this node does not contain its full quota of items we can add the new one forthwith. If it is full, proceed as follows. By definition, the full node must contain an even number of items. If we take these $2d$ items and the one to be inserted, they can be divided into the middle item, the left-hand group of d and the right-hand group of d. The left-hand group is retained, the right-hand group is placed in a new node at the same level, and the middle key is inserted in the parent node. If this is full, the splitting process is repeated: in the worst case, this may lead to the creation of a new root.

As an illustration of B-trees, consider what happens when the following set of items is distributed over a B-tree of order 2.

10 40 20 30 7 35 26 15 18 5 42 22 18 42 27 46 13 8 2 45 9

The first four items go in a single root node:

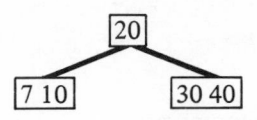

Next we have a new item 7 for which there is no room. Since a full node always contains an even number of entries, when we add one we can always split into two minimal size nodes and a middle value which moves to a level above. Thus

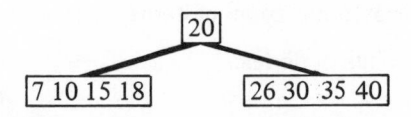

The next four items, 35, 26, 15, and 18, are added without difficulty:

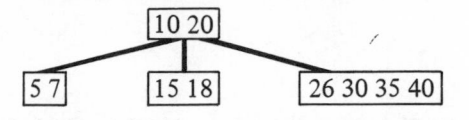

When we add 5, splitting and propagation take place:

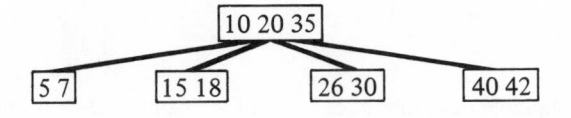

Adding 42 splits the rightmost node:

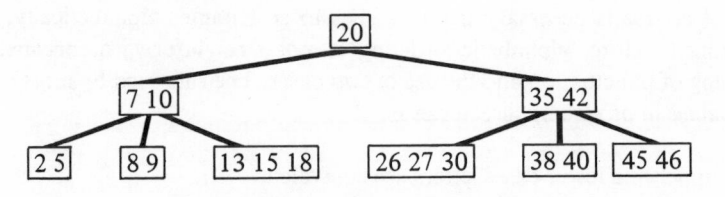

And so we proceed, to the final tree:

Deleting entries from a B-tree resembles the deletion of entries in a binary search tree. We first locate the desired item. If it is in a leaf node it can be deleted; it not we must exchange it with an ordered neighbour that is in a leaf node. Thus having found the item, we first take the pointer immediately to its left, then find the rightmost item in a leaf node in this subtree: this is the candidate. Having exchanged the items, the leaf node may have too few entries, and we try to combine it with one of its neighbours, redistributing the items to achieve more balance. In general these recombination processes may cause the parent node to underflow, in which case the recombination must be repeated at the higher level, and so on until a consistent tree is regained.

This discussion has been couched in terms of a tree in memory: to define a B-tree on a file, we simply have an array of items per node, as in

```
TYPE items = record
            key      : keys;
            data     : ...;
            number,
            successor : itemnumbers;
          end;
          noderange = 1..d;
          nodes = array[noderange] of items;

VAR   Btreefile = file of nodes;
```

and proceed as for a binary tree.

The cost of searching a B-tree grows as the logarithm of the file size; formally, the height of the tree, h, is given by

$$h \leqslant \log_d(n + 1)/2$$

where n is the number of items in the file. This logarithmic cost is very reasonable, even for large files. A B-tree of order 50 which indexes a file of one million records can be searched with only four disc accesses in the worst case.

Key Formation

The humanly readable data that goes onto a file does not always contain a usable key. Although most data processing systems insist on providing every person, car, book, cat, and dog with a number, it is possible to create keys from the data given. This of course is necessary if one wishes to sort names alphabetically. As was mentioned before, alphabetic ordering is not straightforward, because of the mingling of punctuation and the use of two cases. The rule used by most telephone companies in producing directories is:

- upper and lower cases letters are equivalent
- multiple spaces are reduced to one
- spaces come before anything else
- any other punctuation is ignored.

So the following entries would be in order:

Eurocars
Euro-express Travel Agency
Europa Motors
Europair
Europcar
Europe Flooring
European and Eastern Trading
Europe-flooring

Because the rule is arbitrary, it takes a bit of getting used to, but at least there is a defined rule.

A second consideration with alphabetic data is that the names may extend over more than one line of input, and action must be taken when creating the key to ensure that the ends-of-line are handled correctly. Thirdly, the key may be only part of the name, as in the case of searching for key words within a title. In fact, this part of a program can become exceedingly messy, because one is dealing with strings and the string abstraction in Pascal is merely the array—which is not contractible. It would not be a bad thing to make use of any additional string procedures provided by one's system. Alternately, one could make use of another possible abstraction for a string—the file itself, as described in papers by Sale and Bishop in the 1979 volume of *Software—Practice and Experience*.

7.3 File Sorting

We now come to examine the effect of the third reason for files—that of coping with very large amounts of data. It is highly likely that real data will enter our programming systems in unsorted form, and for ease of searching and processing in general, they must be sorted. All the data cannot fit in memory, and so we need to develop a means of sorting which uses files.

The Basic Technique

Let us suppose that we have a file of unsorted items, and that we have an infinite number of temporary files available. (The latter is an unrealistic requirement, but we'll get around it later.) In the sequence of input items, there exist *runs* of items that are in order, even if some of these runs are of length one. For example, given the items

Q W E R T Y U A O P Z X C V B M N I S D

we would have the following nine runs:

Q W
E R T Y

```
U
A O P Z
X
C V
B M N
I S
D
```

If we put each run onto a temporary file, then we can merge them and produce a single sorted file. A *merge* works by considering the current item in each file and choosing for output the one with the key that comes before all the others. That file is then read, and the next item on it becomes available. When a file is finished, it can be excluded from consideration, but it is often easier to grant it an impossibly large key instead. This can then be considered, but will never be chosen. When all the files are finished, the merge is over. Assuming that / is an impossibly large key, then after ten comparisons, the above runs and the output would be as follows:

```
Runs : Q W
       R T Y
       U
       Z
       X
       V
       /
       S
       /
Output : A B C D E I M N O P
```

This process of distributing runs and merging them is known as *merge sort*. The practical problems that must be handled in order to have a sort that does not make unreasonable demands on temporary files, nor takes too many stages, are:

- distributing runs onto a small number of temporary files
- maximizing the length of runs
- coping with the possibility of runs that are too long for the physical files available.

Distributing runs

Distribution of a file into runs works by scanning the file sequentially and switching to a new run whenever the next item has a key lower than the one just written out. So if the number of temporary files is fixed, all we need do is organize the switching process to handle the files in rotation: as soon as we have written a run to each file, and there are still runs coming, we return to the first file and add the new run at the end, and so on. The merge will then produce a new input file

Input :   Q W,E R T Y,U,A O P Z,X,C V,B M N,I S,D

Runs :   Q W, A O P Z, B M N
                 E R T Y, X, I S
                U, C V, D

Merged :   E Q R T U W Y,A C O P V X Z,B D I M N S

Runs :   E Q R T U WY
                A C O P V X Z
                B D I MN S

Merged :   A B C D E I M N O P Q R S T U V W X Y Z.

Figure 7.2   A merge sort with three temporary files

which may well not be sorted, but will have very much longer runs than the original file. Using this file, the process of distribute and merge is repeated until there is only one run—the sorted file. Figure 7.2 shows a merge sort with three temporary files. The runs are indicated by commas.

Maximizing the run length

Distributing the runs in the simple way described above requires only enough memory to hold one item for each file. Just because we are using files there is no reason why we should not make the most of memory as well. One way of doing this is to read in every n items, where n is the maximum that can fit into memory, and perform a straight sort on them, sending this out as a run. Using the above example and an appropriate choice of n as 10, we could straight away distribute the input items into two runs and complete the sort in a single merge, i.e.

Runs: A E O P Q R T U W Y
         B C D I M N S V X Z

Merged: A B C D E I M N O P Q R S T U V W X Y Z

There exists, however, a very much more powerful sorting method known as *heap sort*, which can effectively sort on average $2n$ items in the space for n. Heap sort works by maintaining an array of items, where the first one is always the lowest. At each iteration, this item is output, the new item is read into its place, and then a shuffling takes place to get the lowest item back into first position. Of course, the item coming in could have a key less than that just written out, in which case the usable heap is reduced in size, and the new item is stored in a 'discard heap' which forms at the end. Once the usable heap is down to one item, then a new run is begun with the heap united once again. To complete the description of the sort, we note that the heap is first filled while ensuring that the lowest item lands up in the first position, and it is finally emptied by repeatedly outputting the first item, reducing the heap size, and shuffling.

UCSD Pascal Compiler at Wits University

```
  1   1  1     1 PROGRAM distribute (f0, f1, f2, f3, output);
  2   1  1     3
  3   1  1     3   { Distribution of runs through a heap.
  4   1  1     3     This version produces each run on a new file.
  5   1  1     3     Details of file handling and key formation are
  6   1  1     3     suppressed, as indicated by ... }
  7   1  1     3
 14   1  1   304                                                           {$L+}
 15   1  1   304   CONST maxheapsize = 60;
 16   1  1   304         maxhalfheapsize = 30;
 17   1  1   304         {. . .}
 21   1  1   304                                                           {$L+}
 22   1  1   304   TYPE  heapindex = 0..maxheapsize;
 23   1  1   304         heaprange = 1..maxheapsize;
 24   1  1   304         natural   = 0..maxint;
 25   1  1   304         {. . .}
 38   1  1   304                                                           {$L+}
 39   1  1   304   VAR
 40   1  1   304   { Heap sort variables }
 41   1  1   304       heapsize,
 42   1  1   304       halfheapsize,
 43   1  1   304       usable,
 44   1  1   304       discard      : heapindex;
 45   1  1   308       heap         : array [heaprange] of items;
 46   1  1  2228   { Files}
 55   1  1  4061       {. . .}
 56   1  1  4102                                                           {$L+}
 57   1  1  4102   { Key identification }
 58   1  1  4102       {. . .}
 65   1  1  4153                                                           {$L+}
 66   1  1  4153   { Input control }
 67   1  1  4153       buffer       : items;
 68   1  1  4185       {. . .}
 72   1  1  4188                                                           {$L+}
 73   1  1  4188   { Statistics }
 74   1  1  4188       {. . .}
 77   1  1  4191                                                           {$L+}
 78   1  1  4191
 79   1  1  4191   {Input and key formation procedures
 80   1  1  4191       FUNCTION  endofdata : boolean;
 81   1  1  4191       PROCEDURE selectfile;
 82   1  1  4191       PROCEDURE receive(VAR x : items);
 83   1  1  4191       PROCEDURE give (x : items);}
 84   1  1  4191
345   1 12   138                                                           {$L+}
346   1 13     1   PROCEDURE shuffle (left, right : heapindex);
347   1 13     3   VAR i   : heapindex;
348   1 13     4       j   : natural;
349   1 13     5       x   : items;
350   1 13    37       state : (processing, ended);
351   1 13     0   BEGIN
352   1 13     0     i:=left; j:=2*i; x:=heap[i];
353   1 13    31     state:=processing;
354   1 13    34     repeat
355   1 13    34       if j>right then state:=ended else begin
356   1 13    44         if j<right then
357   1 13    49           if heap[j].key > heap[j+1].key then j:=j+1;
358   1 13    87         if x.key <= heap[j].key then state:=ended else begin
359   1 13   109           heap[i]:=heap[j];
360   1 13   133           i:=j;   j:=2*i
361   1 13   140         end;
362   1 13   149       end;
363   1 13   149     until state<>processing;
364   1 13   155     heap[i]:=x;
365   1 13   170   END;
```

```
366   1 13  184
367   1 14    1   PROCEDURE filltheheap;
368   1 14    0     BEGIN
369   1 14    0
370   1 14    0     {Fill top half of the heap}
371   1 14    0       usable:=heapsize;
372   1 14    9       repeat
373   1 14    9         receive(heap[usable]);
374   1 14   24         usable:=usable-1
375   1 14   27       until endofdata or (usable=halfheapsize);
376   1 14   49       if not endofdata then begin
377   1 14   56
378   1 14   56       {Fill lower half of heap}
379   1 14   56         repeat
380   1 14   56           receive(heap[usable]);
381   1 14   71           shuffle(usable,heapsize);
382   1 14   85           usable:=usable-1;
383   1 14   96         until endofdata or (usable=0);
384   1 14  108       end;
385   1 14  108     END;
386   1 14  124
387   1 15    1   PROCEDURE passrunsthrough;
388   1 15    0     BEGIN
389   1 15    0
390   1 15    0     {Pass runs through full heap}
391   1 15    0       usable:=heapsize;
392   1 15    9       WHILE not endofdata do begin
393   1 15   16         give(heap[1]);
394   1 15   29         if heap[1].key <= buffer.key then begin
395   1 15   47
396   1 15   47           { new item belongs to same run}
397   1 15   47             receive(heap[1]);
398   1 15   60             shuffle(1,usable);
399   1 15   72         end else begin
400   1 15   74
401   1 15   74           { new record belongs to next run}
402   1 15   74             heap[1]:=heap[usable];
403   1 15  100             shuffle(1, usable-1);
404   1 15  114             receive(heap[usable]);
405   1 15  129             if usable <= halfheapsize
406   1 15  132               then shuffle(usable,heapsize);
407   1 15  152             usable:=usable-1;
408   1 15  163             if usable<1 then begin
409   1 15  170
410   1 15  170             {discard heap is full, start new run}
411   1 15  170               usable:=heapsize;
412   1 15  179               selectfile;
413   1 15  181             end
414   1 15  181         end;
415   1 15  181       end; {while}
416   1 15  183     END; {passrunsthrough}
417   1 15  200
418   1 16    1   PROCEDURE emptytheheap;
419   1 16    0     BEGIN
420   1 16    0
421   1 16    0     {Empty the usable heap}
422   1 16    0       discard:=heapsize;
423   1 16    9       repeat
424   1 16    9         give(heap[1]);
425   1 16   22         heap[1]:=heap[usable];
426   1 16   48         shuffle(1,usable-1);
427   1 16   62         heap[usable]:=heap[discard];
428   1 16   90         discard:=discard-1;
429   1 16  101         if usable<=halfheapsize then shuffle(usable,discard);
430   1 16  124         usable:=usable-1;
431   1 16  135       until usable<1;
432   1 16  142
```

```
433   1 16  142     {Empty the discard heap.  Generate last run}
434   1 16  142       if discard>1 then begin
435   1 16  149         selectfile;
436   1 16  151         while discard>1 do begin
437   1 16  158           give(heap[1]);
438   1 16  171           heap[1]:=heap[discard];
439   1 16  197           shuffle(1, discard);
440   1 16  209           discard:=discard-1;
441   1 16  220         end;
442   1 16  222       end;
443   1 16  222     END; {discard}
444   1 16  238
470   1 17  338                                                        {$L+}
471   1 18    1   PROCEDURE initialise;
472   1 18    0   BEGIN
473   1 18    0     heapsize:=maxheapsize;
474   1 18    7     halfheapsize:=maxhalfheapsize;
475   1 18   14     {. . .}
499   1 18  401                                                        {$L+}
500   1 18  401   END;
501   1 18  418
502   1  1    0   BEGIN {Main Program}
503   1  1    0     initialise;
504   1  1   46     selectfile;
505   1  1   48     receive(buffer);
506   1  1   53
507   1  1   53     filltheheap;
508   1  1   55     passrunsthrough;
509   1  1   57     emptytheheap;
510   1  1   59
511   1  1   59     {. . .}
512   1  1   68   END.
```

Figure 7.3   The distributing runs program

The full program to distribute runs in this way is fairly lengthy, so in Figure 7.3
we give only the procedures directly concerned with the sorting process, omitting
by means of comments those concerned with file and key handling. In order to
clarify this rather clever algorithm, Figure 7.4 is an example of a distribution of
the same data as before. The reader should work through the example and the
procedures carefully. For the same data as before, only 2 runs were produced.

Large files on small computers

Although physical considerations are covered in the next section, one concerns us
here. To perform a merge, one needs at least three files: the output file and a
minimum of two temporary run files. Suppose we wish to merge data using a
microcomputer, and that the data occupies several floppy discs. (In reality, this
was the case with the Books-in-Print system discussed in Chapter 4, where 15 000
entries required six discs.) Most microcomputers have only two disc drives. It is
possible to successively load the discs for the input and run files while distributing,
but there is no way of performing the merge with only two drives. How then do we
sort such very large files?

The answer lies in 'divide and conquer'. We know that we can sort one full disc
of data, so we divide the 'one sort of n discs' into 'n sorts of one disc'. We scan

Data : Q W E R T Y U A O P Z X C V B M N I S D

Comment	Buffer	Heap	Output
Fill the heap			
Fill top half	Y	T R E W Q	
Fill other half	U	E T R Y W Q	
while shuffling	A	E U T R Y W Q	
	O	A E U T R Y W Q	
	P	A O E U T R Y W Q	
Pass runs through			
	Z	A P O E U T R Y W Q	
E to lowest	X	E P O Z U T R Y W Q	
O to lowest	C	O P X Z U T R Y W Q	AE
C to discard heap	V	P Q X Z U T R Y W｜C	AEO
Q to lowest	B	Q V X Z U T R Y W｜C	AEOP
B to discard heap	M	R V X Z U T W Y ｜B C	AEOPQ
M to discard heap	N	T V X Z U Y W｜M B C	AEOPQR
N to discard heap	I	U V X Z W Y｜N｜M B C	AEOPQRT
I to discard heap	S	V Y X Z W ｜B N M I C	AEOPQRTU
S to discard heap	D	W Y X Z ｜B S N M I C	AEOPQRTUV
D to discard heap	/	X Y Z｜B D S N M I C	AEOPQRTUVW
Empty the heap			
Y to lowest		Y Z｜B D S N M I C	AEOPQRTUVWX
Z to lowest		Z｜B D S N M I C	AEOPQRTUVWXY
End of main heap		｜B D S N M I C	AEOPQRTUVWXYZ
C to lowest		C D S N M I	B
D to lowest		D I S N M	BC
.....	.....		
S to lowest		S	BCDIMN
End of discard heap			BCDIMNS

Figure 7.4   Distributing runs through a heap

through the entire data and extract only those items with keys in an initial range. For example, with the books, we extract all titles beginning with A, B, or C. This extracted file is then merge-sorted in the usual way. We then scan the whole file again, extracting items in the next range, and sort them, and so on.

Clearly, this is a very time-consuming process. As an illustration, the programs given here, running on a Z80 microcomputer, when applied to the 15 000 book entries took close on 40 hours to complete the sort! And on top of that, the discs had to be changed every half hour or so. There is definitely a moral here:

> If you use a small computer, do not expect it to handle huge files—at least not easily or quickly.

7.4 Files in Practice

Since files in their physical form constitute 'external' storage, consideration must be given to the interface between Pascal and the outside world. To Pascal, the outside world starts at the operating system and continues on to the terminals used for communicating with users, and the users themselves. Full treatment of all these aspects would comprise courses in software engineering or online design, but there are several points which crop up again and again in normal, small programs and these will be dealt with here.

The Interface to the Operating System

The name of a file in a Pascal program is its *internal name*. Associated with this name will be one or more *external names* of the physical files which are under the control of the operating system. All operating systems have some convention for the naming of files, which may include a restriction on the name length and the inclusion of additional information such as the class of file, what kind of device it resides on, and its maximum permissible length. Such information is provided by the programmer in the job control instructions as part of the preface to running a job. The point is, how do we connect up the internal file name with its external counterpart? There are actually three ways:

1. 'Intelligent' program header. The first line of a Pascal program is the program header, and after the name, it is usual (but not compulsory) to list the internal names of all the files used in the program. In the job control instructions, there are commands which associate these names with the external names. For example, on an IBM OS system there would be commands such as

   ```
   //INPUT    DD SYSIN
   //OUTPUT DD SYSOUT=A
   ```

   where SYSIN and SYSOUT are external names for, say, the terminal and printer. The disadvantage of this approach is that there can only be one physical file for each internal name and it is fixed before the program starts.
2. Extensions to reset and rewrite. Many Pascal systems have extended these two procedures by adding an additional parameter for the external file name. The parameter is of some string type and should be a variable although some systems restrict it to a constant. Given this extension, one can then say

   ```
   read (filename);
   reset (f, filename);
   ```

which puts the file association totally under the control of the person running the program.

3. Addition of a *close* procedure. As defined originally, the reset and rewrite procedures, when used on files already open, would cause them to be closed. If we wish to reset a file again, but with a different physical file, then the closing mechanism will have to be explicit. Several systems have added a close procedure with two parameters—one for the internal file name and one for a directive which may instruct the operating system to retain the file or 'throw' it away. Thus we may have something like

```
reset(markfile, 'CS1982');      {Opens CS1982 for reading}
   printresults;
close(markfile,remove);         {Deletes the physical file CS1982}

rewrite(markfile, 'CS1983');    {Creates CS1983}
   readresults;
   printresults;
close(markfile,keep);           {Closes and retains CS1983}
```

Another aspect of file association is what happens if the physical file named in the reset does not exist? The short answer is that the program crashes, but that is not good enough. Once again, an additional procedure or function is required, which can be interrogated immediately after a reset to establish whether the association was successfully made. If it wasn't, the program can take appropriate action, such as asking for another name.

Interaction with the User

Modern programming is geared towards interactive execution, where the user can direct the action of the program from a terminal. Given this freedom, it is no longer necessary to design programs with a sequence of operations in mind; instead we have a set of operations and the user selects from them in any order he chooses. This leads to the idea of a *menu*.

A menu is a list of options displayed on a screen, together with the appropriate commands for selecting those options. Originally, menus occupied several lines and the commands were numbers, as in:

1. Read in a file
2. Extract key words
3. Sort
4. Direct the output to a device
5. List
6. Quit

However, the UCSD Pascal System promoted an approach which is rapidly catching on in user programming. It uses a single line for the menu, with each of the options summarized in a word or two and the command being the one letter given in capitals. This letter would normally be the initial one, but a compromise is made if there is a clash. Thus we have

> CONTROL: Read in, Extract, Sort, Direct output, List, Quit?

Having selected an option, the user may then be presented with another menu such as

> SORT : by Author, Title, Year (or Quit)?

Typing 'Q' for Quit takes him back to the previous menu.

The beauty of this approach is that the control mechanism presented to the user can directly mirror the procedural structure of the program, even down to the association with procedure names. This enhances top-down design (since an option can be included in a menu but actually be 'not implemented yet') as well as modular testing (since the position of an error will be directly related to the most recent command given).

Another important point when designing interactive programs is screen control. It assists greatly in user-friendliness if position on the screen is used to focus the attention of the user. Thus we would reserve the top line for the menu, and jump down to the centre when requesting important information. Such screen control is provided by most systems through the use of the control characters of the underlying character set, and a single procedure to send the cursor to a position given in x, y coordinates. For example, when reading one of the letters from a menu, an invalid letter can be highlighted by ringing a bell and backspacing. The two control characters in the ASCII character set are 7 and 8 respectively. So one can write

> write(chr(7), chr(8));

or even better

> CONST bell = 7; backspace = 8;
> write(chr(bell), chr(backspace));

Designing clever and effective user interfaces for a program is one of the most absorbing tasks, and very time-consuming. There are not many principles to go by—it is mostly a matter of experience and the more programs we read, write, and use, the better we will become. To summarize this chapter we present a double-edged sword:

> A program is only as good as its user interface.
>
> A program is no good if the underlying algorithms have errors.

```
 1   1  1     1   PROGRAM Timetable (input,output);
 2   1  1     3   CONST linemax      = 3;
 3   1  1     3         lecturemax   = 2;
 4   1  1     3         slotsize     = 12;
 5   1  1     3         overslotsize = 13;
 6   1  1     3         space        = ' ';
 7   1  1     3   TYPE
 8   1  1     3     slotcover = 0..overslotsize;
 9   1  1     3     slotindex = 0..slotsize;
10   1  1     3     linerange = 1..linemax;
11   1  1     3     lecturerange
12   1  1     3               = 1..lecturemax;
13   1  1     3     charset   = set of char;
14   1  1     3     times     = (T830,t930,t1040,t1140,t1230,t130,t230,t340,t440);
15   1  1     3     days      = (mon, tues, wed, thurs, fri);
16   1  1     3     lectures  = array [linerange] of string[slotsize];
17   1  1     3     slots     = array [lecturerange] of lectures;
18   1  1     3     periods   = array [times] of slots;
19   1  1     3     weeks     = array [days] of periods;
20   1  1     3
21   1  1     3   VAR week : weeks;
22   1  1  1893       ch   : char;
23   1  1  1894
24   1  2     1   PROCEDURE readch;
25   1  2     0     BEGIN
26   1  2     0       read(ch);
27   1  2    11       if ch in ['A'..'Z'] then ch := chr(ord(ch)+64);
28   1  2    40     END;
29   1  2    52
30   1  3     1   PROCEDURE readoneof(wanted : charset);
31   1  3     0     BEGIN
32   1  3     0       repeat
33   1  3     0         readch;
34   1  3     2       until ch in wanted;
35   1  3    13       writeln;
36   1  3    21     END;
37   1  3    36
38   1  4     1   PROCEDURE readweek;
39   1  4     1     CONST backspace = 8;
40   1  4     1           stet      = '|';
41   1  4     1
42   1  4     1     VAR day     : days;
43   1  4     2         time    : times;
44   1  4     3         lecture : lecturerange;
45   1  4     4         line    : linerange;
46   1  4     5         gap     : slotcover;
47   1  4     6         s       : string[slotsize];
48   1  4    13         dayset,
49   1  4    13         lectureset,
50   1  4    13         answers,
51   1  4    13         timeset : charset;
52   1  4    77
53   1  4     0     BEGIN
54   1  4     0       lectureset:=['1'..chr(lecturemax+ord('0'))];
55   1  4    11       timeset := ['1'..'8','1'];
56   1  4    35       dayset  := ['m','t','w','h','f'];
57   1  4    61       answers := ['y','n'];
58   1  4    87       repeat
59   1  4    87         write('Day (M T W H F)? '); readoneof(dayset);
60   1  4   125         case ch of
61   1  4   130           'm' : day := mon;
62   1  4   135           't' : day := tues;
63   1  4   140           'w' : day := wed;
64   1  4   145           'h' : day := thurs;
65   1  4   150           'f' : day := fri;
```

```
 66  1  4  155        end;
 67  1  4  198        repeat
 68  1  4  198          write('Time (1..8,L)? '); readoneof(timeset);
 69  1  4  234          case ch of
 70  1  4  239            '1' : time := t830;   '5' : time := t130;
 71  1  4  249            '2' : time := t930;   '6' : time := t230;
 72  1  4  259            '3' : time :=t1040;   '7' : time := t340;
 73  1  4  269            '4' : time :=t1140;   '8' : time := t440;
 74  1  4  279            '1' : time :=t1230;
 75  1  4  284          end;
 76  1  4  412          repeat
 77  1  4  412            write('Lecture no. (1..',lecturemax:1,')? ');
 78  1  4  465            readoneof(lectureset);
 79  1  4  474            lecture:=ord(ch)-ord('0');
 80  1  4  484            for line := 1 to 3 do begin
 81  1  4  502              gap := slotsize-
 82  1  4  503                      length(week[day,time,lecture,line]);
 83  1  4  542              write('Line ',line:1,' |',
 84  1  4  583                      week[day,time,lecture,line]);
 85  1  4  623              if gap>0 then write(space:gap); write('|');
 86  1  4  648              for gap:=1 to slotsize+1 do
 87  1  4  668                write(chr(backspace));
 88  1  4  685              readln(s);
 89  1  4  704              if length(s)=0
 90  1  4  708                then week[day,time,lecture,line]:=s
 91  1  4  743                else if s[1] <> stet
 92  1  4  754                  then week[day,time,lecture,line] := s;
 93  1  4  793            end;
 94  1  4  800            write('More? '); readoneof(answers);
 95  1  4  827          until ch='n';
 96  1  4  834          write('More times? '); readoneof(answers);
 97  1  4  867        until ch='n';
 98  1  4  874        write('More days? '); readoneof(answers);
 99  1  4  906      until ch = 'n';
100  1  4  913    END; {readweek}
101  1  4  940
102  1  5    1    PROCEDURE printweek;
103  1  5    1      VAR time    : times;
104  1  5    2          day     : days;
105  1  5    3          lecture : lecturerange;
106  1  5    4          line    : linerange;
107  1  5    5          gap     : slotindex;
108  1  5    6          s       : string;
109  1  5   47          printer : text;
110  1  5  348
111  1  5    0      BEGIN
112  1  5    0        write('To Printer or File? ');
113  1  5   44        readoneof(['P','p','F','f']);
114  1  5   67        if ch='p' then rewrite(printer,'PRINTER:') else begin
115  1  5   96          write('To where? '); readln(s);
116  1  5  137          rewrite(printer,s);
117  1  5  148        end;
118  1  5  148        write('Heading? ');  readln(s);
119  1  5  188        writeln(printer,space:
120  1  5  191                        ((ord(t440)+2)*(slotsize+1)-length(s)) div 2,s);
121  1  5  227        writeln(printer); writeln(printer);
122  1  5  241        write(printer,space:slotsize);
123  1  5  250        for time := t830 to t440 do begin
124  1  5  264          case time of
125  1  5  267            t830 : s := ' 8.30';   t930 : s := ' 9.30';
126  1  5  295            t1040: s := '10.40';   t1140: s := '11.40';
127  1  5  323            t1230: s := '12.30';   t130 : s := ' 1.30';
128  1  5  351            t230 : s := ' 2.30';   t340 : s := ' 3.40';
129  1  5  379            t440 : s := ' 4.40';
130  1  5  393          end;
131  1  5  418          gap := (slotsize-5) div 2;
132  1  5  428          if time<t1230 then ch:=chr(ord(time)+ord('1')) else
```

```
133   1   5   441        if time>t1230 then ch:=chr(ord(time)+ord('0')) else
134   1   5   454                      ch:='L';
135   1   5   458          write(printer,ch,'.',space:gap-2,s,space:gap+2);
136   1   5   510        end;
137   1   5   517      writeln(printer); writeln(printer);
138   1   5   531      for day := mon to fri do begin
139   1   5   545        case day of
140   1   5   548          mon : s := 'Mon ';
141   1   5   561          tues: s := 'Tues';
142   1   5   574          wed : s := 'Wed ';
143   1   5   587          thurs:s := 'Thur';
144   1   5   600          fri : s := 'Fri ';
145   1   5   613        end;
146   1   5   630        for lecture := 1 to lecturemax do begin
147   1   5   650          for line := 1 to linemax do begin
148   1   5   670            write(printer,space:slotsize-7,s,space:3);
149   1   5   700            for time := t830 to t440 do begin
150   1   5   714              write(printer,week[day,time,lecture,line]);
151   1   5   753              gap := slotsize -
152   1   5   754                      length(week[day,time,lecture,line]);
153   1   5   793              write(printer,space:gap+1);
154   1   5   804            end; {times}
155   1   5   811            writeln(printer);
156   1   5   818            s := '     ';
157   1   5   829          end; {lines}
158   1   5   836        end; {slots}
159   1   5   843        writeln(printer);
160   1   5   850      end; {days}
161   1   5   857      close(printer,lock);
162   1   5   865    END; {printweek}
163   1   5   904
164   1   6   1    PROCEDURE saveweek;
165   1   6   1      var filename : string;
166   1   6   42         f : file of weeks;
167   1   6   0      BEGIN
168   1   6   0        write('To where?' ); readln(filename);
169   1   6   51       rewrite(f,filename);
170   1   6   62       f^ := week;
171   1   6   69       put(f);
172   1   6   76       close(f,lock);
173   1   6   84     END;
174   1   6   102
175   1   7   1    PROCEDURE retrieveweek;
176   1   7   1      VAR filename : string;
177   1   7   42         f : file of weeks;
178   1   7   0      BEGIN
179   1   7   0        write('From where? '); readln(filename);
180   1   7   54       reset(f,filename);
181   1   7   65       week := f^;
182   1   7   72       close(f,lock);
183   1   7   80     END;
184   1   7   98
185   1   8   1    PROCEDURE initialise;
186   1   8   1      VAR d : days;
187   1   8   2          t : times;
188   1   8   3          l : lecturerange;
189   1   8   4          i : linerange;
190   1   8   0      BEGIN
191   1   8   0        for d := mon to fri do
192   1   8   11         for t := t830 to t440 do
193   1   8   22           for l := 1 to lecturemax do
194   1   8   39             for i := 1 to linemax do begin
195   1   8   56               week[d,t,l,i] := '';
196   1   8   92             end;
197   1   8   120    END;
198   1   8   140
199   1   1   0    BEGIN {Main program Timetable}
```

```
200   1   1    0     repeat
201   1   1    3       write('Command (Initialise,Read,Print,Save,Get,Quit)? ');
202   1   1   62       readoneof(['i','r','p','s','g','q']);
203   1   1   85       case ch of
204   1   1   90         'i' : initialise;
205   1   1   94         'r' : readweek;
206   1   1   98         'p' : printweek;
207   1   1  102         's' : saveweek;
208   1   1  106         'g' : retrieve;
209   1   1  110         'q' : ;
210   1   1  112       end;
211   1   1  146     until ch ='q';
212   1   1  152   END.
```

Figure 7.5   The timetable program

7.5   Comprehension—A Timetable Keeper

Timetabler is an interactive program for maintaining a class timetable. It illustrates many of the points covered in this chapter, viz:

> menus
> files of records
> file name association
> closing files

Like the program in the previous comprehension on input–output (Section 4.5), it uses a few essential non-standard features of UCSD Pascal. These are:

- the data type string [n] which defines a string of maximum n characters and can be used in the readln procedure to input up to n characters

- the extended reset, rewrite, and close procedures described in Section 7.4.

If possible, set the program up on your computer system, making the necessary changes regarding these two machine-dependencies. Read the program carefully, then carry out the following exercises.

Insecurities

1. There are no checks on the existence of the input file, or on whether the output file should be overwritten. Include these.
2. There is no check on the order in which operations are chosen. For example, one could set about printing a timetable before one had even been read in. Devise a generalized method for controlling the order of commands.

Improvements

1. The various entries are displayed one at a time when a change is to be made. It might be useful to be able to browse through the timetable to see what is

COMPUTER SCIENCE GENERAL TIMETABLE 1982 FIRST TERM

	1. 8.30	2. 9.30	3. 10.40	4. 11.40	L. 12.30	5. 1.30	6. 2.30	7. 3.40	8. 4.40
Mon		AMCSMSI Ferentzy CB142 SHons-System Steele SH1126	CSIIE Mueller GH403 CSHons - AI Layton SH1126	AMCSMSI Machanick CB142 CSIII - PL Bishop BPI016					
Tues	CSII – AP Lazar H208	CSHons-Onlin Crossman SH1126	AMCSMSI Ferentzy CS142 CSHons - AI Layton SH1126	CSHons-Arch Hoogendoorn SH1126		CSII – AP/NA Ypma/Lazar H208	CSII – Tut Lazar/Ypma AMCSMSI-Tut SH3063	AMCSMSI-Tut and Lab Hoog.,Welte, Muel.,Epste.	
Wed	AMCSMSI Machanick CB142 CSIII-Trans Ferentzy BPI016	CSII – NA Ypma OS1 CSHons-Arch Hoogendoorn SH1126	CSHons – AI Hoogendoorn SH1126 CSHons – DB Shochot SH1126	AMCSMSI Ferentzy CB142 CSHons-Comp Mueller SH1126		AMSMSI Machanick SH3063	CSIII – Tut various SH3063 CSIII – PL Bishop SH1125,SHBA SHBB, SHBD	CSIII-Proj. all various AMCSMSI-Tut SH1125,SHBA Mach.,Prins. Korte,Gafin.	
Thur	CSIIE Mueller GLT	AMCSMSI Machanick CB142 OS1 CSHons – PL Bishop SH3063	CSIII – AP Lazar SH1126 CSHons – DB Shochot SH1126	DEPARTMENTAL MEETING or SEMINAR		DEPARTMENTAL MEETING or SEMINAR AMCSMSI Ferentzy CB142	CSIII – Tut Mueller SHWDH AMCSMSI-Tut SH1125, SHBA, SHBB, SHBD	CSIIE – Tut Mueller SHWDH AMCSMSI-Tut and Lab Bish.,Feren. Rods.,Levieu	
Fri	AMCSMSI Ferentzy CB142	CSIIE Mueller SHB2	AMCSMSI Machanick CB142 CSIII – Tran Ferentzy SH3063	CSII – NA Ypma OS1			AMCSMSI-Tut SH125,0C11, Layt.,Lazar, Low,Gowans		

Figure 7.6   Output from the timetable program

booked, without intending to change anything. Investigate the feasibility of adding a browse feature, bearing in mind that the timetable even as it exists now is too large to fit on an 80 × 24 screen. A means of seeing portions of the timetable must be included.

2. The timetable is assumed to fit in memory and the files are only used as storage in between runs (this is why they are declared locally to the retrieve and save procedures). Suppose the program is to be extended to handle timetables for up to a hundred departments, making the total number of entries too large for memory. Design a suitable file structure which will enable the read in method to remain as far as possible the same, and be reasonably efficient.

Chapter 8

Other Languages

For a programmer to call himself 'advanced' is premature if he can only com-municate in one language. As we have seen all along, communicating with people through a program is as important as communicating with the machine, yet not everyone you come into contact with will know Pascal. In other departments and research establishments, it is possible that the *lingua franca* will still be FORTRAN, and in a few years time Ada will be making its mark. In this chapter we shall introduce these two languages, explaining how they differ from the language we have used so far. The speed at which a second and third language can be covered is indicative of the fact that there are certain basic principles which differ from language to language only in syntactic detail.

8.1   An Acquaintance with FORTRAN

History

FORTRAN stands for 'FORmula TRANslator' and was developed during the late 1950s. It was the first high-level language to gain wide acceptance and until the mid-1970s was the accepted teaching language in most computer science departments world-wide. In an effort to halt the growing number of FORTRAN dialects, the American National Standards Institute published a document which defined ANSI Standard FORTRAN IV. Most people try to stick to this standard although the temptation to use the extra goodies provided by a particular system is much greater than it is with Pascal.

FORTRAN, because of its age, is genuinely deficient in many areas. Another problem is that FORTRAN programmers tend to program in the idiom of the 1960s, ignoring many of the advantages of structured programming, modularity, and security that are taught automatically to Pascal programmers. Thus the FORTRAN programs you might have to read will probably be messy: the ones you write should be as good as the language allows.

Recognizing the deficiencies of FORTRAN IV, ANSI set up an investigation into an enhanced language, which culminated in the definition of FORTRAN 77. The improvements included better control structures and additional types for characters. FORTRAN 77 gained some acceptance in the scientific community, but it could not replace FORTRAN 66 (as FORTRAN IV became known) because the new language did not entirely encompass the old, i.e. FORTRAN 66 programs would not necessarily compile and run under a FORTRAN 77 system. As the purpose of this chapter is to enable you to communicate better with FORTRAN programmers, we shall stick to the old standard, which all of them should know. As with Latin and gentlemen, we say that

> No programmer should know FORTRAN IV,
> but every programmer should
> have forgotten it!

Data Structures

There are five scalar types in FORTRAN:

INTEGER

REAL

LOGICAL   (i.e. boolean)

COMPLEX

DOUBLE PRECISION   (i.e. long reals)

Arrays of any of these can be constructed. Records, sets, and pointers are not available, nor can one construct enumerated scalars, subranges, or new types.

Since these are the only type names, there are no separate TYPE and VAR sections and all variables (simple and compound) are declared in lists after one of the above types. Names in FORTRAN can have up to only six characters, the effect of which can be seen in these examples:

INTEGER   I, N, COUNT, LENGTH, LINE(120), DATE(3)

REAL   MATRIX(10,10), SUM, MAX, PERCNT

LOGICAL   FOUND, FINSHD

The arrays have been declared with upper bounds only; this is because all lower bounds are 1. Notice that, in the absence of records, arrays must take their place and the use of the array DATE will rely on some convention for DATE(1) being the day, and so on.

Old-fashioned FORTRAN (Part 1)

FORTRAN has a rule whereby type declarations can be omitted for reals and integers, whereupon their type is decided according to the initial letter of the name. If the initial is I, J, K, L, M, or N, then the variable is integer, otherwise it is real. Thus we find names such as

	KOUNT, IDATE(3)	for integers
and	AMAX, RMATRX(10,10)	for reals.

Since such additional typing letters restrict the useful part of a name to five characters, it does not seem to be a good idea, particularly if one has been brought up to consider declarations as an integral and meaningful part of a program.

In order to declare arrays without specifying real or integer, older programs use

DIMENSION IDATE(3), RMATRX(10,10)

Constants of the five simple types follow expected forms, except for the logical values which have to be enclosed in dots (to distinguish them from identifiers). Examples are:

integer	14, −101
real	3.141592 , 1.OE−12
logical	.TRUE., .FALSE.
complex	(5.1, −2.9)
double precision	0.1698231411022974D4

Expressions are formed as usual, with exponentiation being possible using **. Unlike Pascal, FORTRAN allows the assignment of a real to an integer and truncates it in the process. Also, division of two integers does not automatically give an answer in the real domain. Instead one gets a truncated integer. As an example, if MARKS and N are integers, in

PERCNT = (MARKS/N)*100.0

the division will yield 0 instead of the intended fraction and multiplying by a real does not help at all. The correct form of this statement is

PERCNT = FLOAT(MARKS)/FLOAT(N))*100.0

where FLOAT is a standard function to convert an integer to a real.

Old-fashioned FORTRAN (Part 2)

For some reason, numbers in FORTRAN do not have to start and end with a digit. This allows zeros to be omitted whenever possible, as in

.6   1.   .0006

244

> While .6 is a nice relaxation of the rules, 1. does not have any grounding in maths or arithmetic and should be regarded as definitely sloppy!

Control Constructs

FORTRAN is not well endowed with the control constructs one expects in a modern language, and logical flow has to be built up from primitive components. The major disadvantage is that FORTRAN does not have the concept of a begin–end block. Thus if one wants to group several statements together (after a 'then', say), the grouping has to be achieved by means of labels and GO TO's. Apart from these, FORTRAN has four constructs known as:

1. The logical IF statement
2. The computed GO TO statement
3. The DO statement
4. The arithmetic IF statement

With these and the labels and GO TO's, the standard structured programming constructs can be built up, as shown in Figure 8.1.

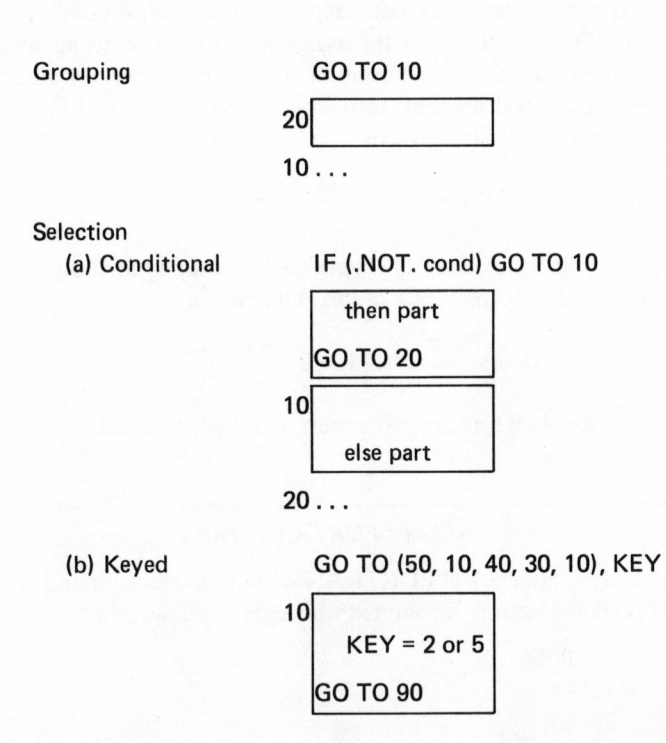

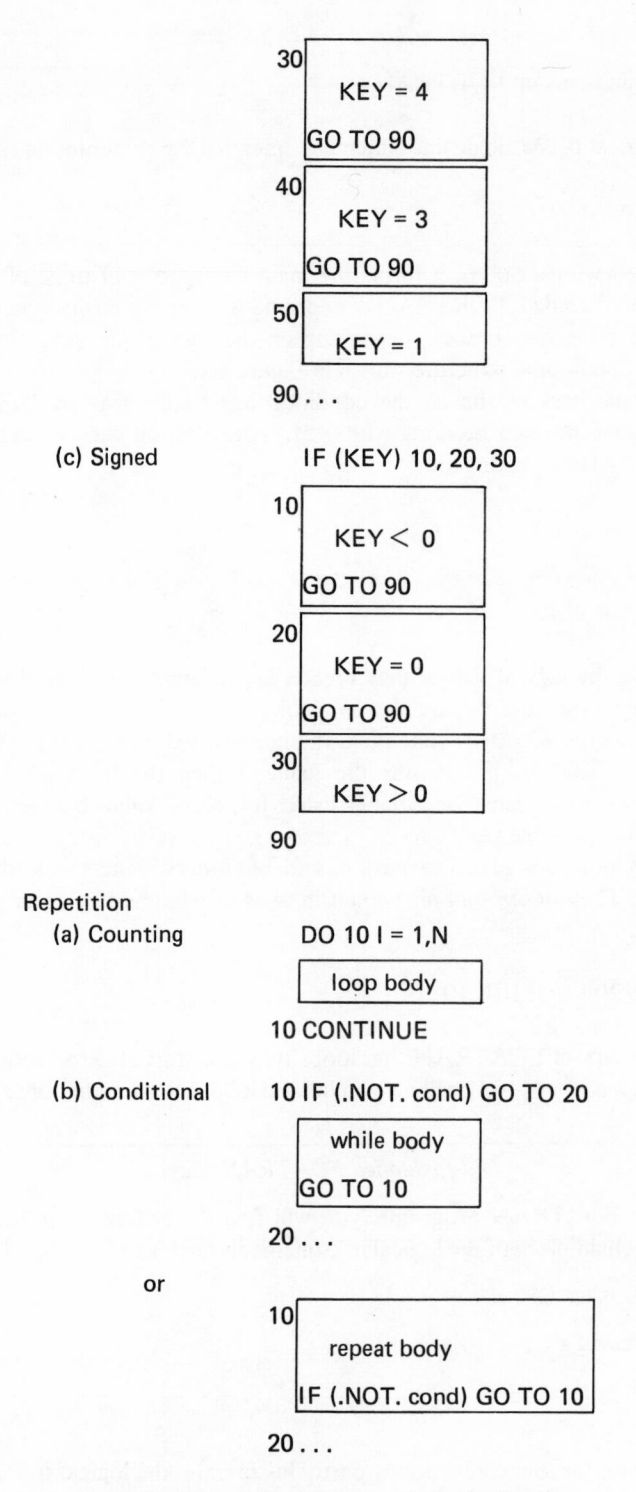

Figure 8.1   Control structures in FORTRAN

Some comments on FORTRAN are:

1. The logical IF is a single line statement, intended for computations such as

   IF (I.GT.N) I = 1

   but used with a GO TO, it forms the main component of most of the control structures needed. FORTRAN also provides an arithmetic IF statement which gives a three-way branch, depending on the sign of the key. This gives the signed conditional structure shown in Figure 8.1.
2. In all the uses of the IF, the condition has to be negated. This does not necessarily have to be done with .NOT.—the relation can be replaced by its opposite. The relations are:

.EQ.	.NE.
.LT.	.GE.
.GT.	.LE.

   and like the logical values they create, are delimited by dots. The relational operators .AND. and .OR. are also available.
3. In the computed GO TO statement, the labels listed in brackets are chosen by position. That is, if KEY has the value 3 then the third label is chosen. Therefore there must be a label listed for every value between 1 and the maximum possible key.
4. The DO-loop uses a label to mark its end, but otherwise acts as a counting loop should. These loops can also count in twos or whatever by specifying a third integer.

   DO 20 J = 1, 101, 10

   It is a quirk of FORTRAN that loops may not start at zero, nor can they be vacuous, e.g. K = 10, 1 will give an infinite loop, not an empty one.

Old-fashioned FORTRAN (Part 3)

In older FORTRAN programs, you will find the arithmetic IF being used extensively in place of the logical IF. Statements such as

   IF (I .GT. 10) GO TO 99

are expressed as

   IF (I–10) 50, 50, 99
   50 ...

The reason for this contortion is partly historical—the logical IF was not in

> the original definition of FORTRAN. Later, when it was added, the word
> went round that it was inefficient, and so the arithmetic IF persisted.

Input and Output

The input/output facilities of FORTRAN differ markedly from those of modern languages. In the first place, the file to be acted upon is known by a number not a name, with 5 being the common choice for input and 6 for output. Then the specifications for the layout of the data are in a different statement to the list of variables to be read or written. Moreover, such specifications (called FORMATs) are compulsory, which is particularly tiresome for input. Finally, each read or write operates on a whole line so that a free and variable arrangement of data is extremely difficult to cope with.

The main stumbling block, though, is the setting up of the formats. Each specification consists of a type letter and a field width, with some typical examples being:

    I4   a four-digit integer
    F6.2 a real in the form +xx.xx
    A1   a single character
    10X ten spaces.

As hinted by the X example, any specification can have a repeat factor, as in 2I4 or 80A1 (a card in character form). Groups of specifications can also be bracketed and given a repeat count, e.g. 10(F6.2,4X). As an example

    READ (5,500) I,N,STAR, SCALE
    500 FORMAT (2I4, 2X, A1, 2X, F6.2)

will expect input of the form

    ⊔⊔331000 ⊔⊔ * ⊔⊔–2.8

One problem with FORTRAN input is that spaces are considered as zeros in numeric fields, so that one must ensure that integers are correctly right-justified in their fields or they may be read as ten times their intended value. For real formats, this need not occur since the appearance of a decimal point overrides the field width given for decimal places. Note the convenient use of the space format on input.

    WRITE (6,600) N, MEAN
    600 FORMAT ('THE MEAN OF ',I3,' NUMBERS IS ',F10.4)

would print something like

The mean of   15 numbers is   60.5000

It is a feature of FORTRAN output that numbers cannot be left-justified, as in Pascal, and so when a small number is printed with a format intended for large ones, gaps result.

Old-fashioned FORTRAN (Part 4)

In the olden days, inputting from cards or paper tape was very slow and much time was spent in saving on 'key-strokes'. Hence spaces in FORTRAN programs were a rarity and in data, real numbers would be entered without a decimal point. The correct value of the number would be calculated according to the field width in the format. For example,

$$-\textsf{\char"2423}\,\textsf{\char"2423}\,218$$

read with F6.2 would give −2.18 but
read with F6.4 would give −0.0218.

The argument against such compression is that numbers cannot be output (readily) in compressed form—the decimal point will always appear. This hinders the working of several programs in sequence, something that was very common on the older, smaller machines.

Arrays can be input or output by mentioning only the array name, but for higher-order arrays, the order of the elements is a_{11}, a_{21}, a_{31}, i.e. column order. This is not always desirable, particularly on output. To change the order, an implied DO-loop can be added to the write statement as in

    WRITE (6, 620) ((MATRIX(I,J), J=1,10) I=1,10)

This begs the question as to what happens when a format runs out before all the variables in the list have been used. The answer is that the format is repeated from the most recent left bracket. Thus

    620 FORMAT ('THE MATRIX IS'/(2X,F6.2/))

will print the heading once only, as required. The slash is a handy way of getting multi-line output in one go as it forces a new line. As with some Pascal systems, one must remember the line control character at the start of each line. Pascal, in fact, inherited the codes from FORTRAN (space for one line, 1 for a new page, etc.)

Subprograms

What put FORTRAN ahead of other early languages (which were called autocodes) was its provision for subroutines and functions. In declaration, these are similar to Pascal with the differences being confined to the parameters (or 'arguments' as FORTRAN calls them). FORTRAN has only variable parameters and their type is specified in declarations following the heading as in

```
SUBROUTINE READDT (D)
INTEGER D(3)
```

However, FORTRAN does not check that the types of parameters match, so be on your guard!

As we already know, parameters are not sufficient for communicating effectively between routines. In Pascal, parameters are supplemented by variables being automatically available through nesting. FORTRAN does not have nesting—all routines are at the same level as the main program. Therefore, blocks of variables that are to be shared between a group of routines are given a name and included at the start of each participating routine. For example:

```
SUBROUTINE NEWLINE (N)
COMMON /PRUNIT/ POSIT, LINE(121)
INTEGER N, POSIT, LINE


    . . . . .


RETURN
END

SUBROUTINE PRINT (CH)
COMMON /PRUNIT/ POSIT,LINE(121)
INTEGER CH, POSIT, LINE


    . . . . .


RETURN
END
```

Unfortunately, there is absolutely no check on corresponding COMMON blocks having sensibly similar lists, and we would get away with

```
COMMON /PRUNIT/ LINE(120), POSIT
```

in one of the routines, then have to suffer the consequences of the mix-up. By

```
 .001       INTEGER I,J,N,ZEROS,COLS
 .002       LOGICAL SYM,TRI
 .003       REAL MATRIX(99,99), PERCNT
 .004 C     ****** READ IN THE VALUES
 .005       READ(5,500) N
 .006 500   FORMAT(I2)
 .007       DO 10 I=1,N
 .008       READ(5,510) (MATRIX(I,J),J=1,N)
 .009 510   FORMAT (10F8.2)
 .010 10    CONTINUE
 .011 C     ****** WRITE OUT WHAT WAS READ IN
 .012       WRITE(9,600) N
 .013 600   FORMAT(' THE MATRIX HAS ',I2,' ROWS AND COLUMNS')
 .014       WRITE(9,610)
 .015 610   FORMAT(//' THE MATRIX IS (FIRST 12 COLUMNS ONLY)')
 .016       COLS=N
 .017       IF (N.GT.12) COLS=12
 .018       DO 20 I=1,N
 .019       WRITE(9,620) (MATRIX(I,J),J=1,COLS)
 .020 620   FORMAT ( 12(1X, F9.2))
 .021 20    CONTINUE
 .022 C     ****** CALCULATIONS
 .023       SYM=.TRUE.
 .024       TRI=.TRUE.
 .025       ZEROS=0
 .026       DO 30 I=1,N
 .027       DO 40 J=1,N
 .028       IF (MATRIX(I,J).NE.MATRIX(J,I)) SYM=.FALSE.
 .029       IF (J.GT.I .AND. MATRIX(I,J).NE.0) TRI=.FALSE.
 .030       IF (MATRIX(I,J).EQ.0.0) ZEROS=ZEROS+1
 .031 40    CONTINUE
 .032 30    CONTINUE
 .033       PERCNT=(FLOAT(ZEROS)/FLOAT(N*N))*100.0
 .034 C     ****** PRINT RESULTS
 .035       IF (SYM) WRITE(9,630)
 .036 630   FORMAT(/' THE MATRIX IS SYMMETRIC')
 .037       IF (TRI) WRITE(9,640)
 .038 640   FORMAT(/' THE MATRIX IS TRIANGULAR')
 .039       WRITE(9,650) PERCNT
 .040 650   FORMAT(/' THE PERCENTAGE OF ZEROS IS ',F6.2,'%')
 .041       STOP
 .042       END
 .043 /DATA
 .044 14
 .045  7.98   0      0      0      0      0      0      0
 .046  0.08   0      9.91   0      0      0      0      C
 .047 13.08   0      0      0      0      0      0      0
 .048  0.48   0      0      0      0      0      0      0
 .049 10.0    1.15   5.42   0      0      0      0      0
```

```
L.050   0       0       0       11.12   4.4   0   0   0   0   0   0   0   0   0
L.051   8.75    7.02    ...
L.052
L.053           2       0       3       4
L.054           0       8       7       6
L.055           0       0       0       0
L.056
L.057
L.058
L.059   18.8    17.7    16.6    15.5    14.4    13.3    12.2    11.1    0   0
L.060
L.061           2       3       4       5       6       7       8       9   0
L.062
L.063
L.064           0       2       3       4       5       6       7       8   9   0
L.065   111111  222222  333333  444444  555555  666666  777777  888888  999999  111111
L.066   222222  0       2       3       4       5       6       7       8   9   0
L.067
L.068
L.069
L.070
L.071
L.072
```

THE MATRIX HAS 14 ROWS AND COLUMNS

THE MATRIX IS (FIRST 12 COLUMNS ONLY)

```
7.98     0.00    0.00    0.00    0.00    0.00    0.00    0.00    0.00    0.00
13.08    9.91    0.00    0.00    0.00    0.00    0.00    0.00    0.00    0.00
10.00    1.15    5.42    0.00    0.00    0.00    0.00    0.00    0.00    0.00
8.75     7.62    11.12   0.00    0.00    0.00    0.00    0.00    0.00    0.00
10.00    20.00   30.00   40.00   50.00   0.00    0.00    0.00    0.00    0.00
90.00    80.00   70.00   60.00   50.00   40.00   0.00    0.00    0.00    0.00
00.00    17.70   16.60   15.50   14.40   13.30   12.20   11.10   0.00    0.00
18.80    16.60   15.50   13.30   12.20   700.20  801.10  906.00   0.00   0.00
100.10   200.20  300.30  400.40  500.50  600.60  700.60  800.80   90.00   0.00
1111.11  2222.22 3333.33 4444.44 5555.55 6666.66 7777.77 8888.88  555.99  1111.11
0.00     0.00    0.00    0.00    0.00    0.00    0.00    0.00    0.00    0.00    2222.22
0.00     0.00    0.00    0.00    0.00    0.00    0.00    0.00    0.00    0.00
0.00     0.00    0.00    0.00    0.00    0.00    0.00    0.00    0.00    0.00
```

THE MATRIX IS TRIANGULAR

THE PERCENTAGE OF ZEROS IS 69.90%

Figure 8.2 A FORTRAN Program

251

'sensibly similar' we mean that the lists must at least refer to the same functional entities, although their names may be different. For example, we could refer to the first element of LINE as the carriage control character directly in

COMMON /PRUNIT/ POSIT, CC, LINE(120)

That concludes our treatise on FORTRAN. There are some features that have not been covered, but these are on the periphery and the serious student will soon find them from studying one of the books mentioned in Chapter 9.

Finally, we give a real example of a simple program written in 'modern' FORTRAN in Figure 8.2. The program reads in a matrix, works out whether it is triangular, and calculates the percentage of zero elements. The matrix (or as much of it as will fit on a page) is then printed out.

8.2   The Significance of Ada

Just as FORTRAN is the language of the past for computer scientists, so is Ada the language of the future. Ada is the general-purpose programming language commissioned by the United States Department of Defense in the late 1970s. Because of the enormous amount of work done by that organization, and the extensive range of its computer equipment, Ada is likely to be available on most computers in the future.

The background to Ada

The development of Ada can be seen against the backdrop of the whole language research effort of the 1970s, which began with Pascal in 1971. Pascal was born out of frustration with the mammoth languages of the late 1960s, namely ALGOL 68 and PL/I. The designer of Pascal, Niklaus Wirth, took as his design goals:

> simplicity
> efficiency
> programming insight

and in all three his language achieved full marks. While simplicity and efficiency rocketed Pascal to the position where it is now available on a wider range of machines than any other language, it was the third goal, programming insight, which made Pascal the accepted starting point for subsequent language design.

After Pascal, two novel ideas evolved in language design. The first was that a data type was not just a definition of a set of admissible values, but that the concept of type was intimately connected with the operations that were meaningful for its objects. The second new idea was that the protection of data need not be left to the good faith of the programmer or the policing role of the operating system, but could actually be built into the language itself. Violations of protection would then be found at compile-time, rather than detected at run-time at far greater cost. A good deal of the impetus for both of these notions was the growing use of high-level languages, particularly Pascal, in large systems projects. As is now understood, large projects have problems of complexity which structured programming alone cannot cope with. What was needed was a new revolution in programming methodology, and by the end of 1977 this movement had a name—*data abstraction*. Data abstraction enabled:

- large systems to be broken up into smaller parts with logical interfaces based on the data being handled;
- these interfaces to stand alone as the specification of the system, with the actual implementations hidden and flexible;
- as much protection as is necessary to be placed on each interface.

By 1977 there were many languages supporting some kind of data abstraction facilities, each of them having a small but keen following. Out of this experience, Ada was born. Data abstraction became the kingpin of the language, governing the underlying structure which, true to its antecedents, looks dominantly like Pascal.

There were also powerful influences on Ada from two other sources, the scientific and real-time communities. For the scientist, the capability to specify and control numerical data was built in, chiefly by Brian Wichmann of the National Physical Laboratory, and based on many years of experience with machine-independent numerical packages such as NAG. For process control, Ada has a rich high-level real-time capability, developed mainly by John Barnes of SPL, who had been involved in real-time languages for many years.

From one point of view, one may say that the design goal of the language which was eventually called Ada was simply to win the tender from the US Department of Defense. However, as a language which was the culmination of years of work all around the world, it had its own destiny to fulfil, as summed up in the single goal of:

> Concern for
>
> MAN—programming as a human activity
>
> MACHINE—efficient use of the resources of today's computers
>
> MANAGEMENT—control and care of large projects.

Data Abstraction in Ada

The data abstraction facilities of Ada can be divided into those that are used in the small, and those that cater for programming in the large. The inner programming effort, where structured programming is now firmly entrenched, is served by the features:

> type definitions
> ranges
> attributes
> access variables

In the large, we have four main facilities:

> packages
> generics
> tasks
> exceptions

Because Ada is Pascal-based, these are all supported by the usual infrastructure of Pascal, including:

> procedures
> functions
> parameters
> control structures
> arithmetic
> relations

and so on. These will not be discussed in detail, and it is hoped that the reader will be interested enough by the development of the other features to pursue the study of Ada with the Reference Manual or one of the books that are now available.

Ada's Type System

Central to the concept of data abstraction is the user-defined type name which enables one to separate the properties of the variable from the various objects needing those properties throughout the program. In Pascal, a typical example is

```
TYPE dates = record
                day : 1. .31;
                month : 1. .12;
                year : 0. .2000;
             end;
      words = array [1. .20] of alfa;

VAR  birth, marriage : dates;
     towns, streets  : words;
```

What does this buy one? When subprograms are set up to deal with the same type of data, only the name need be specified, and all the required properties are automatically brought across. This aids in both ease of programming and maintainability (since changes are confined to one place). Totally erroneous statements such as

```
birth.day := streets;
marrriage.year :=birth.month / 2;
```

should not be allowed, and any such nonsense should be flagged as an error at compile-time. This is called *strict type-checking*. Pascal has it, but does not go far enough, since the second statement above would actually be allowed, both sides being integer-based. Ada's type system endeavours to provide a completely secure environment.

The type system for Ada is summed up in Figure 8.3 and the following explanations:

A *type* in Ada characterizes a set of values and a set of operations applicable to those values. Predefined scalar types are

```
integer  float  boolean  character
```

and there are two possible ways of structuring the values,

```
records    arrays
```

The *values* are denoted by literals or aggregates of the type, and can be obtained as the result of operations.

A *constraint* may restrict the set of possible values without changing the set of applicable operations. There are only four constraints, each applicable to a different kind of type,

```
range constraint          - integers and enumerateds
accuracy constraint       - real
indexed constraint        - arrays
discriminant constraint   - records.
```

A *subtype* is the set of all values satisfying the constraint. The type is then known as the *base type*.

A *derived type* is formed (with an optional constraint) from a type or subtype and inherits all the characteristics,

```
set of possible values
initial default values
```

256

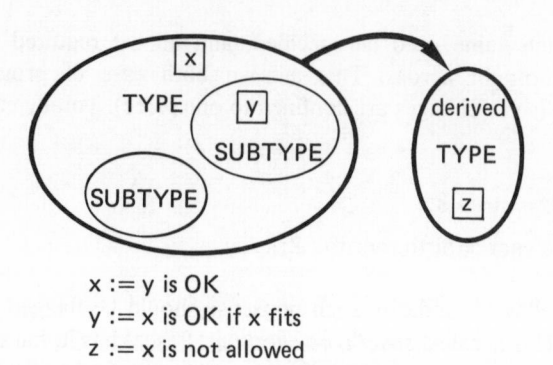

x := y is OK
y := x is OK if x fits
z := x is not allowed

Figure 8.3   Ada's type system

notation for literals and aggregates
notation for components
applicable subprograms and operators.

Before this all becomes utterly confusing, we will embark on detailed examples of how the type system works in practice.

Examples of Types

Integers

The integer type is predefined, so subtypes and derived types can be formed immediately.

```
TYPE      linecover is range 0. .linemax+1;
SUBTYPE lineindex is linecover range 0. .linemax;
SUBTYPE linerange is linecover range 1. .linemax;
```

Here we have set up a type to handle variables on a line, and have introduced two subtypes for those variables that don't need as much freedom as is provided by the full linecover type. Variables of all three can be freely interchanged, provided that the constraints are met. Now if we define

```
TYPE      pagenoindex is range 0. .pageno;
SUBTYPE pagenorange is pagenoindex range 1. .pageno;
```

then variables of these types cannot be mixed with the line ones, although the two sets share a notation for literals and have all the inherited integer operations in common.

Enumerateds

From Pascal, Ada gets the very handy idea of setting up names for specific values in a type. Thus we can have

```
TYPE    days is (Sun, Mon, Tues, Wed, Thurs, Fri, Sat);
TYPE    sex  is (male, female);
```

The range constraint enables us to have subtypes as in

```
SUBTYPE weekdays is days range Mon. .Fri;
```

The character literals are a special kind of enumerated name and Ada permits one to set up new types both by selecting some of them or by a range constraint. Thus we can have

```
TYPE       vowels is ('A', 'E', 'I', 'O', 'U');
SUBTYPE thedigits is character range '0'. .'9';
```

Reals

There is no predefined type called real, since Ada firmly acknowledges that there are two distinct ways of representing reals, i.e. floating or fixed. There is a predefined floating point type

```
TYPE    float is digits D range L. .R
```

where the significant decimal digits that can be held, D, and the range of precision L. .R are implementation-defined. New floating-point types may be created with the same or fewer digits and with a compatible range, e.g.

```
TYPE       coefficients is digits 10 range −1.0. .1.0;
SUBTYPE shortcoeffs is coefficients digits 5;
SUBTYPE positives is coefficients range 0.0. .1.0;
```

The combination of digits and range enables the programmer to specify what trade-off he wants between significance and size. Another example is

```
TYPE    mass is digits 7 range 0.0. .1.0E10;
```

Fixed-point types are specified with an error bound called *delta*. There is no predefined fixed type, but there is an implementation-defined delta which may not be exceeded. Because there is no underlying base type, a range must be given for each new type, though it is optional for subtypes.

```
TYPE      volts is delta 0.125 range 0.0 . . 255.0;
SUBTYPE roughvolts is volts delta 0.5;
```

Volts and roughvolts work over the same range, but volts are given at intervals of 0.125 and roughvolts only on 0.5.

Arrays

The usual way of constructing an array is carried over to Ada. If the bounds are specified in the type, then the array type is called 'constrained', e.g.

```
TYPE    schedule is array (days) of boolean;
TYPE    castlist is array (1. .noofactors) of names;
```

Noofactors may be a variable, but its value must be fixed before the statement of the type using it is encountered. If the bounds are not specified, then the type is unconstrained and variables of that type must give suitable constraints, e.g.

```
TYPE    matrix is array (integer range < >,
                         integer range < >) of real;
TYPE    bitvector is array (integer range < >) of boolean;
```

warrants the variables

```
M       : matrix(1. .100,1. .100);
memory : bitvector(0. .31);
```

The real value of the unconstrained arrays is not in the ability to delay the specification of the bounds, but in defining subtype arrays which will belong to the same groups, as in

```
SUBTYPE square is matrix (1. .n,1. .n);
SUBTYPE addressfield is bitvector (13. .16);
```

Notice that in all these subtype definitions, only the constraints are given: the types of the elements is automatically assumed from the base type's definition.
   There is also a predefined type string, i.e.

```
TYPE string is array (natural range < >) of character;
```

the difference between strings and other vectors is that a string has a special notation for aggregates, and relational operators are defined for it. Here we see the sense of the different types being distinct. It is essential to be able to ask if one string is less than another, but the same question applied to two matrices is quite meaningless (unless defined in detail by a suitable subprogram).

Records

Records are composed in the usual way, with the addition of discriminants. A discriminant is a special field in the record that may cause other fields to vary in one of two ways:

- a discriminant may specify a bound of an array field
- a discriminant may specify a value for a variant tag.

For example,

```
TYPE device is (printer, disc, drum);
TYPE state is (opened, closed);

TYPE peripheral
        (unit : device) is
     record
        status : state;
        case unit is
            when printer ⇒ linecount : lineindex;
            when others  ⇒ cylinder  : cylinderindex;
                            track     : tracknumber;
        end case;
     end record;
```

So peripheral of unit printer will have fields

{unit, status, linecount}

while the others will have

{unit, status, cylinder, track}

We can make subtypes from this general type by specifying a value for the discriminant, as in

SUBTYPE drumunit is peripheral (drum);

Discriminants can have defaults, which is useful when they are used to vary array bounds:

```
TYPE    buffer (size      : natural := 132) is
        record
                position : natural := 0;
                value    : string(1. .size);
        end record;
```

We could then define

```
SUBTYPE cardbuffer is buffer(80);
```

Literals and Aggregates

One of the areas where many languages, including Pascal, have been weak is in the notations for specifying constants. Constants for scalars, known as literals, are fairly standard, but Ada has two improvements

Based numbers : Numbers can be specified to any base i.e. 12 could be

```
12    8#14#    16#C#    2#1100#
```

Unprintable characters: Control characters are given names, e.g.

```
ASCII.CR    ASCII.ESC
```

It is with the structured items that Ada really scores, though. The elements of an array can be listed out positionally, as in

```
daysinmonth : array (months) of days;
daysinmonth := (31,29,31,30,31,30,31,31,30,31,30,31);
```

or using the subscripts to name each element as in

```
daysinmonth := (sept | april | june | nov ⇒ 30,
                feb                       ⇒ 29,
                others                    ⇒ 31);
```

The same applies to records in that we can have

```
birth := (7, oct, 1951);
```

or

```
birth := (year ⇒ 1951, month ⇒ oct, day ⇒ 7);
```

Attributes

One of the most powerful aids to data abstraction is the notion that types have properties, or attributes, that are available for examination via the type name itself. For example, in FORTRAN, one would often write a subroutine to manipulate an array and pass both the array and its upper bounds as parameters, as in

> FORTRAN   SUBROUTINE INVERT (A,N)
>
> DIMENSION A(N,N)
>
> DO 10 I = 1,N
>
> . . .

Even in Pascal, the array bounds are quite unconnected to the array itself and one is forced into defining myriad constants to give names to the limits:

> Pascal   CONST n = . . .;
>
> m = . . .;
>
> VAR   a : array [1. .n,1. .m] of real;
>
> i : 1. .n;
>
> FOR i := 1 to n do

In Ada, the array's properties are given by four attributes:

> FIRST   lower bound
>
> LAST   upper bound
>
> LENGTH   number of elements
>
> RANGE   the subtype FIRST. .LAST

and each can be subscripted for a particular dimension. Now suppose we define a matrix using the unconstrained type as

> mat : matrix (1. .100, 1. .4);

We don't have to define names for 100 and 4 because from now on we can refer to them as

> matrix 'last(1) and matrix 'last(2).

As in Pascal, the size of the matrix is fixed at one place and if we wish to change it, we make the change there. No further changes need to be made as the attributes will reflect the new values automatically. The range attribute is used for indices over the array and when these indices are part of a loop, they do not have to be separately declared. The little example in Pascal above becomes

> a : matrix (1. .100,1. .4);

```
FOR i in a'range loop
   ...
```

There are many attributes serving all purposes and they are listed in Appendix A of the Ada Manual. Some of the more useful ones are

SIZE	the number of bits for an object
IMAGE(X)	the string representation of X ⎫ inline reads
VALUE(S)	the value from the string S ⎭ and writes
DIGITS	the number of digits in the floating type
EMAX	largest exponent
DELTA	the specified interval for the fixed type
POSITION	offset of a field within a record.

Using Types, Subtypes, and Attributes

The power of Ada's type system is illustrated in the following example.

Set up a type called tables which has elements of any type, item, and bounds of any discrete type (integer or enumerated). Write two procedures:

read : reads in a variable number of items until either the table is full or some trailer value is spotted, in which case the table is padded with the trailer.

write : writes out the full table.

A solution to the problem is given in Figure 8.4, and follows the ideas of the 'finding and keeping' algorithm of Section 2.2.

The solution assumes nothing new about the type of the bounds, other than that it is a valid type for an array subscript, and that succ is defined for it.

This level of abstraction is achieved largely by accepting that array bounds should be a data type, and by the extension of this idea to type attributes. However, the logic of the loop and the use of a state variable also contribute to the success of the read procedure.

Examples

These procedures therefore represent quite a powerful piece of programming from the maintainability and protection viewpoints; they are also very useable, as illustrated in these examples.

1. SUBTYPE item is string(8);
            bounds is range 1..20;

    trailer : constant item := '⎵⎵⎵⎵⎵⎵⎵⎵';

```
TYPE tables is array (bounds) of item;

PROCEDURE read (table : out tables) is
    TYPE states is (reading, ended, filled);
    i: bounds := tables 'first;
    state: states := reading;
  BEGIN
    LOOP
      get(table(i));
      if          i = table'last then state := filled;
      elsif table(i) = trailer     then state := ended; end if;
      if     state/= filled      then i := bounds' succ(i); end if;
      EXIT when state /= reading;
    END LOOP;

    WHILE state /= filled loop
      table(i) := trailer;
      if i = table'last then state := filled;
                    else i := bounds' succ(i); end if;
    END LOOP;

  END read;

PROCEDURE write (table : tables) is
  BEGIN

    FOR i in table'range loop
      put(table(i));
    END LOOP;

  END write;
```

Figure 8.4   A simple array iterator

```
streets,
towns: tables;

    read(towns);    -- will read up to 20 towns and pad any
                    -- left-over slots with blanks.
    read(streets);  -- does the same for the streets.
```

2.   TYPE item is real;
         bounds is range 1..100;

```
trailer : constant item := 0.0;
marks: tables;

    read(marks);    -- will read up to 100 marks and pad any
                    -- left-over slots with 0.
```

Packages in Ada

So far we have been concerned with individual data types and how they are manipulated in an easy and secure way, and we end up with features very much at the level of structured programming. Ada's brief extends much further into the realm of large programming projects, with perhaps many programmers involved on different interconnecting tasks. The key to secure management of such a project lies in being able to divide up the tasks logically, and then to use the language to implement them. The facility provided by Ada for this purpose is the *package*.

The structure of an Ada package is illustrated in Figure 8.5. The package starts off with a specification of its data and operations. This is followed by an optional section indicating those parts of the data which will be known to the outside world by name, but cannot be examined in detail. The package body then repeats the specifications, filling out each with the required implementation.

Ada's packages serve data abstraction at three levels:

1. Named collections of declarations. In other languages, this facility is often provided by file 'includes' and a preprocessor.
2. Groups of related subprograms sharing internal declarations. This is the one facility which the traditional block-structured languages could not provide. In Ada, the package idea breaks away from strict nesting.
3. Encapsulated data types with hidden implementations of operations. This is data abstraction in its full sense, providing economy of effort, ease of maintenance, and as much protection as is required.

```
PACKAGE name is

    — types, variable, procedures, and
    — functions for the package.

PRIVATE

    — details of those types which need
    — to be hidden.

END name;


PACKAGE BODY name is

    — local types, variables, etc.

    — expansions of the procedures and
    — functions mentioned in the spec.

END name;
```

Figure 8.5   The structure of a package

The examples that follow illustrate each of these levels. But first we must detail the ways in which packages are actually used. There are three ways:

1. Access to all names in the package by

>   USES table_manager
>
>   IF table_full then . . .

2. Access to only selected names by using dot notation

>   IF table_manager.table_full then . . .

3. Shorthand for selected names by using renames

>   full : boolean renames table_manager.table_full;
>   IF full then . . .

Examples of Groups and Collections

1. Named collections of declarations

```
PACKAGE employeedata is

    TYPE money is delta 0.01 range 0. .100 000;
    TYPE addresses is array(1. .4) of string(1. .20);
    TYPE employee is record
        key             : codehandler.employeecode; - - see 3.
        name            : string(1. .25);
        address         : addresses;
        birth, marriage : dates;
        salary          : money;
    END RECORD;
```

2. Groups of related subprograms

```
PACKAGE printunit is

    PROCEDURE newpage;
    PROCEDURE newline;
    PROCEDURE print (ch : in character);
    PROCEDURE tab   (n  : natural);
    PROCEDURE startprinting;
    PROCEDURE stopprinting;

END printunit;

PACKAGE BODY printunit is
```

```
TYPE lines is array (1..132) of character;
     columns is range 1..4;
     pages is array (pagerange) of lines;

tray          : array(columns) of pages;
currentcolumn : columns;
currentline   : pagerange;
currentchar   : integer range line'range;

PROCEDURE newline is
  BEGIN
    currentline :=currentline+1;
    if currentline = pages'last then newpage; end if;
  END;

  --etc.
```

END printunit;

3. Encapsulated data types

So far, packages have given us the ability to have

> VISIBLE   data in the specification
> and   INVISIBLE data in the body.

Thus in the second example above, only the procedures were relevant to a user; the line positions and the actual storing of the characters to be printed were entirely private and protected. The third kind of abstraction mixes the visibility so that we have

> PRIVATE data which has
>
> > VISIBLE names in the specification
> >
> > and INVISIBLE implementations in the body.

There are several reasons for making this separation. The best one is that it gives the ability to change one's mind about an implementation, without affecting all the other programs that might be using the package.

Suppose a firm sets up codes for all its employees. It may decide after a few years that the code has to be expanded because there are now too many employees. A package can be set up which defines the concept of an employee code, together with the ability to make and compare them, but keeps the actual form of the code hidden.

```
PACKAGE codehandler is
  TYPE employeecode is private;

  PROCEDURE makecode (n : out employeecode);
  FUNCTION "<"          (n,m : in employeecode) return boolean;
```

An application programmer who is writing the programs to set up new employees would be able to declare an employee code, call the *makecode* routine to get a value for it, and store it away. Another programmer who is writing a merge say, would need to compare codes, and could do this using <. He would, of course, get the full details of the whole employee record from another package of the first kind above in which the full layout is defined. A start to such a merge might be

```
USE employeedata, codehandler;
PROCEDURE merge is

  -- declarations of files

  e1, e2 : employees; -- coming from employeedata

BEGIN
  -- open files;
  LOOP
    get(master, e1);
    get(update, e2);
    if e1.key < e2.key then . . .
    . . .
  END LOOP;
END merge;
```

The actual form of the code is declared later in the package, together with the implementations of the two routines.

```
PRIVATE
  TYPE employeecode is
          range 000_000 .. 999_999;
END codehandler;

PACKAGE BODY codehandler is
  currentcode : employeecode;

  PROCEDURE makecode (n : out employeecode) is
  BEGIN
    n := currentcode;
    currentcode := currentcode + 1;
  END makecode;

  FUNCTION "<" (n,m : in employeecode) return boolean is
  BEGIN
    return n < m;
  END "<";

END codehandler;
```

The fact that the code is actually a number is quite hidden from the applications programmers. At a later date it could be changed into an alphanumeric code, in which case the *makenumber* and < routines will become more complex.

The second reason for encapsulating data types in packages is security. Once a type is private, the only valid operations are

declare an object	e.g. c1, c2 : employeecode;
assignment	e.g. mycode := c1;
compare for equality	e.g. if c1=c2 then ...
use as parameters	e.g. PROCEDURE fire (h : employeecode)
packaged operations	e.g. makecode and <

This list excludes the ability to make constants of the type (which would be impossible because the actual form is hidden), access components (if applicable), or do any other operations not in the package (such as writing out the code). Even if a programmer knew or suspected that the code was simply a number, and attempted to say

mycode := 546789;

or

put (mycode); − − i.e. print it.

the compiler would prevent him. Since it may be possible by devious use of assignment, procedures, and equality to fabricate, inspect, and change codes, Ada provides a further level of protection called LIMITED PRIVATE which removes these rights. Limited private objects can only be declared and used with the operations provided.

Generalizing Packages

One of the obvious powers of packages is that they can become like standard utilities which can be used over and over again by many people. For this to be really effective, something must be done about allowing the package to perform its action on data of any kind. For example, we might set up a very efficient merge sort package, but want the details of the records being sorted to remain unspecified in the package itself. Then when a programmer wishes to use the package, he says at that stage what the data looks like. This facility is in fact generalizing the package idea and is provided in Ada through generic packages.

Figure 8.6 shows the structure of a generic package. In the first place, the package is written in a general way and the parts that can vary are specified. When the package is to be used, these parts are filled in and the package is then said to be 'instantiated'. The routines of the package are then executed as required.

A very good example of a package that would benefit from generalization is the pair of routines that we defined earlier. The examples given then showed different

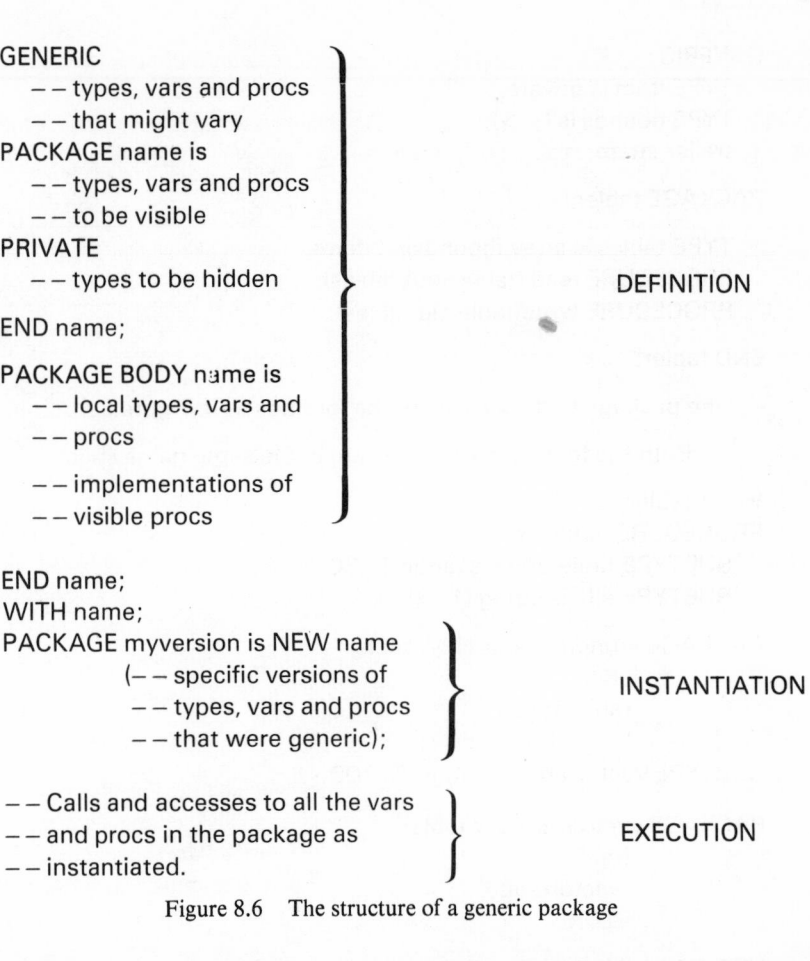

GENERIC
  – – types, vars and procs
  – – that might vary
PACKAGE name is
  – – types, vars and procs
  – – to be visible
PRIVATE
  – – types to be hidden   DEFINITION

END name;

PACKAGE BODY name is
  – – local types, vars and
  – – procs

  – – implementations of
  – – visible procs

END name;
WITH name;
PACKAGE myversion is NEW name
    (– – specific versions of   INSTANTIATION
     – – types, vars and procs
     – – that were generic);

– – Calls and accesses to all the vars
– – and procs in the package as   EXECUTION
– – instantiated.

Figure 8.6   The structure of a generic package

definitions for item and bounds, implying in fact that the procedures would have to be completely written out in each case. Figure 8.7 shows how a generic package would do the trick.

Overloading

In these examples, we have used a facility without explaining it. This is the ability to have the same name for different operations. In the examples of using the *tables* routines of Figure 8.4, *read* was used to read towns and read marks. In fact the actual routines called are quite different, each belonging to one of the instantiations of the tables package. Because towns and marks are of different types, Ada can work out which version of read is required. This is called overloading a name. Notice that overloading is only possible if there is no ambiguity. In the same example when the variables were declared, it was necessary to be explicit about which tables type was being referred to. If the references to *tables* had not been prefixed by the appropriate package name, the compiler would have reported an error.

```
GENERIC
    TYPE item is private;
    TYPE bounds is (< >);
    trailer : item;

PACKAGE tabler is

    TYPE tables is array (bounds) of item;
    PROCEDURE read (table : out tables);
    PROCEDURE write(table : in tables);

END tabler;

- - the package body consists of the routines as in Figure 8.4

    - - Both the following examples are in the same name space.

WITH tabler;
PROCEDURE readin is
    SUBTYPE tablerange is range 1. .20;
    SUBTYPE alfa is string (1. .8);

PACKAGE stringmaker is NEW tabler
                (alfa,
                 tablerange,
            '           ');
SUBTYPE vectorrange is range 1. .100;

PACKAGE vectors is NEW tabler
                (real,
                 vectorrange,
                 0.0);

USE stringmaker, vectors;
streets, towns : stringmaker.tables;
marks, a       : vectors.tables;
BEGIN
read (towns);
read (marks);
END readin;
```

Figure 8.7   Example of a generic package and its use

The Way Ahead

Data abstraction is the key to future programming practice and Ada has excellent facilities for achieving it. Although we have omitted consideration of two of Ada's innovations—real-time packages and exceptions—we have laid the basis for understanding what data abstraction is all about, and what a language that embodies it looks like. Those of you advanced programmers who wish to follow up Ada in detail can now do so with confidence.

Chapter 9

Further Reading

Having got so far, you will no doubt want to learn even more about advanced programming. It is characteristic of the real advanced programmer that he never stops learning about his subject: here we guide you towards some of the rewarding reading that awaits you. The list is by no means exhaustive; it is at best a minimal requirement for any well-educated programmer. We have divided the list up into sections, corresponding to the things you ought to know more about.

About Pascal

You may feel that your grasp of Pascal is not as good as you thought it was. Our favourite introductory text is

L. V. Atkinson, *Pascal Programming*, Wiley, 1980

You will find that the style of programming that he expounds is very similar to what we have been trying to teach you in this book. Other good introductory texts include:

W. Findlay and D. A. Watt, *Pascal: an Introduction to Methodical Programming* (2nd edn.), Pitman, 1981.

Jim Welsh and John Elder, *Introduction to Pascal* (2nd edn), Prentice-Hall, 1982

Arthur Keller, *A First Course in Computer Programming using Pascal*, McGraw-Hill, 1982

About FORTRAN

One of the better books about FORTRAN IS

L. P. Meissner and E. I. Organick, *FORTRAN 77 Featuring Structured Programming*, Addison Wesley, 1980

As the title implies, the book gives a 'modern' view of FORTRAN, emphasizing the ways in which the new features of FORTRAN 77 can be exploited. A particularly valuable feature is that the book includes an extended paraphrase of the FORTRAN 77 Standard as an appendix.

About Ada

Books on Ada are rapidly becoming available. One of the earliest has a ring of authenticity about it, as its author was part of the original design team. It is:

J. G. P. Barnes, *Programming in ADA*, Addison-Wesley, 1982

The ultimate authority on Ada is

J. D. Ichbiah *et al.*, *Reference Manual for the Ada Programming Language*

This is published by the United States Department of Defense (Ada Joint Program Office), reference ANSI/MIL-STD-1815A-1983. It is available in the UK from Castle House Publications Ltd.

About Data Structures

A good general introduction is given in

E. S. Page and L. B. Wilson, *Information Representation and Manipulation using Pascal*, Cambridge University Press, 1983

B-trees are discussed in an excellent survey article

D. Comer, The ubiquitous B-tree *ACM Computing Surveys*, **11**, 2 June 1979

The ultimate authority on the subject is

D. E. Knuth, *The Art of Computer Programming*, Vol. 1: *Fundamental Algorithms* (2nd edn) Addison Wesley, 1973

About this kind of Programming-for-real

The kind of topics we have been discussing are also covered in

G. M. Schneider and S. C. Bruell, *Advanced Programming and Problem Solving with Pascal*, Wiley, 1981

It is always instructive to get a different view of a familiar scene. A view that should on no account be missed is given by the classic

Niklaus Wirth, *Algorithms + Data Structures = Programs*, Prentice-Hall, 1976

About Pascal in the Real World

Programming cannot be taught, but it can be learned, and one of the best ways to learn it is to read other people's programs.

B. W. Kernighan and P. J. Plauger, *Software Tools in Pascal*, Addison Wesley, 1981

is an indispensable collection of well-written programs that should be studied by anyone with pretensions to be a programmer. For an example of a really large program

S. Pemberton and M. C. Daniels, *Pascal Implementation—the P4 Compiler*, Ellis Horwood/Wiley, 1982

lists the whole of the Pascal P compiler, with a commentary.

About Program Design

Program design is a subject in its own right, quite apart from the study of particular problems and languages. Illuminating insights into the subject are to be found in

J. D. Aron, *The Program Development Process*, Addison Wesley, 1974

P. Grogono and S. H. Nelson, *Problem Solving and Computer Programming* Addison Wesley, 1982

About More Formal Programming Methods

We have presented programming as an engineering activity, designing an artefact to meet a specification, subject to constraints. There is another school of thought that regards programming in a much more formal manner as a branch of mathematics. A gentle introduction to this approach is to be found in

N. Wirth, *Systematic Programming*, Prentice-Hall, 1973

and a much more detailed treatment is given in

S. Alagic and M. A. Arbib, *The Design of Well-Structured and Correct Programs*, Springer Verlag, 1978

The theoretical background is brilliantly expounded in

David Gries, *The Science of Programming*, Springer Verlag, 1981

and when you have mastered all these you will be in a position to attempt the classic

Edsger Dijkstra, *A Discipline of Programming*, Prentice-Hall, 1976

A formal approach to the design of programs for commercial data processing is found in another piece of essential reading,

Michael Jackson, *Principles of Program Design*, Academic Press, 1975

About Algorithms

Programs are the realization of algorithms, and it is helpful to know something about the theory of algorithms, especially the analysis of their complexity. A good introductory text is

Sara Baase, *Computer Algorithms*, Addison Wesley, 1978

and the classic text is

A. V. Aho, J. E. Hopcroft, and J. D. Ullman, *Design and Analysis of Computer Algorithms*, Addison Wesley, 1974

General Reading

Finally, there are some classics that everyone in the trade should read and re-read

B. W. Kernighan and P. J. Plauger, *The Elements of Programming Style* (2nd edn), McGraw-Hill, 1978

illustrates good and bad style in a number of programming languages.

F. P. Brooks, *The Mythical Man-Month*, Addison Wesley, 1975

is a collection of essays on software engineering, largely based on the author's experiences as head of the team that developed the software for the IBM System/360 computers. It will teach you a great deal about the problems of writing really big programs.

G. M. Weinberg, *The Psychology of Computer Programming*, Van Nostrand, 1971

was the first book to present programming as a human activity, rather than as a mechanical activity that happened to involve humans. Although it is now quite old, the viewpoint it presents is still valid, and its thought-provoking comments are very relevant to programming today.

D. E. Knuth, *The Art of Computer Programming* (Vols 1 to 3), Addison Wesley

is the fountain-head of wisdom on algorithms and methods. Volume 1 (*Fundamental Algorithms*) has already been mentioned: it covers data structures, trees, linked lists, etc. Volume 2 (*Semi-Numerical Algorithms*) covers random numbers and machine arithmetic, and Volume 3 (*Sorting and Searching*) describes and analyses every sorting and searching method that has ever been invented. (A further four volumes are projected, but there is no firm schedule for their appearance.)

Index